ADVENTURE PATH ✲ PART 2 *of* 6

Rise of the Runelords:

THE SKINSAW MURDERS

Pathfinder™

Credits

Editor-in-Chief • James Jacobs
Art Director • Sarah E. Robinson
Associate Editor • F. Wesley Schneider
Assistant Editor • James Sutter
Editorial Assistance • Mike McArtor
Managing Art Director • James Davis
Production Manager • Jeff Alvarez
Brand Manager • Jason Bulmahn
Marketing Director • Joshua J. Frost
Publisher • Erik Mona

Cover Artist
Wayne Reynolds

Cartographer
Rob Lazzaretti

Contributing Artists
John Gravato
Andrew Hou
Kyle Hunter
JZConcepts
Warren Mahy
Ben Wootten

Contributing Authors
Jason Bulmahn
James Jacobs
Richard Pett
Sean K Reynolds
F. Wesley Schneider

Paizo CEO • Lisa Stevens
Corporate Accountant • Dave Erickson
Technical Director • Vic Wertz
Director of Operations • Jeff Alvarez

Special Thanks
The "Burnt Offerings" playtesters:
Eric Boughton, Joshua J. Frost, Jefferson Hyde, Reid Schmadeka, Joseph Swarner, and Jeremy Williams

"The Skinsaw Murders" is a Pathfinder Adventure Path scenario designed for four 4th-level characters. By the end of this adventure, characters should reach 8th level. This adventure is compliant with the Open Game License (OGL) and is suitable for use with the world's most popular fantasy roleplaying game. The OGL can be found on page 95 of this product.

Paizo Publishing, LLC
2700 Richards Road, Suite 201
Bellevue, WA 98005
paizo.com

Printed in China

TABLE OF CONTENTS

SEND... MORE... ADVENTURERS!

Although he'd already been published at least once, the first time I ever really noticed Richard Pett was a few weeks after I started working at Paizo. As the new guy, one of my glorious duties was doing battle against the slush pile, which at the time also included a sizable mound of manuscript rough drafts that had been requested but not yet accepted for publication.

I got to Rich's "Devil Box," and within two paragraphs of reading it, I was laughing out loud. Which, of course, attracted the curiosity of my fellow editors in the pit, and when I read parts of it aloud, the laughter only spread. Here was an adventure with oversized kobolds and undersized chain devils, freak shows and carnies, and NPCs with names like "Max Muddletude" or "Lumbie the Reptile Boy" or "His Terribleness Duke Chupo, Slayer of Rosie the Seamstress." It was one of the rarest of things—an honestly funny adventure that didn't rely on bad puns or metagame humor.

And the best part about it was that humor wasn't Richard Pett's only strength.

As the years and issues rolled by, Richard Pett's adventures appeared again, and his true strength was revealed—he's got a head full of some of the creepiest things I've ever seen inflicted on the game. Creepy in the same way Grimm's Fairy Tales are creepy. Rich is an expert at confronting you with whimsy and comedy, but then when you look closer, you realize that whimsy is little more than a thin layer over something truly horrific. And then, when the gloves come off, you don't even get the whimsy in a Pett adventure—you get things like haunted Sargasso seas, undead children, spiders that lay their eggs in your throat, and, of course, locations like the polluted and horror-haunted Styes.

When we were building up the outline for Rise of the Runelords, and we realized that we had an adventure involving not only a cult of sicko murderers but an old-school haunted mansion, Richard Pett seemed like the perfect choice. If after you read through "The Skinsaw Murders" you find yourself worried about what might be wearing those old clothes that hang on the cross in the cornfield, or concerned that the strange stain on the carpet might just be a sinister omen if you look at it right, don't say I didn't try to warn you!

MASKED KILLERS AND THE HUNGRY DEAD

Although "Burnt Offerings" had its share of grim and macabre moments, its primary villains were goblins. And goblins are pretty funny critters. In "The Skinsaw Murders," and in the adventures to follow, things grow darker for the Rise of the Runelords Adventure Path. This is mostly by design—after working in the adventure-publishing industry for nearly half a decade, I've noticed that horror-themed and "gritty" adventures are usually the ones that become the most popular. Better writers than I have explored the reasons why horror is such a popular genre across so many forms of entertainment, but I think what it boils down to is this: it's fun to be scared when you're safe. Be it a movie, book, or adventure, exposing yourself to horror causes a rush of adrenaline, and once the entertainment's over, you're back safe in the real world.

One thing to keep in mind about horror in RPG adventures, though, is that the horror is much more personal. In a book or movie, you're confronted with horror that's one person removed; the monster or murderer is after a character that someone else came up with, and you're just along for the ride. In an RPG, though, the monsters and murderers are after your own creation. On some level, at least, even if it's a purely metaphorical level, something horrible is menacing a part of *you*, rather than someone else. Having played in long-term gritty campaigns, I can honestly report that, while they're fun, they get to be overwhelming a lot faster than watching a horror movie or reading a book.

While you're running "The Skinsaw Murders" and the rest of the Rise of the Runelords Adventure Path, make sure that you include some "downtime" for your PCs. Give them opportunities to roleplay encounters with friendly NPCs in Sandpoint or Magnimar, interject encounters with wandering monsters that aren't particularly frightening, and don't be afraid to congratulate them on their victories. Constant fear for a character's survival, relentless menace and mayhem, and unrelenting horror quickly collapses under its own gruesome weight. In order for the horrors that await the PCs in "The Skinsaw Murders" to be their most effective, you need to give the players some contrast. Varying the scenes of horror with light-hearted fare really helps to keep the characters motivated and, more importantly, it helps to make the horror, when it rears its worm-eaten head, to be all the more effective.

Speaking of all things horrible, another good tip for a GM preparing to run "The Skinsaw Murders" is to immerse yourself in the genre. Watch movies like *Se7en* or *Dawn of the Dead* or *Halloween*. Read books like *The Haunting of Hill House* or *Nazareth Hill* or *The Shining*. Movies and books about flesh-eating undead, haunted houses, and masked killers were very much the inspiration for "The Skinsaw Murders," and while these types of entertainment are certainly not to every GM's taste, having a few choice scenes of horror under your belt helps to inspire you when your PCs decide to spend the night in Foxglove Manor, or when they get lost in a certain ghoul-haunted cornfield.

PATHFINDER'S EVOLUTION

You might have noticed a few changes already to the way we're doing things in *Pathfinder*—we're still figuring out how best to present all of this information to you, and as a result, for the first few volumes, change like this is unavoidable. The biggest change is perhaps to the Pathfinder's Journal. *Pathfinder* #1 presented the Pathfinders as an organization, delving into their goals, history, and methods. With this volume, we're shifting to a more first-person approach, and begin following the adventures of one of the organization's newest members—adventurer and sometimes-scoundrel Eando Kline. For now, Eando's adventures will remain in Varisia, but eventually he'll be heading out into the world beyond. We'll be using Eando as a way to explore Golarion, to bring you snapshots of the world as seen through the eyes of one who lives there. In some ways, the Pathfinder's Journal can be thought of as a campaign journal for a campaign that hasn't happened yet.

Next issue, you'll see another change—we'll expand the section on our iconic adventurers (currently Valeros, Seoni, Kyra, and Merisiel) from their one-page formats into a two-page format. Not only will this allow us to keep presenting their statistics as they grow more powerful (and take up more and more space on the page), but it'll give us some room to tell you a little bit about their personalities, histories, and goals. These characters are more than just collections of stats, after all—they've got their own secrets, their own flaws, and their own triumphs. For now, the choices we made in building their stats that might not make sense from a number-crunching standpoint can serve as clues to their personalities: Merisiel's unusually low intelligence for a rogue, Seoni's preference for flashy evocation spells, Kyra's scimitar obsession, and the tankard Valeros carries on his belt next to his swords all have stories waiting to be told!

James Jacobs
Editor-in-Chief
james.jacobs@paizo.com

THE SKINSAW MURDERS

RISE OF THE RUNELORDS: CHAPTER TWO

After slumbering for millennia, Runelord Karzoug woke in the depths of the lost city of Xin-Shalast. Unable to travel far from the source of his power, he conscripted the stone giant Mokmurian as his minion, but Karzoug demanded more. Enslaved giants were well and good for war, but they lacked finesse. Karzoug needed more subtle agents to provide him with both intelligence on this new world and souls to fuel his return to power. He turned his attention to the monstrous creatures that had claimed sections of Xin-Shalast during his long sleep. Of all these, it was the lamias with whom he forged the closest bond.

ADVENTURE BACKGROUND

The lamias' allegiance secured, Karzoug sent his newest minions out into the world. For most, their orders were simply to explore and collect information about what had become of his nation of Shalast, but for a few he had special purposes in mind—these were the lamia matriarchs. He taught them what they needed to know to prepare offerings for his *runewell*—a magical artifact capable of storing power stolen from the souls of those sacrificed during a rite called the Sihedron ritual—and charged them with gathering souls, but left them to their own devices on how best to achieve these purposes. One of these was a lamia matriarch named Xanesha, and after four years of exploring Varisia in her human form, she found a place where greed seemed to rule, where merchants became princes and the lord himself was a paragon of avarice. This was the city of Magnimar.

Before she began her work, though, Xanesha needed a cover. Her investigations led her to an organization called the Brothers of the Seven, a secret society that was itself a cover for a cult of murderers known as the Skinsaw Men. Xanesha insinuated herself into the cult by seducing its leader, a corrupt justice named Ironbriar, and it wasn't long before she took charge of the cult completely.

Xanesha found that running a cult of killers suited her. Themselves worshiping Norgorber, the god of greed, secrets, poison, and murder, the cultists never questioned Xanesha's background and assumed she was a divine agent sent by their sadistic deity. Xanesha never bothered to correct them. Having secured her position as leader of the cult, she began her work of directing her new minions to "harvest" greedy souls—primarily merchants, bankers, moneylenders, gamblers, and adventurers. These poor men and women were brought back to the cult's headquarters within a lumber mill kept as a cover for the cult's sinister truths, where they were marked with the Sihedron Rune and then sacrificed. To further augment her own wealth, Xanesha formed an alliance with a mysterious group called the Red Mantis, a sinister organization of assassins that, among other things, has been developing several horrific diseases to use as weapons. Xanesha suspected that the caverns below a local manor built by a founder of the Brothers of the Seven might hold just such a disease that she can sell to the Red Mantis, and in so doing make a tidy profit for herself. And when a desperate noble named Aldern Foxglove approached her, the lamia matriarch saw a chance to satisfy two goals at once.

Adventure Synopsis

This adventure begins as the PCs become involved in a murder mystery, but what at first seems like an isolated incident is revealed to be the start of a string of murders plaguing Sandpoint. Following the clues, the PCs come to suspect a man they met not long ago, local aristocrat Aldern Foxglove, who has recently been attempting to renovate his old family holdings to the south.

Arriving at Foxglove Manor, the PCs find the mansion anything but renovated. It is, in fact, haunted by Aldern's ancestors churned into activity after Aldern's recent murder of his wife, Iesha. Aldern himself has become a particularly insane ghast, and now dwells in caverns deep below the manor. After the PCs confront him, they discover he was committing his crimes at the request of a larger conspiracy based in the city of Magnimar.

Following up on clues uncovered there, the PCs learn of the existence of a cult of murderers who call themselves the Skinsaw Men. The PCs strike against the cult and expose its leader as one of Magnimar's chief justices, yet even here the puppet strings do not end, for Justice Ironbriar is himself being manipulated by a shadowy mastermind that has moved into an abandoned clocktower in Magnimar's most dangerous district. If they wish to see the Skinsaw Murders come to an end, the PCs must brave this crumbling tower and defeat the powerful lamia matriarch who has claimed it as her lair.

The Foxglove Legacy

Built nearly 80 years ago by a Magnimar merchant prince named Vorel, Foxglove Manor was one of the first homes raised along the Lost Coast. Himself a founding member of the Brothers of the Seven, Vorel was forced to borrow money from his partners to build the manor, and promised them that, after a century, ownership of the manor would revert to the society.

Vorel Foxglove had his own sinister plans—a necromancer by trade, he spent the next 20 years of his life researching methods to become a lich. Yet on the eve of his triumphant transformation, his wife Kasanda uncovered his vile plan. She confronted him, destroyed his phylactery, and triggered a necromantic backlash that destroyed Vorel's body in one horrendous blast of disease and decay. Kasanda attempted to flee the manor with her child, but Vorel's half-completed transformation had an unforseen development. His soul became a part of his manor, treating the house as the phylactery his wife had ruined. It was only a matter of minutes before she, her child, and all of the manor's servants succumbed to a potent and horrific affliction spread by Vorel's vengeful spirit.

When nothing had been heard from Foxglove Manor for days, visitors found the family and servants dead of a mysterious disease. Disposal of the bodies was handled with utmost secrecy by the surviving Foxgloves of Magnimar, but rumor persisted that the bodies were particularly hideous to behold and that Vorel had vanished entirely. The surviving Foxgloves shunned Foxglove Manor for decades, and the estate went through dozens of caretakers—each stayed on at the manor for only a few months before quitting, claiming that the place was somehow "wrong..." that it didn't want anyone living there... that it was haunted.

The building stood vacant for nearly 40 years before Traver Foxglove decided to move his family into the manor to reclaim his heritage and expunge the sour taint of the house's reputation. His wife gave birth to Traver's first (and only) son Aldern not long after they moved in. For six years, it seemed as if whatever was wrong with the manor had corrected itself. Traver's son and daughters were growing into fine young aristocrats and his business seemed to be booming.

Yet Vorel Foxglove remained. His spirit had gone into hibernation after the manor lay empty for so long, but the introduction of Traver's family triggered a slow awakening. In Traver, Vorel found unformed clay he could sculpt, and as the years wore on, Vorel's influence over

Traver grew. His wife Cyralie realized something was amiss but could do little to stop her husband's descent into madness. Before long she became convinced the manor itself was the source. In a fit of desperation, she lit the servants' outbuilding on fire then returned to the manor intending to do the same to it, but Traver, now fully in Vorel's embrace, murdered her before she could light that fire. The shock of watching his wife die freed Traver from Vorel's influence long enough for him to kill himself in despair.

Smoke rising from the fire was seen as far away as Sandpoint, and when folk from town arrived to investigate, they found the servants' outbuilding burnt to the ground and Traver dead by his own hand. His wife's body was found burnt and dashed against the rocks below. Cowering in a second floor bedroom, though, the townsfolk discovered the Foxglove children. Aldern and his older sisters spent time in a Magnimar orphanage before they were claimed by Traver's second cousin and brought back to the city of Korvosa to be raised.

Fifteen years passed before Aldern, now a grown man and a successful merchant himself, returned to the Lost Coast. Rich and popular, he secured a townhouse in Magnimar and set into motion his claim to the family manor. As he reestablished old family connections and worked through the bureaucratic necessities to claim Foxglove Manor, the handsome young noble turned the heads of many of Magnimar's daughters. Although he toyed with a few, his true interest lay in spending nights with the Brothers of the Seven—Aldern found that the society welcomed him with open arms, and it was primarily through their influence that he was able to reclaim Foxglove Manor with such ease.

Yet Aldern Foxglove had trouble finding skilled laborers and servants to aid him in restoring his family estate—Foxglove Manor's reputation as a bad place had decades to take root in local superstition. Worse, the manor's cellars were infested with rats—horribly diseased and aggressive rats that kept to themselves as long as no one ventured too far into the basement. Aldern let none of this deter him. After hiring several desperate, down-on-their-luck carpenters and rat-catchers, he began the painstaking process of rebuilding his home and making it once again fit for living. The job was enormous, from the need to patch the leaky roof in dozens of places to dealing with the strange and repugnant fungus that grew so tenaciously in the basement.

It was about this time that Aldern, returning from a visit to Sandpoint, happened on a group of Varisians upon the moor not far from Foxglove Manor, trapped by the terrible gale he himself was trying to get home in. Seized by an uncharacteristic fit of charity, Aldern did one of the few selfless things of his life and brought the dozen Varisians home with him, inviting them to stay in his manor until the storm had ended. And in doing so, he brought Iesha into his life.

Iesha was surely the most beautiful woman Aldern had ever met, a goddess with raven-black hair and luscious curves, the voice of an angel and the heart of a lion. Aldern fell wildly and passionately in love with the Varisian girl and proposed to her before dawn broke. Overwhelmed by the man's handsome looks, social standing, apparent generosity, and wealth, Iesha accepted and they were married within the week. Alas, as Iesha would soon learn, there was more to Aldern than met the eye.

THE PATHFINDER CHERRY PICK

It's true—not everyone wants to run Adventure Paths. Some people don't even want to run entire adventures. In my own campaigns, I like using elements of published adventures mingled with my own adventures. Having access to PDFs of adventures really fired my imagination—and one thing I've tried in "The Skinsaw Murders" is to include "mini-adventures" tied to the overall plot. You can run this adventure either as part of the whole Rise of the Runelords Adventure Path or as a standalone. You can also dip into the adventure and extract segments of it, using the Hambley Farm encounter as a one-evening side quest, for example.

I was inspired to include these side quests by the messageboards at **paizo.com**. As gamers ourselves, we authors and editors listen to what you have to say. Paizo always had that special relationship with its readers, and that will continue with *Pathfinder* and the GameMastery Modules—both are written by fans of the game, and both display the proud heritage of many years of listening and learning.

—Richard Pett

For Aldern had a mean streak in him, one planted in his soul during his unpleasant upbringing in Korvosa and nurtured by his association with the Brothers of the Seven—in particular by Justice Ironbriar. Aldern's passions and lust for Iesha gave way to jealousy and paranoia, and he grew overprotective of his wife's honor to the extent of locking her in the manor during his business trips to Magnimar. There, Ironbriar continued to work at the man's soul, grooming him for eventual induction into the Skinsaw Cult.

Then, one night after arriving home late from Magnimar, Aldern found Iesha and one of the carpenters together in the library. Making a wildly inaccurate guess at what was going on, he brained the man with a statuette from a shelf, causing Iesha to fly into a frenzy. When Aldern recovered from his rage, he found he'd strangled his wife to death with her own silk scarf.

In a growing panic, Aldern disposed of the carpenter's body by throwing it down the nearby well, but he couldn't bring himself to do the same with Iesha. Instead, he wrapped her corpse in a sheet and hid it in the attic, locking the door and intending to return later to deal with the evidence. He then fled back to the Brothers of the Seven in Magnimar to seek their advice on how to handle this tragic turn of events.

The Brothers of the Seven promised him they'd take care of his problem, asking him to avoid returning to his manor home while they went to work. In the days that followed, Aldern explained to visitors that Iesha was away visiting friends in distant Absalom and that work on restoring his manor had come to a break while he awaited more funds to pay for the final stages of the restoration. He kept up a brave face in public, but in truth, he was slowly being driven bankrupt, both morally and financially, by the Brothers of the Seven. Every week, they demanded more payments in return for their services (implying that if Aldern didn't continue the payments, they would reveal the truth of his murderous acts), while at the same time providing him with the dried flayleaf he had become addicted to, drawing him further and further into their control.

That was when Xanesha decided to involve Aldern in her plans. Promised that his debt to the Brothers of the Seven would soon be paid in full, he was told that he could finally meet the group's mysterious patron. He was taken before Xanesha, who in her human guise informed Aldern that one final task remained before him. It was a simple task, really—return to Foxglove Manor, catch one of the diseased rats that plagued the cellars, and return with it to Xanesha for her to study.

Eager to finally be free of his debt, but nervous about returning to the scene of his crime, Aldern swore off the flayleaf, cleaned himself up, and headed north. He lacked the courage to go directly to Foxglove Manor, though, and instead continued on to Sandpoint, where he attended the Swallowtail Festival. When the goblins raided the town, Aldern's life was saved by the PCs. Aldern grew obsessed with one of these strangers, realizing that here might be someone he could use to climb out of his pit of depression. Ever a master of deception, he maintained his facade of being a successful local noble while he nurtured this new obsession.

Yet when he finally returned to Foxglove Manor (avoiding the upper floors and the sounds of muffled sobbing that he assumed were only in his mind), he had difficulty finding any rats. Vorel's spirit had wakened once again and caused the rats to retreat far underground. When Aldern searched the basement, he heard a strange scratching from under the sagging floor in a central room. Assuming the sounds to be the rats he sought, he dug through the floor and uncovered an ancient stairwell, one that led to Vorel's hidden laboratory under the manor. In these caverns, he finally discovered not only the rats he sought, but the source of their affliction: a disturbing patch of fungus that grew along a cave wall. Harvesting both, he unknowingly exposed himself to latent necromantic contagions, and by the time he returned to Magnimar with the samples secured for Xanesha, he had already all but succumbed to a potent form of ghoul fever.

Xanesha recognized the sickness for what it was and encouraged its growth. Her influence in Foxglove's few remaining hours of life live on in his undeath. She taught him the Sihedron ritual, and once his transformation was complete, sent him back to Foxglove Manor to build an army of ghouls and expand Karzoug's harvest.

PART ONE: MURDER MOST FOUL

A mysterious killer is at large in Sandpoint, but as the adventure begins, few in town know that a murderer stalks their streets at night. The murderer is none other than Aldern Foxglove, transformed into a ghast and told by Xanesha that, by carving the Sihedron Rune upon the bodies of his victims before they are slain, he can someday claim the object of his most recent obsession (one of the PCs) as his own. His first victims—merchants and a farmer—have either not yet been discovered or have been hushed up by Sandpoint's sheriff in an attempt to keep the town from relapsing into the panic that gripped them five years ago when another murderer, a man named Chopper, menaced the town. Yet the night before this adventure begins, the killer strikes again, and this time the gruesome results of his crime cannot be ignored.

An important part of this adventure is the unmasking of the murderer as none other than Lord Aldern Foxglove, the nobleman whom the PCs met at the start of "Burnt Offerings." Keep the pace of events up for the first part of this adventure: a murderer is at large, and as the body count mounts, a tangible sense of fear and frustration grows on the streets. By the time the PCs confront the villain, the discovery of his identity should be all the more shocking.

As Aldern continues to kill, it soon becomes apparent that those he murders are the lucky ones. As this adventure continues, a plague of ghouls in the Sandpoint region quickly drives away memories of goblins. Here is a menace that can't be frightened by dogs or easily defeated by organized resistance, a menace that rises in the bodies of the dead. Without the aid of heroes, the ghoul plague of Sandpoint could have devastating repercussions.

Aldern Foxglove, now the Skinsaw Man, operates from his ruined family seat at Foxglove Manor—a place now called the Misgivings by the locals for its tragic history. Approximately six miles southwest from Sandpoint, Foxglove Manor looms on a remote promontory overlooking the Varisian Gulf. Foxglove's undead state allows him to use the water to mask his tracks, emerging from the surf or rivers to do his horrible work. By using waterways, he makes it impossible to track him to Foxglove Manor—the PCs must piece together the location of his lair by investigating the sites of his murders and the spread of his plague.

Obsession

In the previous adventure, "Burnt Offerings," the PCs rescued Aldern Foxglove from a band of goblins and then accompanied him on a boar hunt—his way of repaying the PCs for saving his life. Although he hid his desperation well, Aldern was deep in debt to the Brothers of the Seven at this point. When the PCs rescued him, he became obsessed with one of them, seeing in this PC a misplaced opportunity for his own redemption. Aldern's obsession stemmed from one of three sins: lust, envy, or wrath.

Lust: If the character is female, Foxglove lusts after the character, intending to replace his beloved Iesha and hoping in a twisted way that, in so doing, he'll somehow redeem the murder of his previous lover. Aldern wants to show the character how powerful he is, how clever he is, and how ruthless he is.

Envy: If none if the PCs who rescued him are beautiful females, Aldern instead becomes insanely jealous of a PC who struck him as particularly brave and powerful. He wants to take that character's place, to prove his own might and wit. Aldern seeks to ridicule and drive out the character, involving him in a web of intrigue in which the PC might even get the blame for the murders himself.

Wrath: Foxglove's obsession with the character has been twisted by his new undead state, and he now hates his rescuer and wants to destroy him. Aldern attempts to implicate the character as the murderer in the hope that the PC will be hanged.

Aldern's obsession with the PC compels him to steal relics and discarded objects from the character. Try to foreshadow the discovery of Foxglove's "collection" in area **B37** by informing the PC that minor personal items go missing now and then.

Sheriff Hemlock's Plea

After the PCs deal with Nualia and the goblins in "Burnt Offerings," give them some time to rest and recover from their adventures. There's no need to start "The Skinsaw Murders" the very same day that they return triumphant from Thistletop. Once you judge that enough time has passed and the PCs are ready for this adventure, they are approached by a sullen and grim-faced Sheriff Hemlock, the commander of Sandpoint's guards and the primary voice of law for much of the Lost Coast. After the PCs aid in defending Sandpoint, Sheriff Hemlock sees them as strong allies for Sandpoint, and the nature of the murders reminds him of Chopper's spree five years ago. He wants help in investigating the crimes before things reach the same level of hysteria that they did then, and that means coming to the heroes of Sandpoint. After greeting the PCs and securing a relatively private place to talk to them, he says the following.

"First, let me thank you again for all you've done for Sandpoint. It's fortunate that you've proven yourselves so capable, because we've a problem that I think you can help us with—a problem that I wish I didn't have to involve anyone with, but one that needs dealing with now before the situation grows worse.

"Put simply, we have a murderer in our midst—one who, I fear, has only begun his work. Some of you doubtless remember the Late Unpleasantness, how this town nearly tore itself apart in fear as Chopper's slayings went on unanswered. I'm afraid we might have something similar brewing now.

"Last night, the murderer struck at the sawmill. There are two victims, and they're... they're in pretty gruesome shape. The bodies were discovered by one of the mill workers, a man named Ibor Thorn, and by the time my men and I arrived on the scene, a crowd of curious gawkers had already sprung up. I've got my men stationed there now, keeping the mill locked down, but the thing that bothers me isn't the fact that we have two dead bodies inside. It's the fact that this is actually the second set of murders we've had in the last few days.

"I come to you for help in this matter—my men are good, but they are also green. They were barely able to handle themselves against the goblins, and what we're facing now is an evil far worse than goblins. I need the help. But I'm afraid you'll need the help too. You see, I'm afraid that this particular murderer knows one of you as well."

At this point, Hemlock passes a bloodstained scrap of parchment to the PC you have chosen to be the target of Foxglove's obsession. That PC's name is written in blood on the outside of the folded parchment; inside is a short message depending on the type of obsession that PC has engendered in Foxglove's diseased mind.

Lust: "You will learn to love me, desire me in time as she did. Give yourself to the Pack and it shall all end."

Envy: "We have spoken of this before, my master. Now it begins. Join the Pack and it will end."

Wrath: "I do as you command, master!"

Whichever note is used, it's signed "Your Lordship" (one of Aldern's three personalities to emerge since his transformation into a ghast). Sheriff Hemlock explains that the note was found pinned to the sleeve of the latest victim by a splinter of wood. He's quick to comfort the PCs with his belief that this note was left at the murder scene to throw suspicion onto them, and that while he certainly doesn't believe that the PCs had anything to do with the murders, if word of this note gets out, he's afraid that the town's reaction might not be as understanding. For this reason, and since he doesn't want to start a general panic, he asks the PCs to keep as quiet as possible about the murders.

Of course, it's possible that the PCs won't want anything to do with the investigation. Sheriff Hemlock won't force them to help, but Foxglove is a cunning foe. New murders occur every few days, and if the PCs let things go for too long, the situation can quickly get out of control, as detailed on page 20 under "Additional Murders." Once things go bad, Hemlock might try to hire the PCs for aid, promising them a 500 gp reward if they can help stop the murders. Worse, the growing number of notes left for one of the PCs by the killer could make it look like the PCs are harboring a murderer themselves.

The Leads

Before the PCs race off to investigate the murders, Sheriff Hemlock runs the current list of clues by them. He informs them that, while he'll be working with them to figure out what's going on, he suspects he'll have his hands full keeping the peace in town. By deputizing the PCs, he hopes that the best possible minds and resources will be focused on solving the murders, leaving him and his guards to the task of keeping Sandpoint from erupting in a panic. He promises the PCs all the support they want, but again asks them to keep their investigations quiet for the town's sake.

Hemlock provides the following list of leads for the PCs.

Sandpoint Lumber Mill: The most recent murders took place here—the bodies are still present, and little has been done with the crime scene itself. Sheriff Hemlock suggests that this be the first place the PCs investigate, since he would like to clean the mill up right away and get the bodies buried.

Ibor Thorn: Sheriff Hemlock has interrogated Ibor, the man who discovered the bodies, and doesn't suspect the frightened miller knows much more.

Ven Vinder: This merchant is sheriff Hemlock's only suspect, although the sheriff is fairly certain that Ven is innocent and that the murders were committed by someone else.

The First Murders: Three con men from the town of Galduria were found murdered in an abandoned barn south of town a few days ago—their bodyguard survived the assault but has gone insane and is being kept at a nearby sanatorium.

The Rune: The star carved on Harker's chest certainly has significance to the killer, but Hemlock's at a loss as to what it means. Perhaps an expert on runes (such as local scholar Brodert Quink) can be consulted?

Sandpoint Lumber Mill

One of the mill's operators, a penny-pinching man named Banny Harker, has of late been engaged in a semi-secret affair with the daughter of a local shopkeeper. He and Katrine Vinder had been meeting at the mill often of late, using the noise of the logsplitter to cover sounds of their trysting. Harker's name was one of many on the list provided to Foxglove by Xanesha, but Katrine was not—she was merely in the wrong place at the wrong time late last night.

After spending a few hours watching activity at the mill from the safety of the marsh across the river, Foxglove crossed the water and clambered up the mill's walls, entering through the upper floor. Therein, the ghast quickly overpowered Harker and set about preparing his body for the ritual to consign his greedy soul to Karzoug, but was interrupted as Katrine entered the room, seeking her lover's arms. A struggle ensued, and after Katrine managed to injure Foxglove with an axe, he pushed her into the log splitter. She died instantly, allowing Foxglove plenty of time to finish his gruesome task and slip back out into the night, returning to Foxglove Manor via the waterways.

The Sandpoint Lumber Mill lies on the shore of the Turandarok River. A sizeable crowd has gathered outside by the time the PCs arrive, and groups of nervous-looking town guards stand at the mill's entrances. A DC 10 Knowledge (local) check is enough to reveal that the mill was working last night—Harker and Thorn, the two millers, often worked late into the night, which had become a bone of contention around town as the noisy mill and its infernally creaky log splitter kept neighbors awake. The guards have already been informed by Sheriff Hemlock of his intent to deputize the PCs, and even if the sheriff doesn't accompany them to the mill, the guards nod silently and step aside to allow the PCs entry.

The mill is a well-built wooden structure with very thick walls. The roof is of wooden shingles, and doors are simple timber and unlocked. The mill machinery has been disengaged, but if it is started again everyone inside the mill makes Listen checks at a –4 penalty due to the noise. There are several points of interest to the PCs as they investigate the site, each detailed below.

The Timber Pier: Timber is delivered to the mill via a small timber pier that extends out into the Turandarok River. A DC 15 Spot check made by anyone investigating the pier reveals a set of muddy footprints that leads from one end of the pier up to the mill itself. A DC 15 Survival check made by a character with Track reveals that a barefoot human man clambered up from the mud under the pier, crossed over to the mill, and then scaled the wall to an upper-floor window.

The Murder Scene: The mill interior is coated with sawdust strewn with footprints and splashes of blood. A DC 15 Survival check reveals what should be obvious—that a desperate struggle took place here several hours ago. If this check exceeds the DC by 10 or more, the character can tell that one set of prints in particular is not only barefoot, but reeks of rotten meat. Harker's body, Katrine's body, a suspicious axe, and a lingering stench of rotten flesh comprise the primary clues here.

The Rotten Smell: The lingering scent of decay in the air is curious—it smells almost as if a small animal had died somewhere in the room and its remains were allowed to ripen. This is the lingering scent of Foxglove's undead body, a smell that is strongest on the blade of the suspicious axe or among a few of the footprints he left behind.

Katrine's Body: Poor Katrine was killed instantly when Foxglove pushed her into the log splitter. Her mangled, ruined remains lie on the mill's lower floor amid heaps of bloodstained firewood. A pale-faced, obviously upset guard stands at attention nearby. The log splitter itself is powered by a waterwheel and consists of a chute in the floor with rotating saw blades that cut logs as they are fed in. While there are no clues among Katrine's mangled remains, try to impress upon the PCs her horrible fate and the cruel efficiency of the log splitter as a deadly weapon—this helps foreshadow events awaiting the PCs later in this adventure.

Harker's Body: Harker's body has been horribly desecrated. The poor man has been affixed to the wall by several hooks normally used to hang machinery. The body is mutilated, the face carved away and lower jaw missing entirely. His bare chest is defaced as well, bearing a strange rune in the shape of a seven-pointed star. This rune (the Sihedron Rune) should be familiar to the PCs, especially if they own the *Sihedron medallion* once worn by Nualia. Its appearance on the chest of a murdered man should drive home its importance to the PCs, yet they should be at a loss still as to what the rune means. A DC 30 Knoweldge (arcana or history) check is enough to identify the marking as the Sihedron Rune, an antiquated glyph that symbolizes arcane magic once practiced in ancient Thassilon.

Closer examination of the body combined with a DC 15 Heal check reveals the presence of several additional wounds. Unlike the deeper slashes on the body, these smaller gashes almost seem to have been made by a claw—a five-fingered, human-hand-sized claw. The rotten scent seems stronger near these wounds. The body is only recognizable as Harker's by a faded tattoo of a raven across his lower abdomen. With his missing face and jaw, his body is in no shape to function for a *speak with dead* spell.

The Suspicious Axe: A handaxe is embedded in the floor near the log splitter, as if it had been dropped there. The handle is covered with bloody finger-marks (left by Katrine), and a close examination of the head reveals two things of note. First, smears of what look like rotten flesh and fragments of bone are caked on its blade, and second, the rotten meat stink is strong on it. Anyone who examines the blade this closely must make a DC 13 Fortitude save to avoid being sickened for 1d6+4 minutes. A character who has fought a ghast before automatically recognizes the distinctive stench—otherwise, someone who makes a DC 25 Knowledge (religion) check can identify the lingering stink of corruption as beyond that which a dead body can normally produce—the axe was likely used within the last 24 hours against some form of corporeal undead.

The Marsh: If the PCs think to investigate the marsh on the other side of the river from the mill, a DC 20 Search check reveals a relatively dry spot that bears a number of barefooted human tracks and a lingering stink of rotten flesh. A DC 15 Survival check made at this point reveals that the tracks lead from and into the river, but never away from the site. The spot is hidden by several low banks of nettles, but offers a perfect view of the mill to anyone hidden here.

Ibor Thorn

Harker's partner Ibor is a young man, handsome if a bit narrow-faced. He is still in shock at having discovered the bodies after he arrived at work this morning. Although the sheriff already interrogated Ibor, Hemlock admits that the PCs might be able to get something out of the miller that he could not. He cautions them to be gentle in their interrogation, though—Thorn's been through a lot in the last few hours.

Ibor waits in a holding cell below the Sandpoint Garrison. His initial attitude toward the PCs is indifferent—unless he's made friendly with a DC 15 Diplomacy check, a successful Intimidate check, or some other means, he refuses to say more about anything, saying that he's already told the sheriff everything he knows.

If the PCs can secure his cooperation, he sighs heavily. Ibor can confirm that Harker had frequent midnight trysts with Katrine, but although Ven's a possessive father, Ibor doesn't think he's capable of doing what was done to Harker. A DC 20 Sense Motive check reveals that Ibor's holding something back. If pressed, or if he is made helpful, he admits that Harker had been "cooking the books" for some time. Ibor's quick to point out that he never took part in the scams, but does admit that Harker might have stashed away quite a lot of money by skimming from the top of sales and business over the past several years. The Scarnettis, the noble family that owns the lumber mill, have a reputation for being ruthless—there are rumors that they're responsible for burning several competing lumber mills in the region, and Ibor wouldn't put it above the Scarnettis to hire someone to kill Harker if they found out he'd been embezzling money.

In fact, the Scarnettis have nothing to do with the murders, and an investigation of Titus Scarnetti and his family should quickly turn into a dead end, even when it becomes apparent that Harker was indeed embezzling from the mill's profits. Feel free to expand on this red herring as you wish—the detail that's important for the PCs to learn is that Harker was greedy, the only tie between all of the eventual murder victims.

Ven Vinder

Ven was the first person Sheriff Hemlock visited after learning of the murders, but after he informed Ven of his daughter's death at the mill, the man flew into a rage. Sheriff Hemlock took him into custody and let him cool off in a cell, but even though Ven fought like a devil, Hemlock's sure that his rage is born from the death of his beloved daughter and not from guilt at being caught. He's prepared to release Ven, but if the PCs wish to speak to him first, he lets them do so.

Of course, if in "Burnt Offerings" the PCs made an enemy of Ven Vinder, the shopkeeper suspects that the PCs have something to do with Katrine's death. In this case, Ven wastes no time in accusing them of murdering his child and calling them jackals, deviants, and worse. His anger flares up again, doing him little good in clearing his name from the list of suspects. Although his accusations have little effect at the time, they take root in the minds of several of Sandpoint's citizens—Ven is well-liked, and if he suspects that the PCs were involved in the murder, many in town are predisposed to accept his accusations. These seeds of suspicion grow as the adventure continues.

The PCs may actually grow to suspect that Ven killed Harker and his own daughter in a fit of wrath at finally discovering proof of their affair. If they do, let them—if it's one thing that any murder mystery needs, it's red herrings. Eventually, the fact that Ven has little connection with the other murders should exonerate him. In any event, Sheriff Hemlock has little reason to keep him locked up once Ven's wife corroborates his alibi that he was at home all evening during both sets of murders.

The Sihedron Rune

Although Sheriff Hemlock doesn't recognize the strange seven-pointed star carved into the dead man's chest, the PCs likely do: it's the same star from the dungeons below Thistletop and the same as on the magic amulet worn by Nualia. A DC 15 Knowledge (local) check is enough for a PC to know that an expert on the ancient ruins that dot Varisia's landscape dwells here in Sandpoint, living in the shadow of the Old Light itself. If the PCs don't make this connection, this expert may seek them out on his own once knowledge of the star pattern leaks into the rumor mill.

This expert is **Brodert Quink** (NG male human expert 7), an expert on Varisian history who moved to Sandpoint recently to study the town's own Thassilonian ruin—the Old Light. Brodert is tremendously excited to be involved in a murder investigation, and does everything he can to aid the PCs. Unfortunately, much of the lore about ancient Thassilon has been lost; what does remain has been gathered from barely legible carvings on the surviving monuments or extracted from the myths and oral traditions of Varisian seers and storytellers.

What he knows about Thassilon is that it was a vast empire ruled by powerful wizards. The sheer size of the monuments they left behind testifies to their power, and the unnatural way many of these monuments have resisted erosion and the march of time testifies to their skill at magic. Most sages place the height of the Thassilonian empire at 7,000 to 8,000 years ago, but Brodert thinks the empire was even older—he suspects it collapsed no sooner than 10,000 years in the past.

Much of what Brodert has to say is vague theory based on conjecture—his belief that the Old Light was once a war machine capable of spewing fire from its peak is relatively unpopular among his peers, for example. Yet he can tell the PCs a few things of interest about the star—namely, that it seems to be one of the most important runes of Thassilon. The star itself is known as the "Sihedron Rune," and signifies not only the seven virtues of rule (generally agreed among scholars to have been wealth, fertility, honest pride, abundance, eager striving, righteous anger, and rest), but the seven schools of magic recognized by Thassilon (divination magic, Brodert points out, was not held in high regard by the ancients). Brodert notes with a smirk that much of what is understood about Thassilon indicates that its leaders were far from virtuous, and he believes the classic mortal sins (greed, lust, pride, gluttony, envy, wrath, and sloth) rose from corruptions of the Thassilonian virtues of rule. In any event, the Sihedron Rune was certainly a symbol of power, one that may well have stood for and symbolized the empire itself. The fact that the killer carved it into the flesh of his victim might point to the fact that the murderer is some sort of scholar—although as soon as Brodert comes to this conclusion, he just as quickly proclaims himself to be innocent. Of course, he is, but the PCs don't know that—having Brodert become an early suspect in the murders can be an interesting red herring.

Messrs. Mortwell, Hask, and Tabe—
A deal has come about that I need capital in. It involves property and gold, and though I am not at liberty to tell you the exact details, it will make us all rich. Come to Bradley's Barn on Cougar Creek tonight. We can meet there to discuss our futures.
Your Lordship

Handout 1

The First Murders

Sheriff Hemlock explains that, two days ago, a patrol of guards along the Lost Coast Road were assaulted by a deranged man near an abandoned barn south of town along the banks of Cougar Creek. The man was obviously sick and insane, his flesh fevered, eyes wild, mouth frothing, and clothes caked with blood. The guards subdued him, but when they checked inside the barn they discovered the mutilated bodies of three men. Although all three bodies were far too disfigured to identify, one of them carried a piece of parchment that Hemlock gives to the PCs to read (reproduced as Handout 1). The note identifies the bodies as Tarch Mortwell, Lener Hask, and Gedwin Tabe, three notorious con men and swindlers known well to Sheriff Hemlock as local troublemakers. He personally forbade the three men from operating their con games and barely legal operations in Sandpoint, and wasn't particularly surprised at the time to find them murdered—it was only a matter of time before they tried to swindle someone worse than them, after all. But in light of the mill murders and the fact that Mortwell, Hask, and Tabe all bore the same seven-pointed marking on their chests that Harker did, Hemlock is convinced there is something worse than revenge afoot.

The bodies of all three men lie in state in a cool basement room below the Sandpoint Garrison, not far from the holding cells containing Ibor and Ven—the PCs are welcome to examine them if they wish. Although decay has set in, a DC 15 Heal check reveals that all three bodies bear claw marks similar to those that the PCs might have discovered on Harker's body.

The insane man has been identified as one Grayst Sevilla, a local Varisian thug. He's been given over to the care of Erin Habe, caretaker of the Saintly Haven of Respite; if the PCs wish to speak to Grayst to learn more, Sheriff Hemlock welcomes them to try but warns them that Grayst is "a bit off his rocker" and they shouldn't expect much. He provides them with a letter of introduction to Habe if they ask.

What the Skinsaw Man Did: Two days ago, the Skinsaw Man lured these three greedy swindlers to Bradley's Barn with a note he knew they couldn't resist. Suspicious, the three men hired a Varisian thug named Grayst to guard them. Unfortunately, even the four of them were no match for the Skinsaw Man, who easily overpowered the group. Foxglove had little interest in slaying Grayst, and instead bound him with rope, letting the man watch as he prepared the three greedy swindlers for sacrifice, a display that drove Grayst mad. As the ghast worked, he spoke to his audience, and when he was done he left Grayst a parting gift—a bite to the shoulder that infected him with ghoul fever. Grayst lapsed into a fever-haunted state of delusion, and only managed to escape his bonds the next day when he heard others passing by—others who turned out to be Hemlock's men.

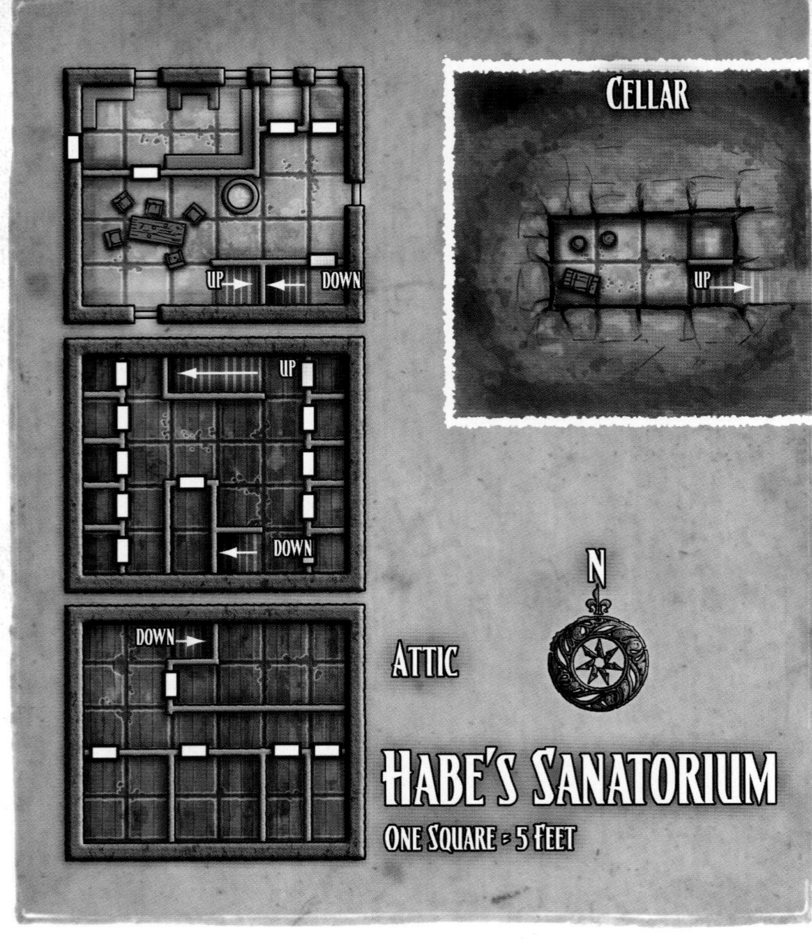

The Thing in the Sanatorium (EL 1)

The Saintly Haven of Respite, better known locally as Habe's Sanatorium, is run by **Erin Habe** (LN male human expert 4), an expert on disease and mental derangement who is as well-traveled as he is knowledgeable. Independently wealthy from his years as a doctor in Magnimar, he chose to build this sanatorium in a remote dale south of Sandpoint for precisely that reason—its seclusion. Here, he hoped his wards would find the peace of mind they needed to heal, and he himself would find the peace to continue his own experiments into what caused their respective dementias without worrying about other folk misunderstanding his sometimes necessarily bloody methods.

When Sheriff Hemlock arrived at the Sanatorium's front door a few days ago, Habe was worried that the man had come to investigate the place. It was with barely hidden relief that he realized Hemlock was merely handing him another patient, a half-crazed man named Grayst Sevilla. In the past few days, Grayst has become Habe's favorite subject. Not only is this man obviously insane, driven so by some still-undiscovered trauma, but he also suffers from a terrible disease causing a hideous physical malaise. Habe has recently determined that Grayst has contracted ghoul fever, and is almost as curious to see how long the Varisian can hold out against the illness as he is to witness his transformation into something undead. Needless to say, Habe is unhappy to receive visitors at this time, and views such as a distraction from his work with Grayst. Yet he doesn't want to arouse undue suspicion, and with a bit of convincing allows the PCs to speak to his patient—under supervision.

The squat, stone building that serves as the sanatorium has three floors under a stout stone-flagged roof, built in the lee of the limestone escarpment known as Ashen Rise. All doors are simple wooden ones, and a brisk sense of cleanliness fills the place—floors are scrubbed and walls are freshly painted white. The somewhat sour smell of burning incense abounds—a scent that Habe has found soothes most deviant minds.

Aside from Habe, two other men work in the building: live-in help that handle much of the daily work of feeding and caring for the building's patients. These two men (both LN human warrior 1) live on the ground floor of a small cottage down the hill from the Sanatorium—Habe himself lives on the upper floor of the same cottage, but spends every waking hour at the sanatorium.

Apart from Grayst, Habe has few patients these days—the majority of his rooms on the second floor of the sanatorium are empty. Only two have occupants, one of whom is known as Blind Sedge (an old farmer who has no family) and the other as Wald (a larger-than-life ninety-seven-year-old man whose tenacious grip on life is matched only by his senility).

Creatures: Habe's initial reaction to visitors is unfriendly—unless made friendly, he refuses anyone entry, claiming that he's in the middle of some frightfully important work and cannot be disturbed. Presenting Hemlock's letter of introduction grants the PCs a +10 bonus on Diplomacy or Intimidate checks. If convinced, Habe begrudgingly allows the PCs entrance into the sanatorium, but asks them to keep their interview of Grayst as short as possible before leading them up to the attic floor of the building, where he's been keeping Grayst in the southwestern room. Both of Habe's orderlies accompany him and the PCs.

Grayst himself is crouched, sobbing, in the corner of the room. His skin is pale and looks gangrenous, hair wild and eyes milky white. Anyone seeing him who makes a DC 14 Heal check realizes he's quite sick and close to death, while a DC 24 success allows a PC to realize Grayst is in the advanced stages of ghoul fever. Grayst is mostly nonresponsive, wrapped as he is in a straitjacket, but a DC 20 Diplomacy check is enough to get him to respond to questioning. Unfortunately, Grayst has little to say apart from incoherent mumblings about "razors" and "too many teeth" and how "the Skinsaw Man is coming."

This all changes as soon as the PC with whom Foxglove is obsessed comes into view—Foxglove spent some time talking about this one, even showing Grayst a cameo painting he'd had done of the character. When he sees this PC, Grayst's eyes bulge and he speaks:

"He said. He said you would visit me. His Lordship. The one that unmade me said so. He has a place for you. A precious place. I'm so jealous. He has a message for you. He made me remember it. I hope I haven't forgotten. The master wouldn't approve if I forgot. Let me see... let... me... see..."

The message Grayst has for the PC depends on the nature of Foxglove's obsession.

Lust: "He said that if you came to his Misgivings, that if you joined his pack, he would end his harvest in your honor."

Envy: "He said you should come to the Misgivings soon, to meet the Pack, for they have something wonderful to show you."

Wrath: "He said that the bodies you are finding are signs and portents; that when he is done, you shall be remembered forever and the Misgivings shall be your throne!"

A DC 15 Knowledge (local) check is enough for a PC to recognize the fact that "the Misgivings" is a local name for a run-down and abandoned estate further south—a place called Foxglove Manor.

At the climax of his speech, the message delivered, Grayst collapses and issues a low moan. One round later, his moan rises to a shriek, and as he lurches to his feet, his arms tear free of the old straitjacket. The man has nearly succumbed to ghoul fever, and although severely ill, remains as strong as he ever was. He lunges at the PC he was speaking to, eager to kill the one whom his "master" loves more than him. The orderlies do their best to get Habe to safety before they step in to help, but anyone who tries to protect the targeted PC is assaulted by the diseased man as well. Grayst's CR has been reduced by 3 to account for his diseased state.

GRAYST SEVILLA **CR 1**

Male human fighter 4
CN Medium humanoid
Init –3; **Senses** Listen +1, Spot +1

DEFENSE

AC 7, touch 7, flat-footed 7
(–3 Dex)
hp 15 (4d10–8)
Fort +2, **Ref** –2, **Will** +2

OFFENSE

GRAYST SEVILLA

Spd 30 ft.
Melee unarmed strike +6 (1d3+3)

TACTICS

During Combat Grayst focuses his anger on the PC he recognizes as being the focus of Foxglove's obsession, ignoring all other targets and even provoking attacks of opportunity in his attempts to reach his target.
Morale Grayst fights to the death.

STATISTICS

Str 16, **Dex** 13 (currently 4), **Con** 14 (currently 6), **Int** 8, **Wis** 12, **Cha** 10
Base Atk +3; **Grp** +5
Feats Diehard, Improved Initiative, Improved Unarmed Strike, Endurance, Power Attack, Weapon Focus (longsword)
Skills Intimidate +7
Languages Common, Varisian

A Varisian Nursery Rhyme

Mumble Mumble Scarecrow,
Alone in the maize.
Sleeping in the daytime,
A stitched man he stays.

But when the moon she rises,
Up Mumble gets.
He shakes his hands at first
And moves his feet the next.

And when the dog is snoring,
And when you're fast asleep,
Mumble Mumble Scarecrow
Will find you good to eat.

Development: After Grayst's outburst, Habe begs for the PCs' forgiveness. He honestly had no idea that the man would react in such a manner, but more to the point, desperately wants to avoid having any bad word of mouth get around about him. Habe admits at this point that he knew Grayst was suffering from ghoul fever, and that he should have turned him over to Father Zantus in Sandpoint for treatment as soon as he made that diagnosis. If Grayst is slain in the battle, Habe loads the body into a cart and delivers it to Father Zantus for purification that same day—otherwise he rebinds the madman and sends for Zantus to make a house call. If one of the PCs can cure Grayst of his illness with *remove disease*, Habe is eternally grateful.

Grayst, unfortunately, remains insane. Barring a *heal* or *greater restoration* spell, he's destined to live the rest of his life here at the sanatorium if cured. Aside from the clues he's given the PCs already, he has little more to offer them.

Farmer Grump

Although the swindlers and the millers were the first victims discovered, they were not the first to fall to the Skinsaw Man. This dubious honor fell instead to a family of farmers who lived relatively close to Foxglove Manor. Old Crade Hambley was well-known among Sandpoint's farmers for being a penny-pincher and a tenacious haggler when it came to selling his crops. His family dwelt in poverty, even though his farms seemed to make as much money (if not more) than those of his neighbors. He was certainly a greedy soul, and perfect grist for Karzoug's *runewell*.

With this first set of murders, the Skinsaw Man was still a bit unsure of his powers. When he invaded the farm, he brought with him several ghouls from the warrens below his manor. When they attacked the Hambley Place, all five members of the family—Crade, his wife Lis, and their three sons—fell to the horrific assault. The next night, when they arose as ghouls themselves, the Skinsaw Man was there to greet them, welcoming them into his pack. He told them them to spread his sickness, to sneak into neighboring farms and attack their livestock, pets, and children.

In the following days, local farmers began talking about walking scarecrows that came out of the fields at night to feed—nothing was seen, but plenty was heard. Screams in the dark, glimpses of people being chased through fields and out over the moors by... things. When neighbors visited farms in the morning, they found them empty. At first, the fiercely independent farmers thought they could deal with the unseen menace themselves, but yesterday it became too much. A group of farmers armed with torches went to inspect the Hambley Place, and only one survived.

A day after this adventure begins, this one survivor, a man named Maester Grump, arrives in Sandpoint breathless and covered with mud and sweat. He seeks out Sheriff Hemlock to tell his tale, and soon thereafter Hemlock tracks down the PCs.

Farmer Grump breaks into nervous babbling as soon as the PCs arrive, frantically chanting a Varisian nursery rhyme about walking scarecrows. Calming him down requires a few minutes of work, at which point he tells a short but harrowing story, speaking of how the southern farmlands have become plagued by foul walking scarecrows that stalk the night. All the farmers knew that the problems were coming from the old Hambley place—things "just ain't been right there for a few days now"—but when a group of locals paid the Hambley farm a visit yesterday evening, they were attacked by folk that looked like corpses but fed like starving animals. At this point in the telling, Grump's worked himself into a lather again and shrieks, "They even ate the dogs!"

Hemlock explains that his men picked up Grump as he ran into town screaming about walking scarecrows. The sheriff asks the PCs if they can investigate, and agrees to provide up to four of the local watch to help them—he would provide more, but daren't leave the town any more exposed than it already is. He hopes that Grump's story has been enhanced by the booze he can smell on the old farmer's breath, but worries that the moonshine may actually have dulled the man's memories of the grim fate that has been visited upon the Hambleys, and that the situation there is even worse than Grump knows.

If the PCs take Sheriff Hemlock up on his offer of aid, use the following stats for the guards he sends with them.

Sandpoint Watchman **CR 1**

Male human warrior 2
NG Medium humanoid
Init +0; **Senses** Listen +1, Spot +1

DEFENSE

AC 16, touch 10, flat-footed 16 (+4 armor, +2 shield)
hp 13 (2d8+4)

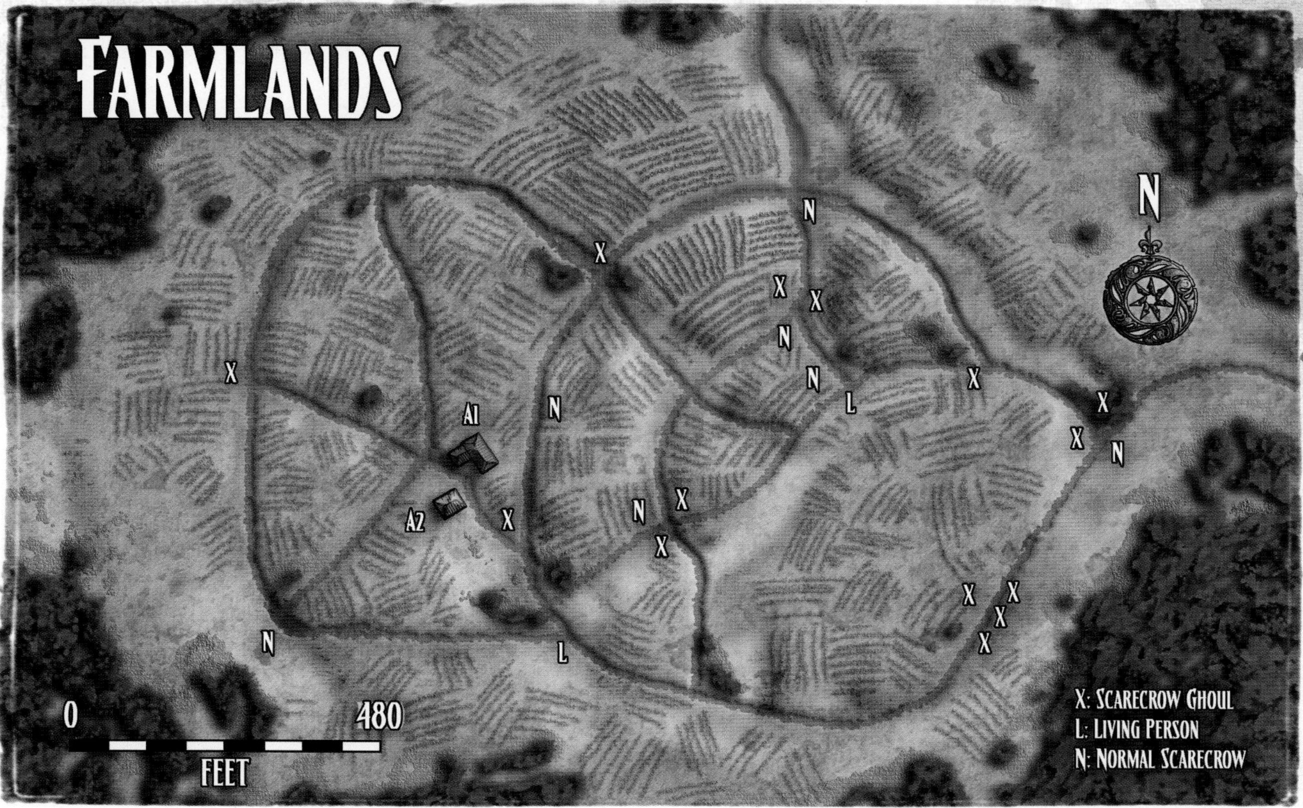

Fort +4, **Ref** +0, **Will** –1

OFFENSE

Spd 30 ft.

Melee longsword +4 (1d8+1/19–20)

Ranged longbow +2 (1d8/×3)

TACTICS

During Combat The watchmen are loyal and brave, and once Hemlock's deputized the PCs, they follow their orders.

Morale Although brave, the watchmen are not foolhardy. If confronted with a foe they can't seem to hurt, or if reduced to 2 hit points or less, a watchman attempts to flee back to Sandpoint to report.

STATISTICS

Str 13, **Dex** 11, **Con** 12, **Int** 10, **Wis** 9, **Cha** 8

Base Atk +2; **Grp** +3

Feats Alertness, Weapon Focus (longsword)

Skills Intimidate +4, Ride +5

Languages Common

Gear chain shirt, light steel shield, longsword, longbow with 20 arrows

The Hambley Farm (EL 7)

The news of walking scarecrows spreads quickly through the farmlands, and PCs stopping to visit farms on the way find the normally friendly locals unwilling to chat with visitors. Over three dozen farmsteads dot the fields and vales southeast of Sandpoint, the furthest being some six miles from town. Farms to the east and north have heard stories of the trouble to the south, but it's not until the PCs move south of Ashen Rise and approach Soggy River that the rumors turn into firsthand accounts.

Footpaths, dusty tracks about 10 feet wide hemmed in by fields of corn and other crops, connect the farmsteads. The Hambley Farm is nestled at the western edge of the Whisperwood, a forest said to be home to capricious gnomes, pixies, and other fey, but now overshadowed by the closer menace. All five of the other farms south of the Soggy River are now deserted, their occupants having either fled north to seek shelter with other farmers or captured by the ghouls. Some of the ghouls created from these farmers have gone on to dwell in the tunnels below Foxglove Manor, but six remain in the vicinity of Hambley Farm, eager to continue their murderous spree.

The layout of the Hambley Farm is shown on the farmlands map. Fields of tall-stalked plants transform the paths between them into oppressive tunnels, making it dangerously easy for visitors to become lost. The Hambley farmhouse and barn sit in the

western portion of these fields. Both house and barn seem unremarkable from the outside, but an exploration of the interiors reveals the true extent of the horror visited upon the region.

A1. Barn: The barn is the larger of the two structures, an L-shaped building constructed around a unique feature—a twelve-foot-high stone head, canted slightly to the left, depicting a helmed warrior, his face a stern model of placid determination. Moss has grown over much of the weathered figure, making his features hard to discern. This head, known locally as the "Stone Warrior," is a remnant of an ancient Thassilonian statue that once stood in the area. Too large to move and too unique to destroy, Hambley decided to use it as a support for his barn and incorporated it into the building's structure. The ghouls themselves have made this barn their lair, and the place has become a macabre tangle of bones and partially eaten carcasses (in most cases cows or horses, but in some, human farmers).

A2. Farmhouse: The farmhouse is in a terrible state as well. It was here that Foxglove murdered Hambley and his family—while his wife and sons have joined the ghoul pack that now dwells in the barn, Hambley's mutilated body lies in the farmhouse's kitchen. Although the corpse is already decaying and swarming with flies, the Sihedron Rune is still plainly visible upon the man's chest, as is a single scrap of parchment pinned to his tunic. The parchment bears the name of the PC Foxglove is obsessed with; the contents depend on the nature of his obsession.

Lust: "Take the fever into you, my love—it shall be but the first of my gifts to you."

Envy: "I fear you. I hate you. You must fear and hate me as well. You may unmask me, so I must unmask you first."

Wrath: "You, and you alone, have brought this fearful harvest. They are dead because of you, and more shall join them soon."

A search of the rotting body uncovers a rusted iron key in one pocket—the key to a footlocker hidden in the master bedroom.

Creatures: In all, there are seven "free" ghouls dwelling in the region—six typical ghouls and one ghoul who was once a caretaker for Foxglove Manor. Once a man named Rogors Craesby, he is the leader of the ghouls here in Aldern's absence. The lesser ghouls dwell in the barn, while Rogors lurks in the farmhouse.

The ghouls have not been idle over the past several days, and have been adding to their number by binding the victims they have chosen not to eat, making scarecrows of them and hanging them up to "ripen" in the surrounding fields. These ghoul scarecrows are marked with Xs on the map and do not count against the total number of "free" ghouls in the area. Bound by baling twine to their frames, they hang confused, blinking through sack-covered faces in the harsh sun, unsure of what has happened to them yet aware of a growing and monstrous hunger. Each of these poor souls is effectively a ghoul now, and if any living creature approaches within 30 feet, they struggle hideously against their bonds, making a Strength check each round in an attempt to break free. It's only a DC 15 check to do so—any ghoul that rips free of its scarecrow frame immediately attacks the nearest living creature with a shriek.

To confuse matters, several normal scarecrows stand in the fields. Worse, two poor souls who haven't yet succumbed to ghoul fever (but surely will within a day) also hang from frames at the locations indicated on the map. These two living people are Horran and Lettie Guffmin, dragged off last night and left bound, gagged, and masked as scarecrows. Both are down to 2 Dexterity and 2 Constituion from ghoul fever; if rescued, they feebly warn the PCs about the ghouls that dwell in the barn before begging to be returned to their families.

If the ghouls become aware of any intrusions (such as might be indicated by a shrieking ghoul leaping off its scarecrow frame), one group of three moves out into the fields to seek out intruders, while the remaining three move into the farmhouse to join Rogors.

Rogors Craesby **CR 4**

Male dread ghoul human expert 4
CE Medium undead (augmented humanoid)
Advanced Bestiary 76
Init +3; **Senses** darkvision 60 ft., scent; Listen +11, Spot +11

DEFENSE

AC 15, touch 13, flat-footed 12
(+3 Dex, +2 natural)
hp 26 (4d12)
Fort +1, **Ref** +6, **Will** +6
Defensive Abilities Dodge, +2 turn resistance; **Immune** undead traits

OFFENSE

Spd 30 ft., climb 30 ft.
Melee bite +4 (1d6 plus paralysis) and
2 claws –1 (1d3 plus paralysis)
Special Attacks command ghouls, create spawn

TACTICS

During Combat Rogors directs his ghouls to focus their attention on foes who are not paralyzed, hoping to catch new living victims to be bound and put up as scarecrows for the sickness to take them.
Morale Rogors fights to the death.

STATISTICS

Str 12, **Dex** 17, **Con** —, **Int** 14, **Wis** 14, **Cha** 13
Base Atk +3; **Grp** +4
Feats Alertness, Dodge, Lightning Reflexes, Track
Skills Climb +9, Craft (carpentry) +9, Gather Information +10, Knowledge (architecture and engineering) +9, Knowledge (local) +9, Listen +11, Search +9, Spot +11, Survival +10
Languages Common, Halfling
Gear key to Foxglove Manor

SPECIAL ABILITIES

Command Ghouls (Su) A dread ghoul can automatically command all normal ghouls within 30 feet as a free action. Normal ghouls never attack a dread ghoul unless compelled.
Create Spawn (Su) Any creature killed by a dread ghoul and lying undisturbed until the next midnight rises as a dread ghoul at that time. The new dread ghoul is not under the control of its creator. A *protection from evil* or *gentle repose* spell cast on the corpse prevents this.
Paralysis (Ex) A creature damaged by a dread ghoul's bite or claw must make a DC 13 Fortitude save or be paralyzed for 1d4+1 rounds. The save DC is Charisma-based.

Ghouls (6) **CR 1**

hp 13 each (MM 118)

Treasure: Rogors was once the caretaker of Foxglove Manor, and an iron key still hangs around his neck on a leather cord. The key bears a heraldic symbol of a curious flower surrounded by thorns. A DC 15 Knowledge (nobility) check identifies the heraldry as the Foxglove family crest. If the PCs don't already know about it, a DC 15 Knowledge (local) check reveals to them the fact that the Foxglove family estate is located on the coast a mere three miles to the west of the Hambley farm.

A DC 22 Search of the master bedroom uncovers a loose floorboard under which Crade Hambley hid a stout wooden coffer. It can be unlocked with the key found on his body or with a DC 25 Open Lock check. Inside, meticulously organized into leather pouches containing 100 sp each, is Hambley's life's savings—a total of 3,400 sp.

Sin and the PC

You should keep an eye on choices the PCs make during the course of this adventure and those to follow. In *Pathfinder #5*'s "Sins of the Saviors," by Stephen S. Greer, you'll be asked several times to adjudicate the effects of certain traps and conditions based on how "sinful" each of the PCs has been. To aid you in this endeavor, you might want to keep a list for each PC, making a hash mark next to each of the seven deadly sins (greed, lust, envy, wrath, gluttony, pride, and sloth) whenever a PC, in your estimation, takes an action that might reflect upon his soul. Don't bother marking minor events, but if, for example, a PC steals the Hambley life's savings and spends it on himself, he might just earn himself a point of Greed (especially if he hides the discovery of the money from his fellow PCs). Likewise, a PC who willingly fell into Shayliss's arms back in "Burnt Offerings" probably earns a point of Lust, and murdering several helpless goblin prisoners is worth a point of Wrath. Again, no need to obsess over these, but once you reach "Sins of the Saviors," these notes should help in determining how the PCs interact with some of the strange and complex areas that await them in that adventure.

Additional Murders

Of course, Aldern Foxglove has no intention of stopping his murder spree with the latest deaths at the Sandpoint Lumber Mill. As this adventure progresses, the Skinsaw Man continues to visit Sandpoint every few nights to look for new victims. He stays away from areas where the PCs are known to be present—he has little wish to confront them now, and would rather they come to his lair on their own. Several clues as to the Skinsaw Man's identity and the location of his lair wait to be uncovered by the PCs in the preceding encounters, but they may not pick up on them. Alternately, they may drag their feet about investigating the region's most notorious haunted house.

If the PCs need additional clues or motivation, you can provide both by having the Skinsaw Man claim additional victims in Sandpoint. Xanesha has done her research, and has singled out nearly a dozen individuals in town whose greed marks them as excellent candidates for the Sihedron ritual. For the most part, these victims should be minor NPCs from town, but if the PCs really need a shot in the arm, you can target one of the NPCs they've grown close to. Titus Scarnetti might be a good choice for a high-profile murder victim. Barring that, one of the local shopkeepers, like butcher Chod Bevuk, grocer Olmur Danvakus, or boutique owner Hayliss Korvaski all make likely victims. Hopefully the PCs head south to Foxglove Manor before Sandpoint runs out of citizens!

Although the results of each murder are similar to those the PCs saw at the mill, you should endeavor to include a new clue at each site. Perhaps they find a bloody, obviously clawed handprint on a wall. They might find a pet, partially eaten and with a few long teeth lodged in the flesh (identifiable as ghast teeth with a DC 20 Knowledge [religion] check). And at each murder, they find new notes penned for Foxglove's obsession, notes that grow increasingly foul and descriptive in their threats and invitations to "become one with the Pack." If the PCs seem to be growing too frustrated, it's probably time to have one of these notes more or less spell out where Foxglove is hiding with a message like this:

Lust: "You continue to ignore my invitations, my love. Did you not sense my need for you that evening after we hunted?"

Envy: "Can this be? Can the fox be outfoxing the hunter? Strange—you seemed so confident against the boars of Tickwood..."

Wrath: "You've let them all die! Their lives could have been spared, but your foolishness doomed them all! Just as you let my dog die on that goblin's blade, I let them die upon my own!"

These increasingly common attacks on the town soon unnerve the citizens of Sandpoint to the brink of chaos. Some folk pack their belongings and move out by daylight, while others bar their doors and shutters at dusk to keep out the "Night Things." The number of ghoul attacks in the outlying regions increases, and before long there can be no denying the nature of this new plague of violence. If the PCs let things go this far, you'll need to improvise, drawing upon the information given about Sandpoint in *Pathfinder* #1 as necessary.

Finally, keep in mind that normally those slain by Aldern Foxglove rise the next night as dread ghasts. The Sihedron ritual disrupts this process—any creature he kills and then offers to Karzoug via the ritual does not rise upon the next midnight. But as his murder spree continues, he might leave other victims unmarked, undead time-bombs that rise a night after their death to wreak even more mayhem on the town of Sandpoint.

Sandpoint Hinterlands

There are numerous locations in the Sandpoint Hinterlands capable of sustaining adventures on their own. The adventure seeds for the following locations will not be expanded upon in future *Pathfinders*, so you can develop them into your own adventures as best fits your campaign needs.

Brinestump Marsh: The Licktoad goblins, goblin snakes, giant geckos, and a few tribes of faceless stalkers are the primary menaces that dwell in this tangled fen, but persistent rumors of Old Megus the Swamp Witch are the primary reason locals avoid this region.

Dragon's Punchbowl: This bowl-shaped island is little more than a series of stony ridges surrounding a small lake; wyverns are said to roost in caves here, and rumors hold that a dragon visits the place once or twice a year for unknown reasons.

The Escarpments: These upthrust limestone pavements are bleak, stony regions. The smaller of the two (Ashen Rise) is relatively safe, but the edges of Devil's Platter are known haunts for the Birdcruncher goblins. Deeper in, it's rumored that the place is controlled by devil-worshiping bugbears that avoid the light of day but emerge at night from caves to light their fires.

Grubber's Hermitage: A notorious generator of shipwrecks, Grubber's Hermitage is a small, isolated thorp of a dozen fishing families. Their ways are their own and they generally don't welcome visitors; Sandpoint citizens theorize that the place is infested with lepers, ghosts, or worse.

The Moors: The moors that stretch through much of the hinterlands consist of poor-quality soil and stony ground. It is devoid of most vegetation apart from thick patches of tall grass and scattered copses of trees, and wolves, worgs, and worse are said to dwell here.

The Pit: Deep in the heart of the Devil's Platter is a sunken area ending in a ten-foot-wide hole that drops down into an inky dark. This is generally agreed to be the most likely lair of the Sandpoint Devil, though no one has yet dared to explore its depths.

Wisher's Well: One of the less-known Thassilonian ruins, this landmark consists of what appears to be a circular stone tower only 30 feet high from the outside, but drops away into a 100-foot-deep shaft ending in a deep pool of water on the inside. Of course, all manner of monsters are said to dwell in the flooded caverns below the well.

PART TWO: MISGIVINGS

The Misgivings is the local name for Foxglove Manor, a region shunned by locals for years as a place of shadowy menace, bad luck, and haunts. Before his transformation into a ghast, Lord Foxglove made attempts to rebuild and reclaim the place, but found few willing to work in the region due to its ill history. Of course, now that he's become undead, the house's reputation has played right into his murderous hands.

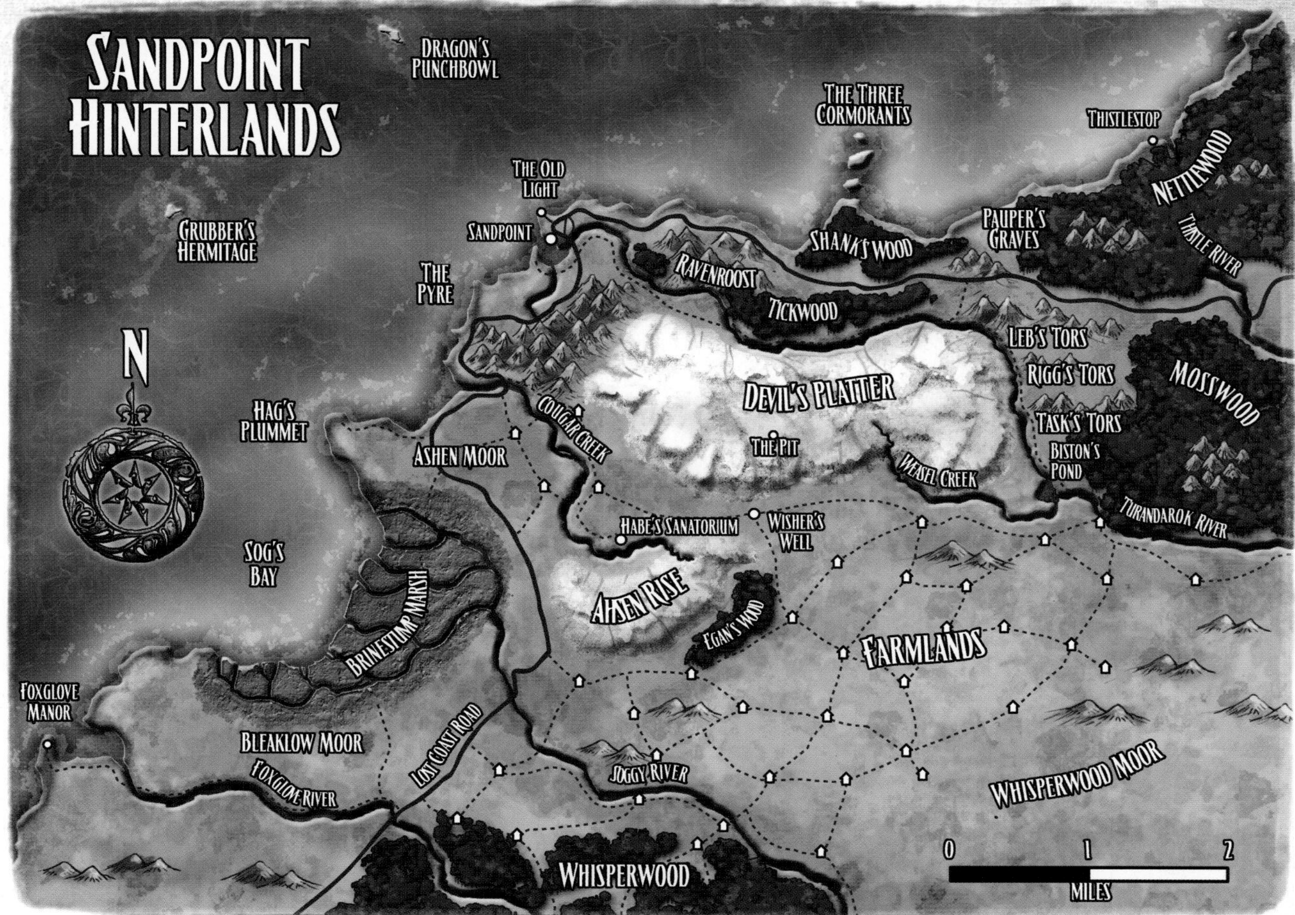

Approaching Foxglove Manor

The route leading out to Foxglove Manor is a three-mile hike along a narrow path that follows the Foxglove river from the covered bridge where it flows under the Lost Coast Road to the dark sea cliffs overlooking the Varisian Gulf. Here, wild sea birds call out to a roaring ocean that churns hundreds of feet below. As the PCs near Foxglove Manor, it almost seems as if nature herself becomes sick and twisted. Nettles and thorns grow more prominent, trees are leafless and bent, and the wind seems unnaturally cold and shrill as it whistles through the cliffside crags. The path slowly rises, turns a steep corner in the cliffs, and then Foxglove Manor looms at the edge of the world.

The strangely cold sea wind rises to a keening shriek as Foxglove Manor comes into view. The place has earned its local nickname of the "Misgivings" well, for it almost appears to loathe its perch high above the ocean, as if the entire house were poised for a suicide leap. The roof sags in many places, and mold and mildew cake the crumbling walls. Vines of diseased-looking gray wisteria strangle the structure in several places, hanging down over the precipitous cliff edge almost like tangled braids of hair. The house is crooked, its gables angling sharply and breached in at least three places, hastily repaired by planks of sodden wood. Chimneys rise from various points among the rooftops, leaning like old men in a storm, and grinning gargoyle faces leer from under the eaves. That the manor clings to the cliff is remarkable, as the whole far side is nothing more than a sheer drop down to the ocean below, a fall of over three hundred feet. Out front, the foundation stones of a long-burnt outbuilding stand sentinel astride the weed-choked approach; a low stone well squats morosely amid these ruins.

Foxglove Manor

Decay abounds inside Foxglove Manor. Ceilings sag, plaster heaves, and timbers rot. Inside, doors are often wedged shut by dampness and rot, requiring a DC 14 Strength check to open. Mold and stains mar walls and floors, often in strangely unsettling patterns (but never more so then in area **B3**). Rooms are unlit except where stated—during the day, the grime and mold encrusting the windows filter the sunlight to shadowy illumination within. When describing areas in Foxglove Manor, take pains to mention the little things now and then; the pervasive smell of decaying wood, the periodic groaning of the house's joists reacting to unaccustomed movement within, and the overall air of ancient neglect.

Foxglove Manor is, in fact, haunted by the spirit of Vorel Foxglove after his failed attempt to become a lich infused the entire structure and the caves below with his life-force. In many

Foxglove Manor
N
B1
B7
B6
B5
B2
B3
B4
B8
B9
Ground Floor

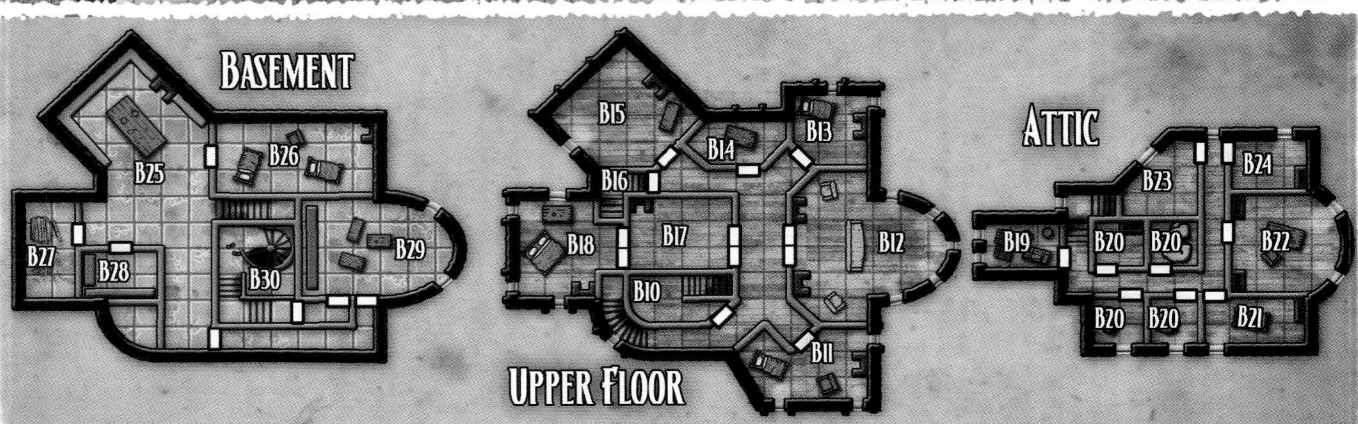
Basement
B25
B26
B27
B28
B30
B29
B15
B13
B14
B16
B18
B17
B12
B10
B11
Upper Floor
Attic
B23
B24
B19
B20
B20
B22
B20
B20
B21

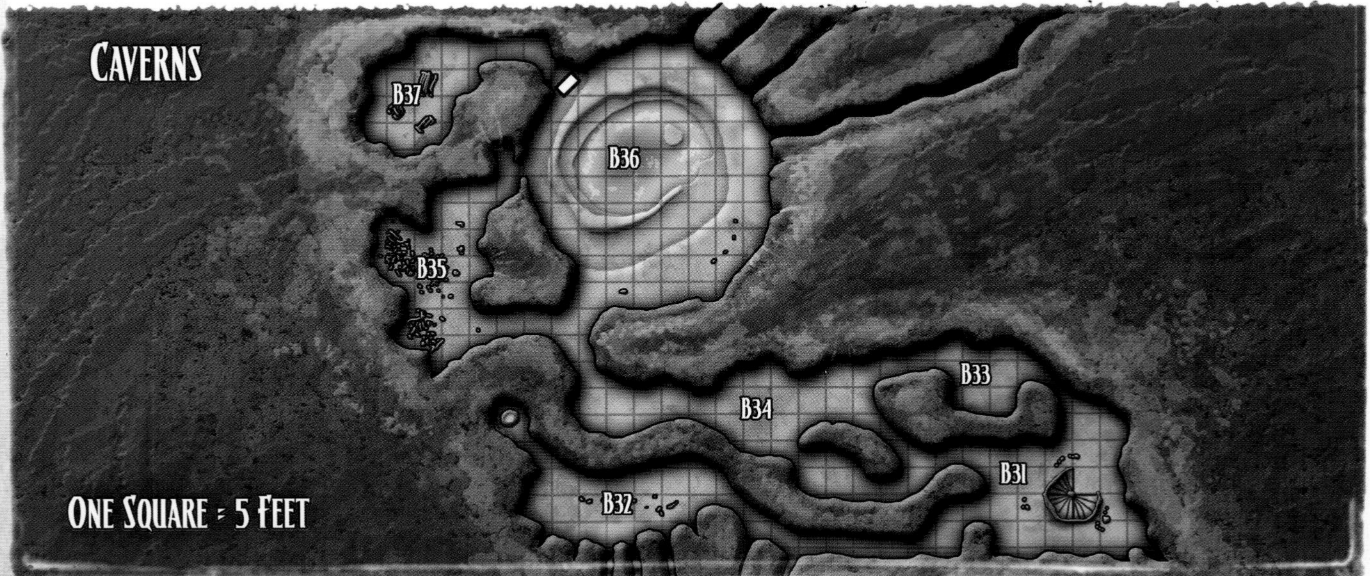
Caverns
B37
B36
B35
B33
B34
B31
B32
One Square = 5 Feet

FOXGLOVE MANOR LORE

Once the PCs realize that Foxglove Manor and its mysterious owner might be behind the murders and the ghoul problems in the farmlands, wise characters probably do a bit of research. The following information can be determined by making a Knowledge (local) check—the character learns all the information for the highest DC he hits as well as the information for lower DCs. Alternately, a character could get the same information by spending 1d4 hours and 1d6 gp in Sandpoint making Gather Information checks.

Check DC	Information Gained
12	Foxglove Manor is 80 years old, and has been the seat of the Foxglove family the whole time. Some sort of tragedy struck the family a few decades ago, and no one's lived there since. Common rumor holds that the place is haunted.
15	Foxglove Manor is known as the "Misgivings" by some locals, particularly the Varisians. It certainly has a bad reputation—sightings of strange lights in the attic windows, muffled sounds of screaming from above and below, and even rumors of a huge bat-winged devil living in caves below the manor are but a few of the tales told about the place. The Foxglove family lived there as recently as two decades ago, but then a fire burned down the servant's building, Cyralie Foxglove was found dead—burnt and dashed on the rocks below the cliffs behind the house—and Traver Foxglove was found in his bedroom, dead by his own hand. The children, including young Aldern Foxglove, were sent away to be raised in Korvosa by distant relations.
20	Aldern Foxglove recently returned to live in the manor, but he had a hell of a time hiring locals to aid him in the reconstruction and repair of the old building. Until Aldern moved back in, the place was cared for by a man named Rogors Craesby who came in three days a week from Sandpoint to air the place out, check for squatters, and make minor repairs.
25	Foxglove Manor was built by Vorel Foxglove, a merchant prince from Magnimar. He and his family lived there for 20 years before the entire family perished from disease. The surviving Foxgloves of Magnimar shunned the place for 40 years, until Traver Foxglove moved back in.
30	The Foxgloves have traditionally been associated with the Brothers of the Seven, a secret society based in Magnimar and consisting of merchants or thieves, depending on who you talk to. Members of the society periodically visited Foxglove Manor at night during the years the manor went unlived in, perhaps to check up on the building and make minor repairs, or perhaps for more sinister pursuits.

FOXGLOVE MANOR TIMELINE

This timeline presents the major events in Foxglove Manor's history. The current year is 4707 AR.

Date	Notable Events
4624 AR	Foxglove Manor built by Vorel Foxglove. Construction is funded partially by the Brothers of the Seven, with the understanding that after 100 years, ownership of the manor reverts to them.
4644 AR	Vorel Foxglove attempts to become a lich, but when his wife Kasanda interrupts the ritual and destroys his phylactery, the botched ritual backfires and consumes him in a storm of disease and tumors. His body destroyed, his life-force becomes infused into the house above. Kasanda tries to escape with her child, but is infected with the disease as well and spreads it to her kids and servants; they all perish within minutes of contracting the horrific disease.
4687 AR	Vorel's great-nephew, Traver Foxglove, and his family move into the manor; Aldern Foxglove is born.
4693 AR	Cyralie burns the servants' quarters but is thrown from the window in the observatory by Traver when she tries to burn the manor. Traver takes his own life, and the children are taken to Korvosa to be raised by relations.
4706 AR	Aldern Foxglove returns to Foxglove Manor and begins restoration work.
8 months ago	Aldern meets Iesha; the two are married by the end of the week.
3 months ago	Aldern murders Iesha and stows her body in the attic. Iesha rises as a revenant that night, but is unable to escape the room she's locked inside. Her periodic sobs and shrieks add a new layer to the rumors that the house is haunted. Aldern seeks help from the Brothers of the Seven to cover up the murder.
1 month ago	Aldern goes bankrupt after being blackmailed by the Brothers of the Seven. To pay off the remainder of his debts to the Brothers, he agrees to return to Foxglove Manor and collect diseased rats for them.
Campaign begins	Before returning to Foxglove Manor, Aldern visits Sandpoint to steel his nerves; he attends the Swallowtail Festival, meets the PCs, and becomes obsessed with one of them.
1 week after campaign begins	Aldern eventually returns to Foxglove Manor; he hears Iesha's sobs in the attic above, but thinking that her body has long since been taken away by the Brothers of the Seven, assumes he's imagining her ghost. His obsession with the PC grows as he toils day and night to dig through to the caverns below. Eventually he enters the caverns, gathers samples of the fungus for Xanesha, and contracts ghoul fever.

ways, Foxglove Manor is Vorel's phylactery, and all who enter its walls are entering the mind of this long-dead murderer and necromancer. Yet Vorel's existence as a haunting presence does not manifest as a single undead monster that can be fought and defeated—he's more like an overall aura or taint that suffuses the entire building. Certainly, his haunting presence makes the place comfortable for the undead, and ghouls have long dwelt in the caverns below. Of course, as long as he dwells within the building's walls and foundations, Vorel can make destroying the manor difficult, to say the least.

Vorel can make his influence felt anywhere inside of Foxglove Manor or in the caverns below the house. For the most part, his presence manifests as small events intended to enhance the unpleasant feeling inside the house, little more than tricks of the light and vague feelings of unease. In certain parts of the house, though, Vorel can create more potent effects. These effects are detailed in the following encounter areas.

There are two obvious entrances into Foxglove Manor, the front doors (which lead into area **B2**) and the side doors (which lead into area **B7**). In both cases, the doors are locked; they can be opened with a DC 30 Open Lock check, or by the key carried by Rogors Craesby. Numerous windows could provide entrance into the manor as well; the unbroken, grime-encrusted panes of glass in their frames speak not only of the Foxglove family's wealth in being able to afford such an extravagance, but also of the manor's notorious reputation—no vandals have dared break them. The windows themselves are curtained from the inside, but it's a relatively simple matter to break most of them and climb into the room beyond. Clambering up onto an upper story or the roof requires a DC 20 Climb check—there are numerous handholds, but of those, many are rotten and crumble under any weight. Finally, characters can attempt to enter the house via the hidden tunnel connected to the well, but doing so places them in immediate danger in area **B32**.

Haunts

Haunts function somewhat like traps, but are difficult to detect since they do not "exist" until they are triggered. When a haunt is triggered, its effects manifest at initiative rank 10 on a surprise round; the haunt effect vanishes as soon as the surprise round is over and things return to normal (haunts never persist into actual round-by-round combat). Any characters haunted by the effect (all creatures for universal haunts, but only single characters for other types of haunts—see below) can make a specific skill check to notice the haunt in time to react—if he notices it, he may make an initiative check to determine when he acts in the round. Once a haunt is active, a successful turn undead attempt against the haunt's effective Hit Dice ends it immediately, although the character making the turn attempt must notice the haunt and act before it in the surprise round it is activated. If the turning attempt results in a destruction result, that particular haunt is exorcised and permanently disabled. Given many years, Vorel's sprit could rebuild an exorcised haunting, but in the short term it remains harmless. Once a haunting is triggered, it does not trigger again for 24 hours.

Each haunt is given a subcategory; before the PCs enter Foxglove Manor, you should assign one of these categories to each PC, jotting down their assignments on a piece of paper (do not reveal them to the PCs). When a haunt of a certain category occurs, it only affects those PCs—other characters can aid the PC in question, but can't interact with or observe the haunting as it occurs (although *detect evil* and *true seeing* allow non-haunted individuals to notice or observe the haunting's effects). When assigning haunts to your PCs, try to keep one PC to a haunt—if you have more than six PCs in your group, though, you'll either need to double up on some of them or invent new categories of your own. No PC should be assigned to more than one haunt; if you have fewer than six PCs in your group, unassigned haunts become universal haunts.

Universal Haunt: These haunts affect everyone in the vicinity—they represent the most emotional and primal of Vorel's undead rages. All PCs experience universal haunts.

Festering Haunt: These haunts are associated with Vorel's painful death, consumed by the necromantic backlash that unleashed a thousand diseases in his flesh. This haunt should be assigned to a PC who has a history of disease, a fear of sickness, or who is the most accepting of necromancy and the undead.

Wrathful Haunt: Linked to Vorel's wife, this haunt is infused with Vorel's rage and hatred of women, fueled by his wife's betrayal and disruption of the lichdom ritual he attempted moments before his death. This haunt should be assigned to a female PC, or to a character who has had some form of betrayal affect him in the past.

Burning Haunt: This haunt is linked to Cyralie Foxglove. She tried to burn Foxglove Manor down when she realized it was driving her husband Traver mad, but succeeded only in burning down the servants' building before she was slain by Traver. This haunt should be assigned to the most violent character, the character with the greatest obsession with fire, or the character most prone to loneliness and depression.

Insane Haunt: Traver Foxglove, an accomplished hunter and loyal husband, managed to resist Vorel's influence for many years but was eventually driven to deeper and deeper madness. This haunt should be assigned to the most impulsive character, or to the character regarded by the players as the least trustworthy or most prone to unexpected actions.

Obsessed Haunt: Linked to Aldern, this haunt plays off of Aldern's obsession with one of the PCs as much as it does Vorel's obsession with endless life. This haunt should be assigned to the PC who Aldern is obsessed with.

Vengeful Haunt: This final haunt is associated with Iesha, Aldern's murdered wife, and carries with it a burning need for revenge and retribution. This haunt should be assigned to a PC who has expressed a need for revenge, or who is currently involved in a romantic relationship.

Any character foolish enough to sleep in Foxglove Manor exposes himself to Vorel's presence even more. Such creatures experience disturbing dreams, either of being trapped in a crumbling house with no exits that grows smaller and smaller with each breath (for male characters) or of being stalked through a house by a shapeless monster that wishes to do them harm or drive them to kill themselves by exposing their mistakes and weaknesses in the form of horrific visions (for female characters). In either case, a sleeping character must make a DC 15 Will save upon waking to avoid taking 1d4 points of Wisdom damage from the horrific dreams—a character that takes Wisdom damage also wakens fatigued.

Each haunt is assigned a CR score, calculated as if it were a trap. For experiencing and surviving a haunt, award the entire party experience points as if they had defeated a creature of that CR. All haunts are mind-affecting fear effects, even those like the burning manticore in area **B2** that produce physical effects like fire damage.

B1. Ruined Servants' Quarters (EL 5)

It's impossible to tell how many floors the outbuilding that stood here once had, for all that remains are the crumbling stones of its foundation. The stones still bear scorches and cracks from the fire that destroyed the building long ago. To the east, a four-foot-wide stone well sits, partially collapsed, in the corner of the ruins.

The well drops 100 feet into a 50-foot-deep pool of rainwater. Just above the level of the water, a passageway leads southwest into area **B32**. An overhang makes it difficult to notice this opening from above—if the PCs can see this far into the darkness, it's a DC 25 Spot check to notice the passage from the surface (this DC accounts for distance modifiers).

Creatures: The first time the PCs pass by this area, a few sickly looking ravens are perched atop the foundation stones; they fly clumsily away once approached. The second time the PCs pass by (likely on their way out of the manor), hundreds upon thousands of ravens sit quietly in this area, covering every square foot of the ruins. These ravens are disturbingly silent and still, watching as one as the PCs approach. As soon as anyone comes within 30 feet, the ravens take to the air and swoop to attack, only then revealing their true natures. These ravens are, in fact, three swarms of undead birds known as carrionstorms, created when carrion birds feed upon ghoul-tainted flesh. The carrionstorms can sense Vorel's influence in the area, and although the evil spirit cannot control them directly, the birds do their best to kill anyone attempting to escape the manor. They pursue foes as far as the Lost Coast Road, but do not follow those who flee back into the manor—their goal, after all, is to return the intruders to Vorel's cradle for him to deal with personally.

Carrionstorms (5) **CR 1**
hp 13 each; see page 83

B2. Entrance Hall (EL 3)

The sound of the house straining and creaking gives this long, high-ceilinged room an additional sense of age and decay. The place smells damp, the unpleasant tinge of mold lacing the air as surely as it stains the wooden floor, walls, and furniture in pallid patches. A curving flight of stairs to the south winds up to the upper floor, while a pair of large stone fireplaces brood to the north and south. Heavy dark-blue curtains hang over the windows, and the frames above each of the two doors are carved with dancing gargoyles and skeletons. Trophies hang on the wall to the northeast: a boar, a bear, a firepelt cougar, and a stag, their glassy eyes staring from fur crusted with mold and cobwebs, yet they pale in comparison to the monster on display in the center of the room. Here crouches a twelve-foot-long creature with the body of a lion, a scorpion's tail fitted with dozens of razor barbs, huge bat-like wings, and a deformed humanoid face. The stuffed beast's poorly maintained fur has fallen away in places, allowing the sawdust filling it to sift out into tiny mounds on the platform below.

Nothing major occurs the first time the PCs enter this room, although you should allow the PCs a DC 20 Listen check—success indicates that they hear what sounds like a brief set of sobs coming from somewhere upstairs. These noises come from Iesha in area **B24**—feel free to ask the PCs to make additional Listen checks now and then to catch a brief snatch of her sobbing as they explore the manor.

Haunt: The first time the PCs enter this area, the PC haunted by burning catches a momentary whiff of burning hair and flesh. The second time the PCs pass through this area, the haunting manifests in a much more dramatic manner, as the manticore (killed and preserved by Traver Foxglove) lurches to sudden life, its face shifting to resemble that of Cyralie Foxglove and its fur erupting into flame. Its tail strikes forward against the victim in an attempt to burn him, then returns to normal.

Burning Manticore **CR 3**
Type burning
Notice Spot DC 20; **Effective HD** 6

EFFECTS

Trigger proximity; **Reset** automatic (24 hours)
Effect Atk +8 touch (burning stinger against one target in area **B2**, 4d6 fire damage); Reflex DC 15 to avoid catching on fire (these flames burn only the haunted target, and cannot spread to other creatures or objects)

B3. The Spiral Stain

A rather gruesome antique—what appears to be a mummified monkey head—hangs on the northern wall here. A bellpull extends from the monkey's gaping mouth. A ratty throw rug partially obscures a foul stain of dark-colored mold on the floor.

The stain under the rug is about ten feet across, a swirling pattern of dark blue, sickly green, and black mold that grows in a spiral. If examined closely with a DC 20 Search check, it looks almost like an image of a spiraling staircase descending downward, with each step littered with skulls and bones. The stain itself is a harmless manifestation of Vorel's spirit, a clue to the entrance to the caverns below—it grows back within 24 hours if scrubbed away. Traver and his family took to covering it with a throw rug.

Treasure: The monkey head is actually a minor wondrous item called the *hungry decapitant*. When the attached rope is pulled, the head gives out a shrill simian shriek akin to an *alarm* spell. The strange curio, one of the few remaining from Traver's time in the house, was used to signal the start of dinner. It can be removed from the wall easily, and continues to function thereafter. It's worth 500 gp.

B4. Dining Room

A large mahogany table surrounded by high-backed chairs sits in this room. The table is covered by a moldy white cloth, and a cobweb-choked chandelier hangs from the ceiling above. Twin fireplaces loom to the west, while to the east, a bank of stained glass windows obscures what could have been a breathtaking view of the Lost Coast. Each of the windows depicts a stylized monster rising out of smoke pouring from an intricate seven-sided box covered with spiky runes. From north to south are depicted a gnarled and tangled tree with an enraged face, an immense hook-beaked bird with sky-blue and gold plumage, a winged centaur-like creature with a lion's lower body and a snarling woman's upper torso, and a deep blue squid-like creature with evil red eyes.

Here, as in areas **B12**, **B22**, and **B29**, stained glass windows look out over the Varisian gulf. A DC 15 Knowledge (architecture and engineering) check notes that it was an unusual design choice to fit the rooms with arguably the best view of the Lost Coast with windows one cannot see through—this hint speaks to the importance of the images, constituting a set of hidden clues left by Lord Vorel Foxglove.

The route to lichdom is a personal quest. While each prospective lich can build upon the discoveries and methods of previous necromancers, the actual formula varies from soul to soul. Proud of his accomplishments, yet knowing he couldn't brag of them to most folk, Vorel instead decided to commemorate his personal path to lichdom with the banks of stained-glass windows in these four rooms, using symbolism and metaphor instead of facts and figures. The four stages of his process are meant to be read from attic to basement; the stained glass windows here depict the third step of his procedure—the construction of his phylactery. Vorel built his phylactery from body parts harvested from four exceptionally long-lived monsters, and each of these stained-glass windows depicts one of the four—a treant, a roc, a sphinx, and a kraken. A DC 25 Knowledge (arcana) check is enough to note that the runes on the box are necromancy-related, that the monsters seem not to be emerging from the boxes but rather being drawn in, and that perhaps their snarling visages aren't of rage but of fear.

B5. Lounge (EL 4)

This dusty room features a long couch, its cushions caked with white sheets of wispy fungus. The couch faces a stone fireplace with capering imps and birds carved along its mantel. Eddies of dust skitter along the warped floorboards as if caught up by a slight breeze, yet no wind is noticeable in the air.

Haunt: Any character who examines the dust closely and makes a DC 20 Spot check notices that the dust seems to be being disturbed, as if an invisible person were pacing violently back and forth before the fireplace—footprints even manifest momentarily in the dust with each step before fading from view. A character who attempts to pass through the path of the unseen pacer exposes himself to a brief flash of memory—a woman's memory filled with worry about what her husband might be doing on those late nights spent in the basement. An instant later, the character is suddenly convinced that one of the other PCs is his child, and develops a powerful urge to escape the house with that PC before something horrible happens.

WORRIED WIFE — **CR 4**

Type universal

Notice Listen DC 20 (to hear a woman's voice whisper, "Lorey"—this was the name of Vorel's and Kasanda's daughter) **Effective HD** 8

EFFECTS

Trigger proximity; **Reset** automatic (24 hours)

Effect spell effect (*suggestion* to drag another PC out of the house to area **B1**, likely into the gathering mass of carrionstorms; Will DC 14 resists; CL 8th)

B6. Washroom (CR 1/3)

This is a simple washroom. An ancient metal washtub stands to the west, a ring of mildew crusting its inner surface. A strange, furtive scratching comes from inside the tub.

Creature: Rats have always been a problem in Foxglove Manor, especially now. The creatures nest in the walls and caverns below, and most of them have been exposed to the dangerous mold growing in area **B37**. One such rat has fallen into the tub and cannot escape. The creature is a horrific and pitiful sight, a rodent the size of a cat whose face and back are a dripping, pulsing mass of raw tumors and sores. The rat is blind; the tumors have grown over its eyes, but it can still use scent to locate anyone nearby—if it does so, it begins shrieking and squeaking in a frenzy, making a DC 25 Climb check each round in a desperate attempt to clamber out of the tub and feed on anyone it smells.

DISEASED RAT — **CR 1/3**

hp 1 (MM 278)

AC 10, touch 10, flat-footed 10

SPECIAL ABILITIES

Blind (Ex) The rat is blind, and while this makes it immune to sight-based attacks, it also takes a –2 penalty to its AC, loses its Dexterity bonus to AC, moves at half-speed, and takes a –4 penalty on Search checks and most Strength- and Dexterity-based skill checks. Its scent ability negates concealment for its foes.

Disease (Su) Vorel's Phage—bite, Fortitude DC 10, incubation period

1 day, damage 1d4 Cha and 1d4 Con. The save DC is Constitution-based, unlike the source fungi in area **B37** which have a static DC.

B7. Dancing Parlor (EL 3)

This oak-paneled chamber must have once been breathtaking, but is a sad sight now—the floorboards are warped with moisture and the paneling scratched and splotchy with mold. A once-magnificent crystal chandelier lies smashed on the floor, while frescoes depicting dancing scenes have been ruined by rot and are barely recognizable. A grand piano, its surface splotchy and keys warped, leans tiredly in the southeast corner.

Haunt: Foxglove Manor was too small for a full-sized ballroom, so this dancing parlor saw much use in the relatively few years the home was inhabited. In particular, Aldern's wife Iesha enjoyed dancing here for her new husband, spinning in ever-increasing pirouettes of Varisian ecstasy to the sounds of the piano. An investigation of the piano with a Perform (keyboard) check reveals that the piano seems unnaturally decayed, as if it had been standing unattended here for decades, yet if any keys are depressed, they are in perfect tune.

As soon as any of the piano's keys are pressed, the instrument explodes into sudden music, playing a catchy but discordant Varisian song. A character in the room with the vengeful haunt is suddenly swept into a series of rapidly increasing pirouettes, and leaps across the room in the arms of an invisible dance partner. The haunted PC can, of course, see his partner: Iesha in all her vibrant beauty. Unlike most of the haunts, this one persists for several rounds. Each round that passes, Iesha's beauty grows less as her neck darkens into an angry blue-and-black bruise, her eyes bulge and water, her mouth twists in pain, and her tongue protrudes as if she were being invisibly strangled. In the final round of the haunt, she crumbles away into rot in her partner's arms.

DANCE OF RUIN **CR 3**
Type vengeful
Notice Listen DC 15; **Effective HD** 6

EFFECTS

Trigger touch; **Reset** automatic (24 hours)
Effect The haunted character is caught up in a whirling dance and spins wildly through the room for 1d6 rounds, taking 1 point of Strength damage each round (a DC 15 Will save ends the dance early); once the dance ends, the character becomes fatigued. If the character can be successfully grappled and pinned, Iesha shrieks in rage as the haunt ends prematurely; her shriek causes 1d2 points of Wisdom damage to all in the room (DC 15 Will save negates).

B8. Drawing Room

This cozy-looking drawing room is marred by the unnatural dampness and the thick sheets of mold that cling to the curtains closed over the southern window.

VOREL'S PHAGE

This hideous malady can be contracted from the bites of the diseased rats that infest Foxglove Manor, or by touching or eating the fungus growing on the wall of area **B37**. To those who are of Vorel's blood, the disease works at the victims' minds, slowly driving them insane—and eventually causing death and transformation into a dread ghast or other undead menace. To most victims, though, the phage causes a painful and hideous outbreak of facial tumors and a sickening deterioration of the skin across the entire body.

Infection—contact or ingestion; Fortitude DC 20; Incubation 1 day; Damage 1d4 Charisma and 1d4 Constitution.

A character who opens the curtains sees a brief glimpse of a forlorn woman's face reflected in the window beyond—Iesha's. The reflection vanishes an instant later and does not remanifest.

B9. Library (EL 5)

This library features a pair of chairs, one of which lies on its side, set before a stone fireplace. Every available inch of wall space features floor-to-ceiling bookshelves filled with books, their spines riddled with

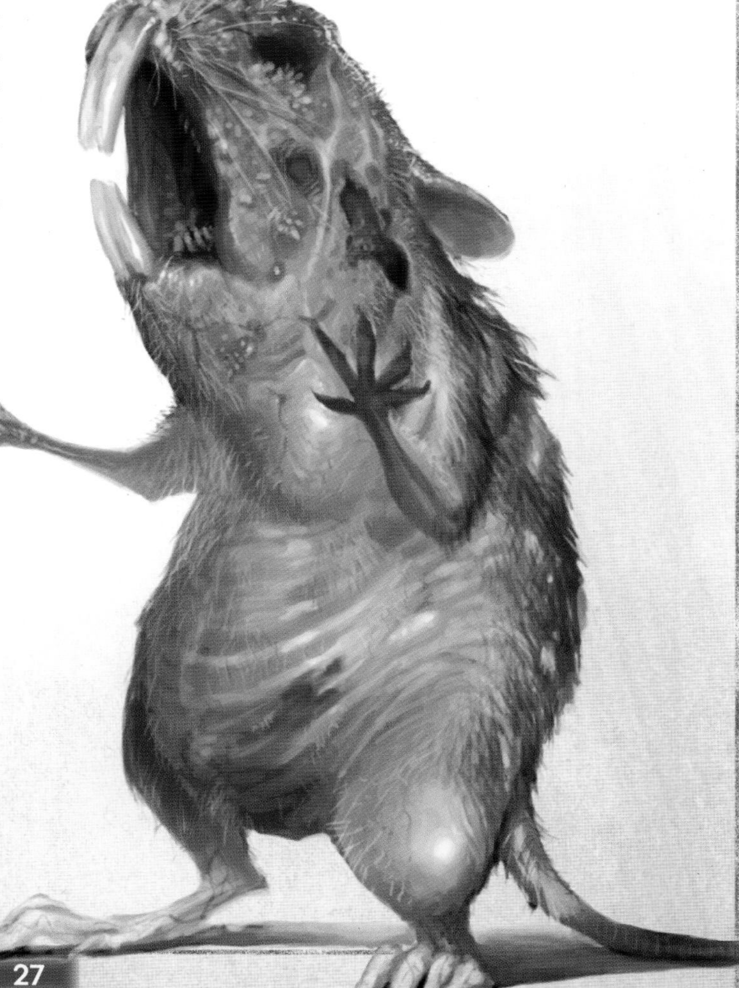

mold. A brightly colored scarf, its reds and golds contrasting sharply with the drab, moldy palette of the room, is draped over the side of the fallen chair. A single book, open and face-down, sits on the floor between the chairs. A stone bookend, carved to look like a praying angel with butterfly wings, lies on its side in the fireplace itself.

An investigation of this room reveals some disturbing clues. A splash of dried blood stains the back of the northernmost chair, and an examination of the bookend reveals more blood, clots of hair, and bits of skull and flesh—in addition, part of one wing has been broken off and is missing.

Haunt: This room was where Aldern murdered his wife and an innocent carpenter only a few short months ago. Already under Vorel's growing influence, he returned home drunk one night and found the two here, huddled in the chairs by the fire, their heads almost touching as they leaned toward each other. Aldern mistook their shared examination of a book on Varisian history for passion and roared into the room, sweeping up a stone bookend from a shelf as he approached. He brained the carpenter with the bookend, knocking him senseless, then dropped the bookend and strangled Iesha with her own scarf. He hid her body upstairs and dumped the carpenter down the well (where he survived only long enough to be killed by the dread ghoul dire bat in area **B32**).

This room's haunt activates as soon as the PC haunted by vengeance approaches within 5 feet of the scarf. At this point, a horrific shriek fills the room as the scarf flies into the air to wrap around the haunted PC's throat.

IESHA'S VENGEANCE **CR 5**

Type vengeful

Notice Spot DC 15 (to notice the scarf moving on its own); **Effective HD** 10

EFFECTS

Trigger proximity; **Reset** automatic (24 hours)

Effect When Iesha's scarf unerringly wraps around the haunted character's throat, he must make a DC 16 Will save to avoid being paralyzed with fear as a ghostly image of Aldern manifests before him and appears to be using the scarf to choke him to death; at the same moment, the haunted character loses sense of himself and believes he has become Iesha. He must then make a DC 16 Fortitude save—success indicates he merely takes 3d6 points of nonlethal damage, but failure indicates he is immediately reduced to –8 hit points and is dying.

Treasure: Once the haunt is over, Iesha's scarf settles to the ground, lifeless. It is a work of art worth 100 gp, and can be used to influence Iesha's revenant in area **B24**.

B10. Stairwell

As PCs traverse this flight of stairs, their footsteps echo back at them a round later, as though an invisible person were following them. Although this might seem like a supernatural haunting, the effect is purely natural—the noise is simply the floorboards settling back after they are walked upon.

B11. Aldern's Bedroom (EL 3)

This bedroom features a child-sized bed, a chair next to a toy box, and a looming stone fireplace big enough for a child to get lost in.

Haunt: When Cyralie Foxglove tried to burn down the manor, she started (and succeeded) with the servants' quarters. She then moved back into the house, intending to reach area **B22** to light her second fire in Traver's favorite room. Her children saw her, wild-eyed and brandishing a torch, and when they saw their father attack their mother in that room, they ran down here to hide.

FRIGHTENED CHILD **CR 3**

Type obsessed

Notice Listen DC 15 (to hear the sound of a child sobbing); **Effective HD** 6

EFFECTS

Trigger proximity; **Reset** automatic (24 hours)

Effect The haunted character suddenly becomes convinced that his parents are trying to kill each other, and that whichever of them survives will be coming to kill him next; he has a vision of his mother, wielding a torch, and his father, festering with tumors and wielding a long knife, both struggling to kill each other. The vision passes as fast as it occurs, at which point the haunted PC must make a DC 14 Will save to avoid taking 1d4 points of Wisdom damage from the mind-numbing terror of the sight.

B12. Musicians' Gallery

This large room features two padded chairs and a long couch facing a wide alcove lined with stained-glass windows. Several music stands lean against the southern wall next to a violin, two flutes, and a large harp; all three instruments are in poor condition. The windows themselves depict a diverse array of animals and plants—from north to south are a large pale and ghostly scorpion, a gaunt man holding out his arms as a dozen bats hang from him, a moth with a strange skull-like pattern on its wings, a tangle of dull green plants with bell-shaped flowers, and a young maiden sitting astride a well in a forest while a spindly spider the size of a dog descends along a string of webbing above her.

A DC 20 Knowledge (arcana) check identifies all five of the subjects in the windows as classic spell components for necromancy magic (scorpion venom, vampire's breath, the tongues of deathwing moths, belladonna, and the heart of a maiden slain by poison); if the check exceeds this DC by 10 or more, those spell components are recognized as having ties to several known lich apotheosis formulas.

B13. Guest Bedchamber (EL 3)

This entire bedroom is caked with a thick, spongy layer of dark green, blue, and black mold.

Although disgusting and foul-smelling, the mold in this room is a harmless manifestation of the evil spirits in Foxglove Manor; if destroyed, it regrows within 24 hours.

Haunt: After disrupting Vorel's attempt to become a lich, Kasanda fled back up from the caverns below Foxglove Manor to seek out her daughter and then escape, yet by the time she reached this room (her daughter's bedroom), Vorel had already suffused the walls of the place with his evil. Kasanda realized she was being overtaken by his phage when her daughter saw her face and screamed in terror; the disease quickly spread to her daughter and their servants. Every living thing in Foxglove Manor was dead within only a few minutes, their bodies deformed and twisted.

Both Kasanda and her daughter perished of the phage in here, and when the PC associated with the festering haunt enters the room, he suddenly feels an itching on his face. Although to his companions nothing seems amiss, the PC feels as if his face has suddenly erupted into a tangled mess of tumors and boils, lasting just long enough for him to attempt to claw the offending sickness from his skull.

Phantom Phage **CR 3**

Type festering

Notice Listen DC 15 (to hear a child's voice, quivering with fear, ask "What's on your face, mommy?"; **Effective HD** 6

EFFECTS

Trigger proximity; **Reset** automatic (24 hours)

Effect The haunted character must make a DC 14 Will save; failure indicates he claws desperately at the flesh of his own face, dealing 1d6 points of damage and 1d4 points of Charisma damage.

B14. Upstairs Washroom (EL 1)

An iron tub sits in the middle of this room, the floorboards around it sagging with the tub's weight.

Trap: The floor in this room has grown unstable recently—any Medium or larger creature that enters the room triggers a collapse that drops him down into area **B6**.

Collapsing Floor **CR 1**

Type mechanical

Search DC 20; **Disable Device** DC 25

EFFECTS

Trigger location; **Reset** repair

Effect 10-foot fall (1d6); multiple targets (all creatures in area **B14**); DC 15 Reflex save avoids.

B15. Master Bedroom (EL 3)

This once-fine chamber has been destroyed. The bed is smashed, mattress torn apart, walls gouged as if by knives, chairs hacked apart, and paintings on the walls torn to pieces—with one exception. A portrait hanging on the northwest wall seems to be untouched, although it hangs backward, its unseen subject facing the wall.

The master bedroom was destroyed by Aldern after he hid Iesha's body in the attic, although in his fit of rage he couldn't bear to destroy the portrait of his wife he'd commissioned a few months before. If turned around, the portrait reveals a beautiful dark-haired woman in a thoughtful pose.

Upon seeing the portrait, a PC haunted by obsession experiences a sudden wave of sadness, and a PC haunted by vengeance a sudden wave of fear. These emotions pass quickly without any real game effect.

Haunt: Although the room was recently destroyed by Aldern, the haunt that suffuses the chamber is keyed to the room's first inhabitants—Vorel and Kasanda Foxglove. Only 1d4 rounds after a character haunted by wrath enters this room, he suddenly becomes dizzy and staggers, even if he has since left the room. An instant later, the dizzy spell passes but he becomes filled with an overwhelming hatred of women, and for 1d4 rounds is driven by an urge to attack the closest woman.

Misogynistic Rage **CR 3**

Type wrathful

Notice Listen DC 15 (to hear the sound of a woman's shrill voice saying, "What do you get up to down in the damp below?"; **Effective HD** 6

EFFECTS

Trigger proximity; **Reset** automatic (24 hours)

Effect The haunted character must make a DC 14 Will save or be compelled to attack the closest female, using all of his capabilities in an attempt to kill the target—this haunting continues beyond the surprise round for 1d4 rounds. If no suitable target is within sight he instead attacks himself, leaping out the window if no weapon is handy.

B16. Stairwell

These stairs lead up to the attic. The door to this stairwell is locked but can be picked with a DC 25 Open Lock check or smashed down with a DC 24 Strength check—the key to the lock is long lost.

B17. Gallery (EL 3)

A stone fireplace sits in the northwestern portion of this chamber. Paintings hang on the walls to the north and south, each covered over with a thick sheet of dusty cobwebs that obscures its subject from view.

Wiping away the dusty cobwebs over the paintings reveals them to be portraits of the previous tenants of Foxglove Manor. The three to the north depict Vorel and Kasanda Foxglove and their daughter Lorey. Vorel is a tall, middle-aged man with long dark hair, a clean-shaven face, and dark blue noble's clothes, while Kasanda is a stern-faced brunette woman with wisps of gray in her short hair and a flowing blue dress. The five to the south show Traver and Cyralie Foxglove, their son Aldern, and their two daughters Sendeli and Zeeva. Traver, like Vorel, is tall and thin, but with an even narrower face and a thin mustache. Cyralie is a young woman with long red hair and an impish smile. Each painting bears a plaque that identifies those pictured within.

Haunt: As soon as all of the portraits have their cobwebs cleared away, the temperature in the room drops dramatically. Breath frosts in the air and fingers of rime slither across the walls. The figures depicted in the portraits suddenly shift from paintings of living people to those of dead folk. Kasanda and Lorey slump into misshapen tumor-ridden corpses. Traver grows pale as a long cut opens in his throat and blood washes down over his chest. Cyralie blackens and chars, and her arms, legs, and back twist as if broken in dozens of places. Aldern's flesh darkens with rot, his hair falls out, and he deforms into a ghoul-like monster. Both Sendeli and Zeeva's portraits frost over but otherwise remain unchanged. Vorel's entire portrait, frame and all, erupts into a sudden explosion of fungus and tumorous growth. This wave of fungus and disease washes over the entire room in seconds before the room suddenly reverts to normal.

THE STRICKEN FAMILY **CR 3**

Type universal

Notice Wisdom DC 10 (to notice the room start to grow cold); **Effective HD** 6

EFFECTS

Trigger proximity; **Reset** automatic (24 hours)

Effect When the room explodes into rot and fungal decay, every PC in the room must make a DC 14 Fortitude save to avoid contracting Vorel's Phage (see page 27). Once the room reverts to normal, those characters who failed their saves can see tiny splotches of mold and tender red bumps on their flesh, but until the disease has a chance to incubate, these symptoms remain invisible to others.

B18. Bedroom (EL 4)

The furniture in this bedroom, while dusty and unkempt, does not exhibit any major signs of water or mold damage. The one exception is a dark stain on the desk near the northern window.

Haunt: After Traver Foxglove killed his wife in area **B22**, the shock of watching her burning body plummet into the waves below allowed him to regain control of his mind and body. He could feel Vorel out there still, trying to claw his way back into his flesh, but for a few moments at least, Traver was his own man again. In a desperate (some might say cowardly) move, he fled to here, the room he and his wife had shared, sat down at his desk, and slit his own throat with his dagger.

As soon as a PC haunted by insanity enters this room, he shudders and is suddenly overwhelmed with the conviction that he has just killed the person he loves most. Overwhelmed with despair, he moves to the desk, retrieves what appears to be a silver-handled dagger from it, and tries to cut his own throat. Anyone who attempts to stop him is instead attacked. If he survives, the "dagger" reverts to its true form—a splintered but very sharp length of wood.

SUICIDE COMPULSION **CR 4**

Type insane

Notice Spot DC 20 (to notice the appearance of a dagger on the desk that, an instant before, was not there); **Effective HD** 8

EFFECTS

Trigger proximity; **Reset** automatic (24 hours)

Effect The haunted character must make a DC 15 Will save. Failure indicates he moves over to the desk and attempts a coup de grace action on himself with the jagged length of wood, dealing 2d4 (plus twice his Strength modifer) points of damage on himself. He must make a Fortitude save (DC 10 + the damage dealt) to avoid being slain by this suicide attempt. If anyone tries to prevent the attempt, the haunted character makes a single attack against that person with the "dagger." If he hits, the supernaturally guided strike automatically scores a critical hit. After this attack, the "dagger" turns back into wood.

B19. Workroom

A large number of planks of wood, rope, and other repair supplies are stored here. The ceiling above sags noticeably; in several areas patches of the sky above are visible. Dozens of ceramic urns and metal pots sit on the floor below to catch leaks.

This room was partially repaired by Aldern and his hired assistants, but they didn't finish the job before Vorel's spirit manifested.

B20. Storerooms

Each of these rooms is stacked with old furniture, sheets and linens, boxes and crates, and other bits. Nothing of value can be found here.

B21. Loft

The ceiling of this room angles down steeply, leaving only four feet of headroom to the southeast. A low cot and a dresser are the room's only furnishings.

This loft was once the home of the manor's head butler, but hasn't been lived in since Vorel's time.

As the PCs round the corner in the hallway beyond the entrance to this door, a sudden and unmistakable shriek of pain echoes through the attic. The sound obviously comes from the door to area **B24**.

B22. Observatory (EL 4)

A desk and a chair sit in the middle of this drafty room. Chimneys rise to the west, while to the east, two intricate stained-glass windows are set into the wall. The northern window depicts a dark-haired woman with pale skin, large green eyes, and a black-and-red gown; with both hands she wields a jagged iron staff. The southern window has been broken on its lower half and patched with canvas; what remains of its upper half depicts a handsome man dressed in regal finery and a crown of ivory and jade. Small scorch marks mar the wood near the broken window. A battered and ruined telescope lies on its side near the desk and a large trapdoor in the roof has been tied shut by several lengths of rope.

The trapdoor in the roof could once be raised and lowered, exposing a slice of the sky for observation, but the pulley system has long since fallen apart. The trap door can now be opened only with a DC 24 Strength check. The broken telescope on the floor was once a magnificent piece of equipment but is now beyond repair.

The stained glass windows here once depicted the two wizards who most directly inspired Vorel's research into the secrets of lichdom. Each figure can be identified by a DC 35 Knowledge (history) check—since both wizards attained notoriety after becoming liches, their pre-undeath appearances are more obscure. The northern window depicts Arazni, the Harlot of Geb, while the southern one depicts Socorro, the Butcher of Carrion Hill.

Haunt: This room is where Cyralie confronted Traver about his encroaching madness, hoping one last time she could convince him to leave the manor with her before it was too late. Unfortunately for her, that time had already passed. Traver attacked her, and when she tried to light the room on fire, he redirected the flow of the fire using magic to ignite her instead. Burning to death, Cyralie staggered across the room and threw herself through the window to plummet to her death on the rocks below. This sight caused Traver to finally snap out of his madness long enough for him to retreat to area **B18** and kill himself.

When the PC assigned to the burning haunt enters this room, he suddenly feels uncomfortably hot. A second later, he believes he has suddenly caught on fire, and that the only way to put the flames out before he burns to death is to throw himself through the unbroken window and, hopefully, into the sea below. The haunted character attempts this self-destructive act only once; if restrained from leaping through the window for 1 round, he recovers his wits to some extent.

PLUMMETING INFERNO **CR 4**

Type burning

Notice Wisdom DC 10 (to notice the sudden stink of burning flesh); **Effective HD** 8

EFFECTS

Trigger proximity; **Reset** automatic (24 hours)

Effect The haunted character must make a DC 16 Will save. If he fails, he is compelled to hurl himself through the unbroken window, taking 2d6 points of damage from the shattering glass and a further 1d6 points of damage from the fall onto the rooftop below. A weather vane on the roof makes a single +8 attack against the falling character; if it hits, the character takes another 1d6+7 points of damage, but his fall ends. If it fails to hit him, the character must make a DC 15 Reflex save. If that fails, he slides off the steep roof over the course of one round, whereupon he may make a final DC 10 Climb check to catch himself before falling 300 feet to the rocky surf below, taking 20d6 points of damage in the process.

B23. Private Study (EL 3)

Although this chamber is cluttered, it seems to have remained undamaged, avoiding the decay and vandalism present in other rooms. Shelves of books line the walls, interspaced with curious objects such as skulls fitted with stubs of candles, tribal fetishes, and decorative scroll cases. An empty birdcage lies near the southern wall beside a small desk and a fine leather chair. Statues and sculptures grin outward from all corners of the room.

Aldern's father Traver often spent time here, poring over old accounts of safaris, expeditions, and the odd excerpt from the *Pathfinder Chronicles*. Between this room and the observatory, Traver rarely visited other parts of the house after Vorel's influence started to take hold of his mind in the last few months before his death.

Haunt: When the PC haunted by insanity enters this room, dozens of memories of expeditions, sea voyages, and travels to exotic locales race through his mind, remnants of Traver Foxglove's journeys before he settled down here in Varisia. As the memories build momentum, they become increasingly infused with a sense of bitter disappointment and regret, and the character becomes increasingly aware that he is now receiving memories that never were, memories of fantastic discoveries he could have made had he not chosen to settle down with a shrill harpy of a wife.

UNFULFILLED GLORIES **CR 3**

Type insane

Notice Listen DC 20 (to hear the sound of pages rustling, as if a book were being read rapidly); **Effective HD** 6

EFFECTS

Trigger proximity; **Reset** automatic (24 hours)

Effect Once the memories grow bitter and culminate in an overwhelming sense of depression and loss, the haunted PC must make a DC 14 Will save to resist taking 1d6 points of Wisdom damage.

Treasure: The oddments include several dozen curious fetishes and masks, but the most impressive piece is an old painting of a bullfight. The painting bears a plaque that reads "Throwdown in Swynetown," and in the painting, vast crowds leer and cheer the bullfighter on, the huge bull aurochs towering over him, its cruel forward-jutting horns each the length of a spear. Dozens of bodies lie in the streets—the aurochs has clearly rampaged through them already, and although a score of brightly colored spears jut from the creature's flanks and back, it still rages on. This painting is, in fact, an original work by renowned Magnimarian artist Andosalu, worth 600 gp.

The books are mostly on tribal cultures and history (most of it local and relating to the Shoanti tribes), along with numerous maps of mysterious realms and ship charts. None of the books are particularly valuable. The scroll cases contain more maps, along with two arcane scrolls—*lightning bolt* and *keen edge*.

B24. Iesha's Prison (EL 6)

The door to this room is locked, but the unmistakable sound of a sobbing woman can be heard beyond it. The door can be unlocked with a DC 25 Open Lock check, or battered down with a DC 24 Strength check.

This room is cold and damp; a few crates sit near the north wall. The ceiling slopes down to only four feet high to the northeast, leaving little room for a small window, while to the southeast, a mold-encrusted pillar of brick marks the passage of a chimney. A full-size mirror in a dark wooden frame of coiling roses leans against these bricks, angled toward the tiny window.

Creature: After he murdered Iesha, Aldern Foxglove moved her body into this corner storeroom, wrapped it in a sheet torn from their marital bed, and hid it behind the crates. He locked the door and handed the key over to the Brothers of the Seven, assuming they would need it to clean up the situation for him. Of course, they did no such thing, and so Iesha remained here, dead. But not for long.

The night after her murder, the woman rose as an undead creature known as a revenant. Driven by a powerful desire for vengeance against Aldern Foxglove, Iesha is not without her weaknesses in her new, undead incarnation—for one, the sight of her own reflection has rendered her helpless with self-loathing. Moving the mirror (or destroying it) causes her to instantly recover—she stands up and unleashes a baleful shriek, then cries out, "Aldern! I can smell your fear! I'll be in your arms soon!"

Unless the PCs get in her way or attack her, Iesha then begins to unerringly seek out her murderous husband using her ability to locate creatures—Aldern is currently lurking in area **B37**, and if the PCs can keep up with Iesha, she'll lead them right to him.

If any PC is openly carrying her scarf from area **B9** or the portrait from area **B15**, Iesha must make a saving throw to avoid being overwhelmed by self-loathing; if she resists, her wrath is momentarily turned away from Aldern to the one who carries the object that reminds her of her life. Handing over the object to her can stop her rage—she immediately destroys the item, then continues on her relentless march toward Aldern.

IESHA FOXGLOVE, REVENANT **CR 6**

hp 69; see page 90

TACTICS

During Combat If Iesha ends up attacking the PCs, she fights them until they either hand over whatever item it was that triggered her wrath or everyone in the group spends a round not attacking her or getting in her way; at this point, she breaks off the attack and continues on her march toward Aldern.

B25. Kitchen (EL 5)

A large oak table, its surface covered with moldy stains and rat droppings, sits in the center of this large kitchen. Shelves line the walls, and an oversized fireplace dominates the northeast portion of the room. The shelves in the southwest wall are in a much greater state of disarray, and two one-foot-wide cracks in the wall near the floor lead south into the earth beyond the basement walls.

The two cracks in the walls are short tunnels that lead over to area **B27**, fissures that allow the rat swarms in there to move in and out of the place as they please. Several of the tunnels wind up and provide access into the wooden walls of the manor above as well.

Creatures: Any substantial noise in this room is enough to attract the attention of the two diseased rat swarms in area **B27**. The rapidly growing susurrus of oily diseased rat bodies slithering through tight confines, combined with the rising wave of rodent squeaks, gives the PCs 1d3 rounds to prepare for the onslaught before the swarms pour out into area **B25**, one after the other.

RAT SWARM (2) **CR 3**

hp 13 each (MM 239)

AC 10, touch 10, flat-footed 10

TACTICS

During Combat Once enraged, the swarms continue to pursue intruders throughout the house. They do not follow prey outside.

SPECIAL ABILITIES

Blind (Ex) The rat swarm is blind, and while this makes it immune to sight-based attacks, it also takes a–2 penalty to its AC, loses its Dexterity bonus to AC, moves at half-speed, and takes a –4 penalty on Search checks and most Strength- and Dexterity-based skill checks. Its scent ability negates concealment for its foes.

Disease (Su) Vorel's Phage—bite, Fortitude DC 10, incubation period 1 day, damage 1d4 Cha and 1d4 Con. For more details, see the sidebar on page 27. The save DC is Constitution-based.

Treasure: In a cupboard near the oven sits a very fine silver dinner set, with an exceptionally large silver salver and a dozen crystal decanters. The set as a whole is worth 1,000 gp. A DC 15 Search check discovers a small clay urn hidden in a nook behind a loose brick on the chimney. The urn is stuffed with some dried pine cones and three small violet garnets worth 100 gp each.

B26. Kitchen Staff's Quarters

Two bunks stand in this room, their sheets relatively free of dust and mold. A single chair lies on its side between them.

This room was where the kitchen staff lived back in Traver's day. Aldern was going to rebuild this room as a new servants' quarters, but the rat problem even a year ago was enough that he didn't make much progress on this front. Since he abandoned the manor again, leaving Vorel's spirit waxing powerful, the rat problem has only increased.

B27. Pantry

Although once a pantry, this room has become a filthy, reeking lair of what must be hundreds, if not thousands, of rats. Swaths of fur cling to everything, and mounds of rat droppings cover the floor. Numerous cracks in the walls doubtlessly allow the rats that live here access to a wide network of tiny tunnels beyond the basement walls.

Development: If the PCs haven't already disturbed the rat swarms and fought them in area **B25**, they are encountered here.

B28. Wine Cellar

Two wine racks line the walls here, their shelves empty and dusty. Mounds of broken glass bottles clutter the floor.

Treasure: A DC 20 Search check of the top shelf of the western rack reveals a hinged and hidden compartment at the back. Beyond is a narrow nook in which are hidden eight fine vintages of wine from the famed Vigardeis vineyard in distant Cheliax. Each bottle is worth 100 gp.

B29. Vorel's Workshop (EL 3)

The door to this room is locked and made of iron, and while patches of rust mar its face, it remains quite stout. It's a DC 30 Open Lock check to pick the lock, or a DC 28 Strength check to break it down. Aldern Foxglove carries the key.

This room looks to have once been some sort of arcane workshop, although little remains but broken glassware, shattered jars of pottery that contain dust and mold, and several rusty instruments and tools. A row of soggy books sits on the northern end of a workbench along the western wall. At the other end of the workbench, what looks like three iron birdcages sit, each containing a dead diseased rat. To the east, two stained-glass windows loom. The northern window depicts a thin man with gaunt features drinking a foul-looking brew of green fluid, while the southern one shows the same man but in an advanced state of decay, as if he had been dead for several weeks. His arms raised and head thrown back in triumph, his rotting body turns to smoke and spirals into a seven-sided box.

The stained-glass windows look out over the Varisian Gulf; although the basement itself is underground, the curved eastern wall of this room extends beyond the side of the cliff face. These final windows depict Vorel Foxglove taking the potion he brewed to catalyze his transformation into a lich (recognizable for who he is with a DC 25 Knowledge [nobility and royalty] check, by any PC who has examined the portraits in area **B17,** or by PCs haunted by festering or wrathful haunts), and then showing his new undead body bonding with his phylactery.

The books are in sorry shape, but a look through them reveals that they all cover various arts of necromancy and the creation of undeath. Worm-eaten and crumbling, they won't stand up to much investigation, but a character who looks through them and makes note of where the previous owner had glossed the text with marks and observations can make a DC 25 Knowledge (arcana) or Knowledge (religion) to realize that whomever studied these books was curious about the transformation of mortal into lich.

The iron cages each contain a dead rat that suffered from Vorel's Phage. Physical contact with one of these rats is not enough to expose a character to the disease, but eating one certainly does. Close examination of any of these cages reveals a small symbol of a pig with a mouthful of lockpicks peering at a keyhole; under the pig is a guildsign that says "Pug's Contraptions—Magnimar." These cages were left here by Aldern—he's already delivered a sample of the fungus from area **B37** to the Brothers of the Seven, and he intends to deliver these three dead rats sometime soon.

Haunt: Kasanda finally discovered the depths of her husband Vorel's plan here; forbidden by him to enter this room, she managed to do so one fateful night by using a *wand of knock* she'd purchased for just this purpose. While Vorel prepared the final stages of his lich transformation ritual, Kasanda found his books and realized what he was up to. Enraged and horrified, she moved down to the caverns below to confront him.

The PC haunted by wrath experiences a sudden urge to cross the room to read the books on the workbench as soon as he sees them. If he touches them, he freezes in place as a flood of information flows through his mind. He experiences a series of visions chronicling the various stages Vorel went through in his quest to become a lich, from researching the works of previous liches, to gathering the components for the lich transformation potion, to building his phylactery, finally culminating in a vision of Vorel taking his potion and doubling over in agony as his body began to rot away. All of these visions take place as if in a realm of animated stained-glass

windows, which should obviously explain the true nature of the windows in Foxglove Manor. As Vorel doubles over, the PC is filled with blinding shame that a loved one would do this to himself, followed by a burning rage that he must be stopped before he finishes his ritual. These visions take only a few seconds to occur; once they end, the PC doubles over in an agony of anger.

Origins of Lichdom **CR 3**

Type wrathful

Notice Spot DC 20 (to notice subtle movement in the stained-glass windows, as if the man depicted therein were sneering at the observer); **Effective HD** 6

EFFECTS

Trigger touch; **Reset** automatic (24 hours)

Effect Once the haunted character receives the vision described above, she must make a DC 14 Will save or suddenly be filled with terror at the knowledge that Vorel has already succeeded in transforming himself into a lich, and must flee at top speed upstairs to try to find her "children" and rescue them. Anyone who gets in her way or tries to stop her suddenly seems to transform into Vorel, and the haunted character must attack that character to the best of her ability until she can continue on her flight up to area **B13**. *Calm emotions*, *dispel evil*, and *protection from evil* can end this effect before the character reaches **B13**, as can any effect that removes a fear effect.

B30. The Pit (EL 4)

Piles of broken stone, dirt, and a few ruined pickaxes line the edges of this room. The floor in the middle of the room has been torn up to reveal an ancient set of stone spiral stairs, obviously of much older construction than the surrounding basement, winding deep into the bedrock below. A foul stink, like that of rotten meat, wafts up on a cold breeze from the darkness.

These stairs existed before Foxglove Manor, once leading down into an ancient complex devoted to the worship of Urgathoa, goddess of undeath. The complex has partially flooded and eroded into what looks like little more than a series of caves today. Vorel knew about the complex and incorporated the stairs into his design, but he kept their existence secret from his wife. After the manor fell vacant, Justice Ironbriar made a search of the place. He hired a priest to use *stone shape* to conceal the entrance to the caves, hoping to keep them from whomever would come to dwell here later until legal ownership of the manor reverted to the Brothers of the Seven. It wasn't until Xanesha sent Aldern back here to gather samples of the fungus she suspected grew deep below that this entrance was reopened.

The stairs descend 80 feet to area **B31**.

Haunt: When the obsession-haunted PC enters this room, she experiences a sudden vision of Aldern, sweaty, filthy, and wild-eyed, digging away at the stone floor of this room with a pickaxe. With each swing, he grunts out two words: "For you." The PC knows that Aldern is speaking of her. As the vision ends, Aldern breaks through into the room beyond, and a horde of shrieking ghouls rises up to pull him into the darkness below before they turn their lambent eyes to the PC.

Ghoulish Uprising **CR 4**

Type obsessed

Notice Wisdom DC 13 (to notice a sudden increase in the stink of rotten flesh); **Effective HD** 8

EFFECTS

Trigger proximity; **Reset** automatic (24 hours)

Effect As the ghouls reach for the haunted PC, she must make a DC 16 Will save to shake off the vision and regain her senses. If she fails, the ghouls grab her and begin to tear and bite at her flesh. Observers see the haunted PC jerk and thrash in the air as if she were being shaken by a mob, and suddenly deep red claw and bite wounds appear on her flesh. The haunted PC takes 6d6 points of damage from the assault (half on a DC 16 Fortitude save), and must make a DC 16 Fortitude save to resist catching ghoul fever (MM 118).

B31. Landing

The stairs end in a limestone cavern. The walls drip with moisture, and swaths of black and dark blue mold grow in spiraling, tangled patterns on the floor, ceiling, and walls. Bits of rubble and broken bones clutter the floor, and a rhythmic sound—as of the breathing of some immense creature—echoes through the cave from three tunnels, one to the north and two to the west. Of the two western tunnels, the southernmost one seems to be a relatively new creation.

The tunnel leading to area **B32** is only a few months old—observing the wall's cracks and crumbling sandstone, Aldern had his ghouls use pickaxes to create a second entrance to the tunnels.

The breathing sound is nothing more than the sounds of the surf echoing strangely through various other fissures that connect area **B32** and **B36** to the cliffs overlooking the Varisian Gulf.

Development: Characters who make excessive noise or light here quickly attract the attention of the ghouls in area **B34** and **B35**, who come to investigate.

B32. Feeding Cave (EL 5)

This long cave stinks of rotten meat. The source of the horrific smell is readily apparent in the swath of carcasses strewn about the floor of this place. Most seem to be of small animals and fish, but at least three humanoid bodies and one partially eaten horse lie in the mess as well.

Creature: A single dire bat took residence in this cavern in the years before Aldern returned. The creature came and went by squeezing up and down the well shaft, emerging nightly in area **B1** to feed until it was savaged by Aldern and his ghoul minions. Now, the bat has become a dread ghoul itself, and one of the cavern's most horrific guardians.

Ghoul Bat **CR 5**

Advanced dire bat dread ghoul (MM 62; *Advanced Bestiary* 76)

CE Large undead (augmented animal)

Init +8; **Senses** blindsense 40 ft., scent; Listen +10, Spot +9

DEFENSE

AC 24, touch 17, flat-footed 16 (+8 Dex, +7 natural, –1 size)

hp 52 (8d12)

Fort +6, **Ref** +14, **Will** +10

Defensive Abilities +2 turn resistance, undead traits

OFFENSE

Spd 20 ft., climb 20 ft., fly 40 ft. (good)

Melee bite +13 (2d6+6 plus paralysis) and 2 claws +8 (1d4+2 plus paralysis)

Space 10 ft.; **Reach** 5 ft.

Special Attacks command ghouls, create spawn

TACTICS

During Combat Although it rarely needs to, the ghoul bat can squeeze to clamber in and out of this cave via either exit. It pursues intruders as long as it is able to scent them.

Morale The ghoul bat fights to the death.

STATISTICS

Str 18, **Dex** 26, **Con** —, **Int** 4, **Wis** 18, **Cha** 8

Base Atk +6; **Grp** +14

Feats Alertness, Improved Natural Attack (bite), Stealthy, Track, Weapon Finesse

Skills Climb +12, Hide +6, Listen +10 (+14 with blindsense), Move Silently +10, Spot +9 (+13 with blindsense), Survival +12

Languages Common (cannot speak)

SPECIAL ABILITIES

Command Ghouls (Su) A dread ghoul bat can automatically command all normal ghouls within 30 feet as a free action. Normal ghouls never attack a dread ghoul unless compelled.

Create Spawn (Su) Any creature that is killed by a dread ghoul bat and lies undisturbed until the next midnight rises as a dread ghoul at that time. The new dread ghoul is not under the control of its creator. A *protection from evil* or *gentle repose* spell cast on the corpse prevents this.

Paralysis (Ex) A creature damaged by a dread ghoul bat's bite or claw must make a DC 13 Fortitude save or be paralyzed for 1d4+1 rounds. The save DC is Charisma based.

Treasure: Two of the three dead humans among the bat's victims are long-dead Varisian nomads with nothing of much value on their remains. The third, however, is the corpse of notorious bandit Shaz "Redshiv" Bilger, suspected of organizing the robbery of nearly two dozen merchant convoys along the Lost Coast Road over the past decade. His partially eaten remains can be identified with a DC 20 Knowledge (local) check. Proof of his demise presented to the law at Magnimar is worth a 500 gp reward.

Of more immediate monetary gratification, though, is his surviving gear, which consists of a pearl ring worth 300 gp, an adamantine longsword, a *hat of disguise*, and a scattering of 56 gp.

B33. Dangerous Mold (EL 6)

The mold seems to grow particularly thick in this portion of the tunnel. Several pickaxes have been tossed into the corner of the room—one of them looks particularly well-made.

After widening the tunnel to area **B32**, the ghouls abandoned their digging tools here, barely even noticing the poisonous cloud of spores the act kicked up at the time. The southern two five-foot-squares here are thick with fungus, much of it yellow mold (DMG 76).

Treasure: Of the six picks abandoned here, five are ruined from the mold and the damp. The sixth, however, happens to be a *+1 heavy pick* that has weathered the conditions rather well.

B34. Ghoulish Guardians (EL 3)

Creatures: This otherwise nondescript cave is always watched over by three ghouls, stationed here and commanded to act as guardians by Aldern. The ghouls hide in the shadows: one in the nook to the north, one in the shadows of the southeast entrance, and one in the shadows of the western entrance. If they're spotted, they attack at once. Sounds of combat here draw the attention of the ghouls in area **B35**, but not the denizens of area **B36**; the additional ghouls from area **B35** arrive in 3 rounds.

Ghouls (3) — **CR 1**
hp 13 each (MM 118)

B35. The Grave (EL 4)

The western half of this foul-smelling cavern is heaped with bones, each scarred by the scraping of teeth. Most of the bones have been cracked open for the marrow within. The horrific stink of the place seems to mostly come from a wretched pile of body parts—some animal, some humanoid—heaped in a dismaying mound to the east.

Creatures: Another four ghouls dwell in here, crouched upon the macabre heaps of bones as they chew the last remaining tatters of flesh from the rapidly diminishing pile of body parts. If the PCs take the time to look closely, one of these ghouls has a partially smashed-in skull from which a strangely shaped chunk of stone protrudes. This ghoul was once a carpenter in Aldern's employ—the same one he caught with his wife Iesha. The bit of stone protruding from his head matches the missing wing from the statuette in area **B9**.

Ghouls (4) — **CR 1**
hp 13 each (MM 118)

B36. The Vent (EL 6)

The cramped tunnel opens into a vertiginous gulf here, a cathedral-like cavern with a roof arching thirty feet overhead and dropping into a sloshing pool of foamy seawater fifty feet below. A steep stone ledge winds down to these surging depths, its slope glistening with moisture and mold. Narrow fissures wind into the rock face to the northwest, rivulets of water dripping down from them across the sloping ledge into the pool below. A stone door stands in the northern wall about halfway down the slope.

The sloping ledge is difficult to navigate; a character who doesn't climb along its surface (doing so is a DC 5 Climb check) must make a DC 12 Balance check each round. Failure by 5 or more sends the character sliding down the ramp all the way to the bottom, taking 1d6 points of damage per 20 feet slid until he plunges into the cold waters at the bottom.

The pool at the bottom is one hundred feet deep. At its bed, it opens into a large cavern that eventually connects to the sea via several underground tunnels that wind for nearly a half mile to the south. The sound of the water surging and sloshing is the source of the strange "breathing" sound heard throughout these caves. It's a DC 15 Swim check to navigate the pool's waters due to the churning currents. The stone door leading to area **B37** is unlocked and untrapped.

Creatures: The characters might have come to think that they've seen the last of the Lost Coast's goblins by this point, but in fact a pack of four goblin commandos from the Toadlick tribe to the north wandered a little too close to Foxglove Manor a few weeks ago and were set upon by the dire bat ghoul while it was on one of its increasingly rare forays outside. Aldern found the goblins later that evening and rescued their bodies from the ghoul bat, and when the four goblins woke as dread ghouls later that evening, he put them to work here as the final guardians of his realm.

Goblin Ghouls (4) — **CR 2**
Dread ghoul goblin ranger 1 (MM 133, *Advanced Bestiary* 76)
CE Small undead (augmented humanoid [goblin])
Init +5; **Senses** darkvision 60 ft., scent; Listen +7, Spot +7

DEFENSE

AC 21, touch 16, flat-footed 16
(+3 armor, +5 Dex, +2 natural, +1 size)
hp 6 (1d12)
Fort +4, **Ref** +5, **Will** +2
Defense +2 turn resistance

OFFENSE

Spd 30 ft., climb 30 ft.
Melee bite +5 (1d4+3 plus paralysis) and
2 claws +0 (1d2+1 plus paralysis)
Special Attacks favored enemy +2 (animals)

TACTICS

Aldern—

You have served us quite well. The delivery you harvested from the caverns far exceeds what I had hoped for. You may consider your debt to the Brothers paid in full. Yet I still have need of you, and when you awaken from your death, you should find your mind clear and able to understand this task more than in the state you lie in as I write this.

You shall remember the workings of the Sihedron ritual, I trust. You seemed quite lucid at the time, but if you find after your rebirth that you have forgotten, return to your townhouse in Magnimar. My agents shall contact you there soon—no need for you to bother the Brothers further. I will provide the list of proper victims for the Sihedron ritual in two days' time. Commit that list to memory and then destroy it before you begin your work. The ones I have selected must be marked before they die, otherwise they do my master no good and the greed in their souls will go to waste.

If others get in your way, though, you may do with them as you please. Eat them, savage them, or turn them into pawns—it matters not to me.

—Your Mistress, Wanton of Nature's Pagan Forms

Handout 2

During Combat The goblin ghouls focus their attacks on one target, attempting to overwhelm their victim with their claws and bites.

Morale The goblin ghouls fight to the death.

STATISTICS

Str 16, **Dex** 21, **Con** —, **Int** 10, **Wis** 16, **Cha** 10

Base Atk +1; **Grp** –1

Feats Mounted Combat, Track

Skills Climb +11, Handle Animal +4, Listen +7, Move Silently +9, Ride +13, Spot +7, Survival +15

Languages Common, Goblin

SQ command ghouls, create spawn, wild empathy +0

Gear studded leather

SPECIAL ABILITIES

Command Ghouls (Su) A dread ghoul goblin can automatically command all normal ghouls within 30 feet as a free action. Normal ghouls never attack a dread ghoul unless compelled.

Create Spawn (Su) Any creature that is killed by a dread ghoul goblin and lies undisturbed until the next midnight rises as a dread ghoul at that time. The new dread ghoul is not under the control of its creator. A *protection from evil* or *gentle repose* spell cast on the corpse prevents this.

Paralysis (Ex) A creature damaged by a dread ghoul goblin's bite or claw must make a DC 13 Fortitude save or be paralyzed for 1d4+1 rounds. The save DC is Charisma based.

B37. Vorel's Laboratory (EL 7)

This damp cavern contains several items of furniture. A rickety table sits in the middle of the cave, its damp surface cluttered with all manner of what appears to be garbage: empty bottles, bits of clothing, crumpled bits of paper, and more, lying in neatly organized rows. A painting leans against the far side of the table, facing a large leather chair that sits nearby. This chair's high back and cushion are horribly stained by smears of rotten meat and its arms are sticky with blood. A smaller table sits against the southern wall, its surface heaped with silver platters, fine porcelain plates, and crystalware. The "food" on these plates and platters is rotten meat, in some cases humanoid in source, and in all cases writhing with maggots. Thick, rotting blood gels in the crystal. Yet the horrific stench of the room seems somehow even thicker and more overwhelming than this gruesome display can account for on its own. The stench seems strongest to the west, where the cave's wall has been overtaken by a horrific growth of dark green mold and dripping fungi. At the center, a patch of black tumescent fungus grows, its horny ridges and tumor-like bulbs forming what could almost be taken to be a humanoid outline. What appears to have once been an exquisite puzzlebox the size of a man's fist lies smashed on the ground at the fungoid shape's feet.

A closer inspection of the collection on the table should be enough to worry one of the PCs, for this is Aldern's collection of relics from that PC's life. You should tailor the list of things found here to the PC Aldern is obsessed with, ranging from mundane things like used potion bottles and scrolls on up to objects as personal as an envelope of hair (perhaps harvested from the PC as she slept or from a discarded comb) or, if you can engineer such an event earlier in this adventure, even small personal objects that have gone missing. The only objects here that weren't taken from the stalked PC's garbage are a stack of charcoal drawings on water-damaged parchment depicting the character, drawn by his hand. The nature of the drawings varies (erotica for lust, idealized perfection for envy, or pictures of the PC killed in numerous manners for wrath), but the subject remains the same throughout the collection of several dozen pages. Mixed in with these drawings is a letter written in a graceful hand. Addressed to Aldern, the letter is presented here as Handout 2, and provides the PCs with the strongest link to Magnimar they are likely to find in Foxglove Manor.

The portrait that leans against the table's far side is of Iesha, but Aldern has used his own waning artistic skills in a clumsy attempt to repaint the portrait with blood and bits of runny rotten flesh into a caricature of the PC he has become obsessed with. The painting can be cleaned with a DC 25 Craft (painting) check and a day of work to reveal its original subject. This painting was done in Foxglove's townhouse in Magnimar, and although Iesha fills the piece, an open window over her shoulder shows a portion of a city skyline that can be identified with a DC 15 Knowledge (local) check as Magnimar.

The fungus on the wall comprises of the remains of Vorel Foxglove—after his wife disrupted the ritual he was performing here to become a lich, the necromantic energy lashed back and destroyed his physical body, transforming it into the embodiment of contagion and fungoid corruption that grows on the wall here. Anyone who touches the foul black fungus must make a DC 20 Fortitude save or immediately contract Vorel's Phage (the incubation period, in this case, is immediate—the character takes the ability damage at once). Actually ingesting a portion of the fungus imparts a –4 penalty on the saving throw.

The shattered box on the ground is the remains of Vorel's phylactery. A DC 20 Knowledge (arcana) check identifies it as being associated with necromancy; if this check exceeds this DC by 10 or more, the character realizes it is an incomplete and ruined lich phylactery.

Creature: Aldern Foxglove, once a handsome and cultured nobleman who had a way with the ladies, is now condemned to an unlife of unending hunger, driven to eat the flesh of those he once might have called friends or lovers. The transformation into a ghast has ruined his mind, yet his former personality was not completely destroyed—at least, not at first. To deal with his increasing madness, Aldern developed a split personality. He alternately refers to himself as his Lordship, the Skinsaw Man, and the Hurter. He spends his days conversing with himself as his Lordship, fearing the arrival of the Hurter, whom he regards as an entirely separate person. His Lordship is a frightened creature with a nervous twitch and quick excited voice. The Hurter appears in times of stress or excitement—a hateful, murdering cannibal who seeks to continue his harvest of living flesh. It is this personality that is most tied to Vorel's spirit, yet despite its feral and savage hunger, it is the Skinsaw Man that is, perhaps, the most dangerous. This personality seeks to find salvation and purpose among the Skinsaw Cult and is slowly becoming the dominant face in this tortured soul. In time, Aldern the Hurter and Aldern the Lord will be gone, and Norgorber will have a powerful new minion to call his own.

Aldern sits in his chair as the PCs arrive, his Lordship in control for a few moments. When he sees the PCs, his eyes widen in a mixture of fear and delight, but when he sees the PC that is the object of his obsession, he staggers to his feet. His proclamation to that PC depends on the nature of his obsession.

Lust: "You! You've come to me! I knew my letters would sway your heart, my love! Let us consumate our... our... hunger!"

Envy: "No! You were supposed to die! You still live! You still live!"

Wrath: "You live! Well and good, for now I shall have the reward of tasting your heart while it is yet warm..."

No matter the nature of his obsession, the Hurter takes over and Aldern attacks. As soon as he is injured, his Lordship takes over. At this point, Aldern drops to his knees, sobs, and begs for the PCs to save him. He is terrified that the Hurter will come again, and is willing to say anything to convince the PCs to aid him. While in this state, he can reveal much of his story to the PCs, including his association with the Brothers of the Seven.

Unfortunately for the PCs, as his Lordship begins revealing the secrets of the Brothers of the Seven, the Skinsaw Man arrives. He suddenly breaks into a wide grin, stands slowly, bows before the PCs, and says, "I wonder how your deaths shall affect your friends. What things might you have done that will go unfinished? What will those broken promises spawn? How will your murders shape the world?" He attacks with a renewed fury at this point, gaining a +2 profane bonus on attack rolls and damage rolls and fighting to the death.

ALDERN FOXGLOVE, THE SKINSAW MAN — CR 6

Male dread ghast human aristocrat 4/rogue 3
CE Medium undead (augmented human)
Init +8; **Senses** darkvision 60 ft.; Listen +1, Spot +1
Aura stench (20 ft.), unnatural aura (30 ft.)

DEFENSE

AC 19, touch 15, flat-footed 15
(+1 deflection, +4 Dex, +4 natural)
hp 87 (7d12)
Fort +8, **Ref** +10, **Will** +6; evasion
Defensive Abilities +4 turn resistance, undead traits

OFFENSE

Spd 30 ft., climb 30 ft.
Melee *+1 war razor* +10 (1d4+3/18–20) and
bite +4 (1d8+1 plus paralysis) and
claw +4 (1d6+1 plus paralysis and ghoul fever)
Special Attacks command ghasts and ghouls, create spawn, paralysis, sneak attack +2d6

TACTICS

During Combat Aldern's tactics in combat are influenced to a certain degree by his personalities, as detailed above. When the Skinsaw Man takes over, he puts on his mask and assumes the form of his obsession, attacking that character to the exclusion of all other targets.
Morale Aldern fights to the death.

STATISTICS

Str 17, **Dex** 18, **Con** —, **Int** 14, **Wis** 12, **Cha** 22
Base Atk +5; **Grp** +8
Feats Improved Initiative, Lightning Reflexes, Persuasive, Weapon Finesse
Skills Balance +6, Bluff +18, Climb +11, Diplomacy +20, Hide +9, Intimidate +20, Jump +20, Knowledge (local) +8, Knowledge (nobility and royalty) +9, Ride +11, Sense Motive +11, Sleight of Hand +12, Tumble +10
Languages Common, Elven
SQ trapfinding, trap sense +1
Gear *+1 war razor*, *ring of jumping*, *ring of protection +1*, *stalker's mask*, extravagant noble's outfit worth 200 gp, cameo worth 100 gp containing tiny portrait of PC, key to area **B29**

SPECIAL ABILITIES

Command Ghouls (Su) Aldern can automatically command all normal ghasts and ghouls within 30 feet as a free action. Normal ghasts and ghouls never attack a dread ghast unless compelled.
Create Spawn (Su) Any creature killed by Aldern that lies undisturbed until the next midnight rises as a dread ghast at that time. The new

dread ghast is not under the control of its creator. A *protection from evil* or *gentle repose* spell cast on the corpse prevents this.

Ghoul Fever (Su) Disease—bite, Fortitude DC 19, incubation period 1 day, damage 1d3 Con and 1d3 Dex. An affected humanoid who dies of ghoul fever rises as a ghoul at the next midnight. A humanoid that becomes a ghoul in this manner retains none of the abilities it possessed in life. It is not under the control of any other ghouls, but it hungers for the flesh of the living. A humanoid of 4 Hit Dice or more rises as a ghast, not a ghoul.

Paralysis (Ex) A creature damaged by Aldern's bite or claw must make a DC 19 Fortitude save or be paralyzed for 1d4+1 rounds. The save DC is Charisma based.

Stench (Ex) Any breathing creature within 20 feet of Aldern must make a DC 19 Fortitude save or become sickened for 1d6+4 minutes. A creature with the scent ability must make this save at a range of 40 feet and takes a –2 penalty on the save. The save must be repeated each round, but once the sickened condition has been applied, further failed saves merely reset its duration. Creatures resistant to poison may apply their bonus to this saving throw, and creatures immune to poison are immune to this ability as well.

Unholy Fortitude (Ex) Aldern gains bonus hit points equal to his Charisma modifier times his Hit Dice, and a bonus to his Fortitude saves equal to his Charisma modifier.

Unnatural Aura (Su) Any animal within 30 feet of Aldern automatically becomes panicked and remains so as long as it is within this distance.

Haunt: The patch of fungus on the wall presents an additional hazard to a PC associated with the festering haunt. When he sees the strangely humanoid shape on the wall, he realizes the shape matches that of his own shadow exactly, and suddenly experiences a sensation of vertigo as he feels compelled to feed on the fungus to reclaim his stolen shadow.

THE SKINSAW MAN

Vorel's Legacy **CR 4**

Type festering

Notice Spot DC 15 (to notice the phylactery shards rattle and shake); **Effective HD** 8

EFFECTS

Trigger proximity; **Reset** automatic (24 hours)

Effect Spell effect (*suggestion* to eat the fungus, Will DC 15 resists).

Treasure: If cleaned, the portrait of Iesha is worth 200 gp. A small silver key ring worth 10 gp sits on the table amid the rotten meat, with two keys on the ring. The larger of these two is a tarnished iron key set with a round opal worth 100 gp—this is the key to Foxglove's townhouse in Magnimar. The smaller key is made of bronze and has an unusually long tang ending in a set of three notched blades. The head of this key resembles a roaring lion. This key opens the hidden cache in area **C11** of the townhouse. Finally, a DC 25 search of the fungus south of the dangerous black patch uncovers a mold-encrusted but still functional *wand of knock* (18 charges); the same wand used 60 years ago by Kasanda Foxglove to enter her husband's secret world.

Development: The patch of dangerous fungus can be temporarily destroyed by fire, acid, or the application of at least five vials of holy water, but the foul stuff simply regrows in 24 hours unless the site is subjected to a *hallow* and a *consecrate* spell or a *dispel evil*. Casting these spells here causes the fungus to suddenly animate and tear free from the wall. The thing howls in a sloshy, barely human voice, then crumbles to dust—the haunt of Foxglove Manor is thusly exorcised, and while the building retains its unwelcoming aura, it is no longer haunted.

Ad Hoc Experience Award: If the PCs manage to exorcise Vorel's spirit, award them experience points as if they had defeated a CR 7 creature.

PART THREE: WELCOME TO MAGNIMAR

After the PCs finish exploring Foxglove Manor, defeat Aldern, and discover the link between his actions here and the actions of the

Stalker's Mask
Aura faint illusion; **CL** 5th
Slot head; **Price** 3,500 gp

Description

This mask is crafted from leathery preserved sections harvested from several different human faces, draped one over another almost like scales and leaving the eyes and mouth exposed—the overall effect is similar to that of a scaled skull. When worn, the mask desaturates the wearer's color, making him appear insubstantial and shadowy and granting a +5 competence bonus on Hide checks. Once per day, the wearer may cause the mask's features to slither and take on the appearance of any creature within 60 feet that he observes, allowing the wearer to use a *disguise self* spell to take that person's appearance. As long as he wears this guise, the wearer gains a +2 bonus on attack rolls and weapon damage rolls made against the person he is disguised as, as the mask builds upon the wearer's rage and jealousy of the target's appearance.

Construction

Requirements Craft Wondrous Item, *disguise self*, *rage*; **Cost** 1,750 gp, 140 XP

Bolstering the Undead

Although undead are immune to critical hits, their lack of a Constitution score ends up being one of their biggest weaknesses—especially in the case of corporeal undead. This is particularly a problem for "boss undead," like Aldern Foxglove. Built as a standard dread ghast human, he ends up with a paltry 45 hit points, barely enough to last a round against mid-level characters. Aldern's Unholy Fortitude ability is a way to address this problem—by allowing Aldern to apply his Charisma bonus to his hit points, he ends up with 87 hit points and goes from a one-round wonder in a fight to the memorable villain he deserves to be.

—James Jacobs

Brothers of Seven in Magnimar, allow them time to recover from their ordeals. They should be 6th level by the time they head into Magnimar, so if they're falling behind after Foxglove Manor, consider running some side adventures for them. If the PCs still haven't shut down the *runewell* below Sandpoint or haven't defeated Malfeshnekor under Thistletop, now would be a good chance to head back to *Pathfinder* #1 and finish off those stories.

Although the Lost Coast is remote and quiet, news travels fast. Word of the murders in Sandpoint reach Magnimar quickly, and there are those who are pleased with Aldern's work. Yet others see these murders in an entirely different light—for Magnimar has had trouble with killings of late as well.

Haldmeer Grobaras, Lord-Mayor of Magnimar, is a bombastic and self-serving nobleman who sees his stewardship over the city as a reward for his hard work as a young aristocrat and not as a service to his people. Normally, the plight of the poor isn't his concern—he has people who have people to take care of problems beyond the Summit. Yet this new plague of slayings is something else. Merchants, nobles, bankers, and recently the proprietor of one of Haldmeer's favorite gambling dens are being slain, and it's no longer possible to discount theories that an entire cult of madmen might be involved. Angry demands to stop the slayings fill the streets and taverns by day, and Haldmeer isn't sure that the frightened silence of the nights is much better.

Unfortunately, his rule of Magnimar has left the bureaucratic machine in bad need of a tune-up. Magnimar's guards aren't equipped to handle a cult as crafty and sneaky as the Brothers of the Seven, especially with one of the city's own Justices living a double-life as one of the cult's leaders. This man, Justice Ironbriar, works behind the scenes to defeat and distract organized attempts by the government to handle the situation, sending guards and investigators on wild goose chases and wasting resources so the cult can continue its work. And just as fast as news of the Sandpoint murders travels to Magnimar, so too does news of heroes standing against and defeating Foxglove. By the time the PCs come to Magnimar and begin their investigations there, Ironbriar is ready for them.

Welcome to Magnimar

Magnimar is a sprawling city—any number of adventures can begin (or end) in the City of Monuments, but this adventure focuses only on those things pertinent to "The Skinsaw Murders." Player characters, being what they are, will certainly get distracted by the sights and sounds of the city—in this case, consult the accompanying section on the city that begins on page 56. You should also consult that section for details to present to the PCs, depending upon where they go.

As the PCs explore Magnimar, they'll certainly hear rumors and news about a disturbingly similar spate of murders plaguing the City of Monuments of late. Stories of merchants, politicians, crooked guards, and moneylenders showing up dead—their bodies mutilated, faces missing, and chests carved with seven-pointed stars—seem to be on everyone's lips, just as it seems that every week brings a new victim to light. The crime scenes are now tightly controlled by the city government—the PCs should have little or no chance of getting into one of them to investigate. Which is just as well, for the Skinsaw Cultists are quite adept at leaving behind no traces, and little remains behind at these sites to incriminate them.

Unfortunately for the cult, Foxglove hasn't been so careful about hiding his trail. Despite their best efforts to preserve their secrets, clues remain hidden at the townhouse to send the PCs on their way to disrupting the Skinsaw Cult completely.

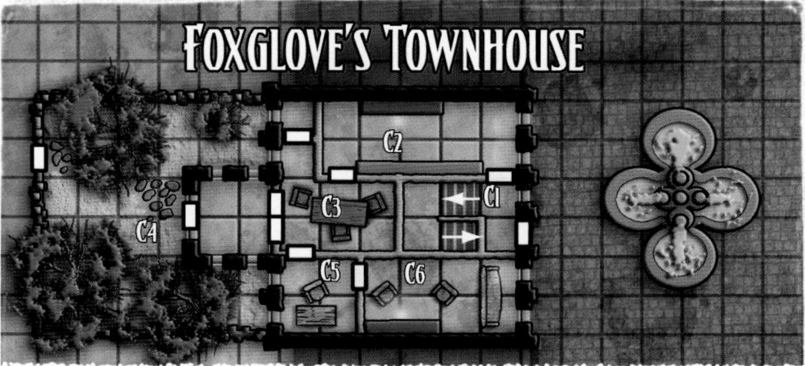

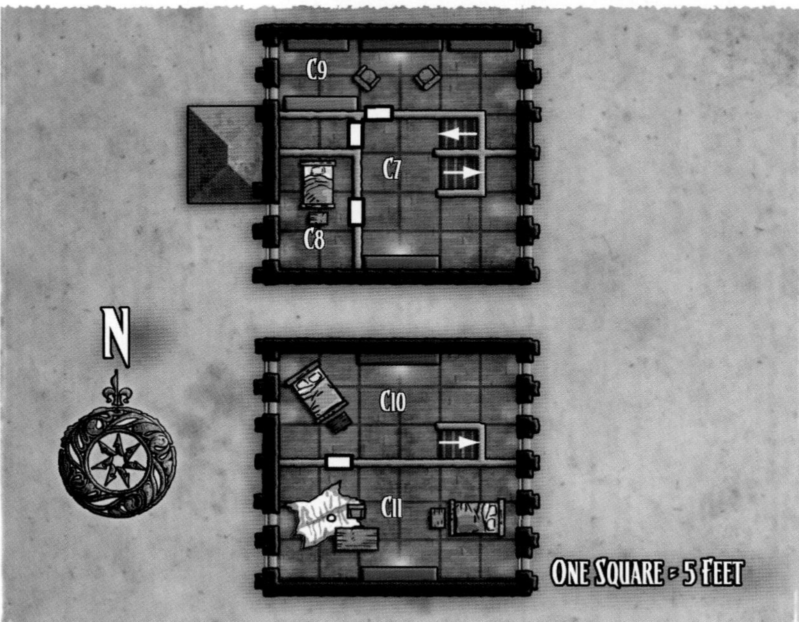

Foxglove's Townhouse

C1. Entrance: Dry mud covers the floor.

C2. Trophy Hall: The north and south walls here once featured shelves of hunting trophies—primarily elk, boars, and bears. All have been ripped from the walls and lie scattered on the floor.

C3. Dining Room: The room to the west is a small kitchen.

C4. Garden: Overgrown with tangled vines, the door here is boarded over. The high wall obscures observation from the nearby alleys; the walls can be climbed with a DC 5 Climb check.

C5. Study: The desk here is empty, its drawers pulled out and scattered on the floor.

C6. Lounge: The chairs and sofa here have been slashed and ruined.

C7. Landing: Several paintings have fallen here.

C8. Guest Room: The bed's mattress is slashed open, and the footlocker upended and emptied of its contents.

C9. Library: Hundreds of mundane books litter the floor.

C10. Master Bedroom: This large room has been thoroughly ransacked.

C11. Master's Study: The exotic zebraskin rug on the floor here is worth 35 gp. The bed and chair are torn apart, and the desk and footlocker have been looted. A secret cache is hidden in the fireplace mantel.

Foxglove's Townhouse (EL 6)

While Aldern Foxglove might have mentioned his townhouse to the PCs in "Burnt Offerings," they can also learn of its existence from the letter in the caverns below Foxglove Manor. It's the logical first stop in town for PCs seeking more clues about the brotherhood mentioned in the letter, but unfortunately it's also the logical place for the Skinsaw Cult to make its first attempt to murder the PCs.

The townhouse is located in the Grand Arch District, not far from Starsilver Plaza. Its facade faces a small courtyard in which stands a fountain consisting of four pools, each fed by one of four long-necked iron wyvern heads.

Aldern's townhouse hasn't been lived in for months, although Aldern still owns the property. Since he's not yet been declared dead, the building has stood empty for that time. Justice Ironbriar has had copies of the building's keys made, and while the cult ransacked the house for valuables and destroyed any clues they could find that might point back to their association with Aldern, they overlooked a hidden cache that Foxglove used to store personal oddments. If the PCs have Aldern's key, the design on its head should give them the clue they need to discover this cache.

The building itself is three stories tall. Boards have been nailed over the windows on the ground floor, courtesy of the Skinsaw Cult. A DC 20 Gather information check made in the vicinity reveals that the house was boarded up by workmen one night not all that long ago. The back door is boarded over, but the front door is only locked (Open Lock DC 30). Attempts to enter the building by force during the day invariably draw the attention of the city guards, but no one questions PCs who enter the house using a key.

Within, Foxglove's townhouse is cold, dark, and empty. The rooms are dusty and in disarray, as if someone ransacked the place several months ago. The townhouse overview on page 41 lists the basic contents and functions of the rooms, but there's really only one thing of interest to the PCs here—a cache hidden in the fireplace mantel in the Master's Study (area **C11**). This mantel is decorated with two roaring lion heads at either end; if the PCs found Aldern's key ring in Foxglove Manor, the lions match the one on the mysterious bronze key. A DC 20 Search check of the left lion reveals a tiny keyhole deep in the back of its throat, while a DC 30 Search of the right lion reveals that it is cleverly hinged to open (although no external mechanism for opening it is apparent).

Creatures: Justice Ironbriar is no fool. He suspects that, after the PCs finished with Aldern, they'd follow up on any clues they found at the manor by visiting this building. As a result, he's prepared an ambush using several dangerous creatures known as faceless stalkers, swamp-dwelling aberrations capable of assuming humanoid form. Ironbriar ordered the two creatures, on "loan" from his new mistress Xanesha, to take the shapes of Aldern and Iesha Foxglove, and to await the PCs' arrival here. Both bide their time in area **C6**, but once they realize their "home" has visitors, they call out to the PCs and track them down, eager to treat their guests to a home-cooked meal in the kitchen. Of course, this is a ruse; the faceless stalkers are merely trying to size up the PCs. Once they're ready, the monsters assume their true forms and attack.

FACELESS STALKERS (2) CR 4

hp 42 each; see page 88

TACTICS

During Combat The faceless stalkers attempt to keep one foe flanked at all times, fighting near walls if possible to prevent the same happening to them.

Morale The faceless stalkers fight until one is killed, whereupon the other attempts to flee. It does not return to its lair in the Shadow Clock, as it is terrified of Xanesha's likely response to its failure—instead it tries to flee the city entirely to return to the Mushfens.

Treasure: The hidden cache contains one of Foxglove's nest eggs: a bag of 200 pp along with a shallow wooden case containing a number of legal papers pertaining to the townhouse, as well as the deed to Foxglove Manor. The deed indicates that the Foxglove family only financed two-thirds of the manor's construction 80 years ago; the remainder was financed by a group called the "Brothers of the Seven." The deed also bears an unusual clause near the end that indicates that after one hundred years, ownership of Foxglove Manor and the lands within a mile "around and below" reverts to the brothers.

Under the case is a thin black ledger—the majority of the purchases and payments recorded are mundane, but several near the end of the ledger should catch the PCs' attention. These are nearly a dozen entries over the past three months labeled as "Iesha's Trip to Absalom," each indicating Foxglove was paying someone referred to as "B.7" 200 gp a week for her "trip," dropping off the payment every Oathday at midnight at a place called "The Seven's Sawmill."

PART FOUR: THE SEVEN'S SAWMILL

The cult of Norgorber is a complex organism, but the god of murder, secrets, greed, and poison would have it no other way. Many thieves' guilds include small shrines to his guise as the "Gray Master." Hidden sects of conspirators who venerate him as the god of secrets know him as the Reaper of Reputations. And those who see divinity in the poisonous know him as "Blackfingers." Yet the most sinister and dangerous of his followers are the Skinsaw Men—they know Norgorber as Father Skinsaw. These fanatic murderers are not assassins—they kill, not for wealth, but for the sick joy of it. The Skinsaw Men hold that all of their murders serve a greater cause, their leaders receiving visions of victims which they believe to be divine messages from Father Skinsaw. With each murder, society is shaped—deeds the victim might have accomplished go unrealized and the lives of those who knew the dead shift and change in subtle ways. Over the course of years, or even centuries, murders can shape nations and write the future's history. And when the Final Blooding occurs, then shall Father Skinsaw reveal to his flock the purpose of this shaping of society by death.

The Skinsaw Men of Magnimar come from old blood, a master cult that has existed for hundreds of years in the decadent Chelish city of Vyre. Yet today, the Magnimar cult is very much its own entity. An elf named Ironbriar has served as the cult's master since Vorel Foxglove's disappearance—the long-lived cleric leads a double life as one of the city's Justices and has used the ironic cover to great effect. Few would suspect a Justice, one of the city's ruling judges, of being a cultist of the god of murder, after all. He helped established the semi-secret Brothers of the Seven society (with the aid of six other merchants, among them Vorel Foxglove) as a cover for his cult, and over the decades, Ironbriar has taken advantage of his growing (but always small) cadre of murderers, using them now and then for additional income. The commission from the Red Mantis to deliver samples of Vorel's Phage is one such bit of moonlighting, but his involvement with the beautiful Xanesha is more personal. At first, he believed she was interested in him for his connections among the Justices of Magnimar, but in fact it is his Skinsaw Men she wants. Xanesha is, in fact, a lamia matriarch in the service of Karzoug; she charmed Justice Ironbriar and has maintained her magical control over the man for many months. She uses this influence to send his cultists out to kill not those whom Norgorber wills, but those whose greedy souls will more rapidly fill Karzoug's *runewell*.

Although himself a reprehensible murderer and traitor to Magnimar, Ironbriar's involvement in these new murders is not his own doing, and if the PCs can free him from Xanesha's control he might even be able to lead them to her lair. If not and he is killed, there are plenty of clues awaiting the PCs at the Seven's Sawmill.

Sawmill General Features

The Seven's Sawmill is one of several mills that operate along the shores of Kyver's Islet. The mill is intended to look from outside like a standard lumber mill, but while it does indeed produce lumber, the structure's primary purpose is to give the Brothers of the Seven a cover and a safe place to meet. The walls are made of wood, and all doors are standard unlocked wooden affairs, with the exception of the actual entrances to the building, both of which are locked (Open Lock DC 30). Floors are wood and worn smooth by the passage of feet. The mill itself is powered by four water wheels in the undermill (area **D3**).

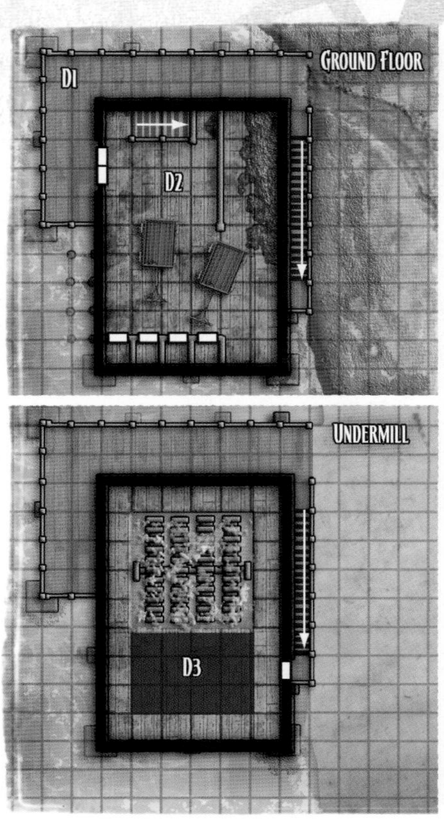

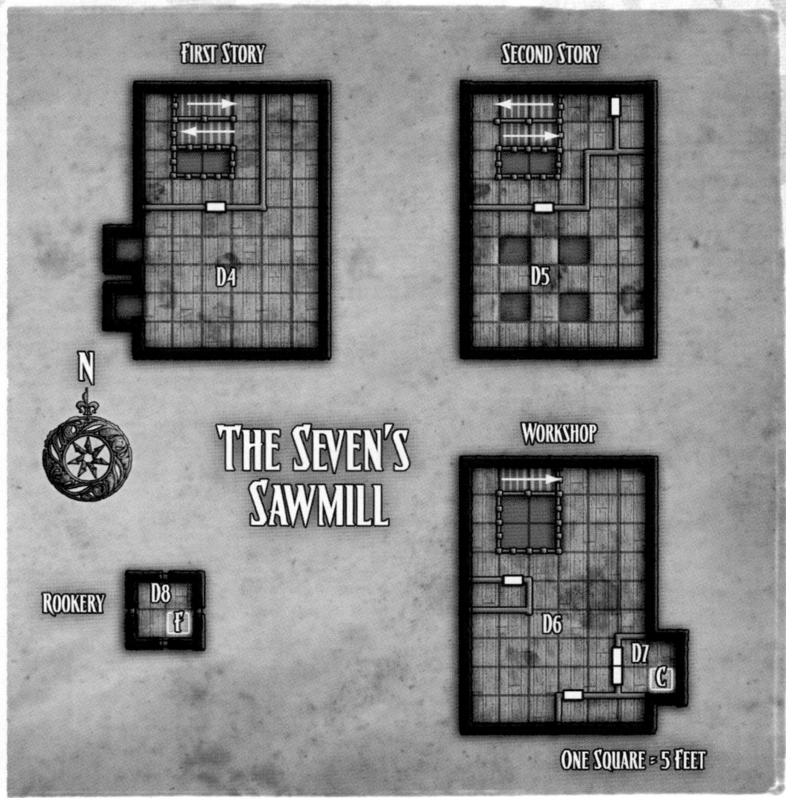

D1. Outer Walk

Built over the Yondabakari River, this wood building sits on massive wooden pilings driven into the riverbed below. A wooden boardwalk wraps around the northern rim of the building, and a flight of stairs leads down to a door on the east side just above the water level. The churning of four large water wheels under the mill fills the air with sound and mist.

Characters who stake out the mill see that, from outward appearances, it seems normal. Deliveries of new lumber arrive in a holding pond near the mill and are pulled up through two chutes into area **D4** by ropes and pulleys. Shipments of processed timber or firewood ship out once every three days, hauled by horses in large wagons.

D2. Loading Bay

The entirety of this first floor consists of a loading area. An opening in the ceiling into the floor above is filled with a tangle of ropes and slings for lowering timber. Nearby, a flight of stairs ascends to the next floor. Two sturdy wagons sit to the south, next to a bank of machinery accessed by four low doors; the grinding and creaking of the machinery fills the room.

A character can climb up into the upper floor via the hanging ropes and slings with a DC 10 Climb check, but the stairs provide a much easier way to reach the same location. The four low doors to the south open into workspaces where the waterwheel-driven machinery that powers the logsplitters and saws on the upper floors runs up along the southern wall of the mill. As long as the waterwheels are running, Listen checks are made at a –2 penalty in this room.

D3. The Undermill (EL 5)

This is a place of mist and noise. Four immense waterwheels churn steadily in the northern part of this large room, while to the south, whirring belts of leather, gears, pulleys, and thick ropes spin and churn, using the eternal motion of the river below to power pistons that rumble along the southern wall.

Levers at the west and east end of the four waterwheels once provided emergency stops, but they have long since rusted in place; an attempt to pull either simply results in the lever breaking off. To stop the wheels, characters must either make a DC 20 Disable Device check or physically destroy them. Alternatively, a DC 25 Disable Device check can sabotage the machinery elsewhere in the room (indicated by shaded squares on the map). Failure at either of these checks by 5 or more indicates the character is caught by the machinery and takes 1d6 points of damage; he must also make a DC 15 Reflex save to avoid being pulled into the gear works for another 3d6 points of damage. Each round, he can attempt a new saving throw (or a DC 20 Escape Artist check) to escape, otherwise he continues to take 3d6 points of damage per round. Attempts to destroy the waterwheels or the machinery via melee attacks force a DC 15 Reflex save each round to avoid being caught up in the machines. Stopping the wheels renders the log splitters in area **D5** harmless.

Waterwheels (4)
hp 120 each
Hardness 5; **Disable Device** 20; **Break** DC 30

Machinery
hp 60 per five-foot square
Hardness 8; **Disable Device** 25; **Break** DC 26

Creatures: The machinery here needs near-constant upkeep and maintenance. This task falls to three cultists who work in shifts day and night. The cultists do not wear their robes while working, but their razors and masks are never far away. They respond to intruders with feigned friendliness at first, warning them that this room is no place for visitors and that, if they need assistance, they should contact the mill manager. If the PCs demand to know the manager's name and address, the cultists smile calmly, claim that they aren't allowed to hand out that type of information, and slowly move to surround the intruders. Once they're flanking foes, they don their masks and attack.

As long as a character is in a square bordered by an outer wall, he's safe. If he moves through any other squares during combat, he treats that square as difficult terrain and must make a DC 15 Reflex save, as detailed above, to avoid being caught in the machinery or waterwheels. A character caught in the waterwheels is dumped into the river below after 1d3 rounds. The cultists are intimately familiar with the workings of the room and can move through these squares safely (although it still counts as difficult terrain for them).

Skinsaw Cultists (3) **CR 2**
Human rogue 1/cleric 1
NE Medium humanoid
Init +6; **Senses** Listen +2, Spot +6

DEFENSE

AC 14, touch 12, flat-footed 12
(+2 armor, +2 Dex)
hp 12 (1d6+1d8+2)
Fort +3, **Ref** +4, **Will** +4

OFFENSE

Spd 30 ft.
Melee mwk war razor +2 (1d4+1/18–20)
Special Attacks death touch 1/day (1d6 damage), sneak attack +1d6, rebuke undead 2/day (–1, 2d6)
Spells Prepared (CL 1st)
1st—*command* (DC 13), *disguise self*[D] (DC 13), *shield of faith*
0—*light, mending, virtue*
D domain spell; **Domains** Death, Trickery

TACTICS

During Combat A Skinsaw Cultist casts *shield of faith* on the first round of combat if he has a chance, saving *command* for emergencies if he needs to slow down pursuit. Here in the undermill, a cultist might attempt to trip or bull rush a character not armed with a melee weapon into the machinery.
Morale If one of the cultists is slain, the others attempt to flee upstairs to join their brothers in defending the mill.

STATISTICS

Str 12, **Dex** 15, **Con** 13, **Int** 10, **Wis** 14, **Cha** 8
Base Atk +0; **Grp** +1

Skinsaw Cultist

Skinsaw Mask
Aura faint necromancy [evil]; **CL** 3rd
Slot head; **Price** 1,500 gp

DESCRIPTION

This hideous mask resembles a patchwork deformed face, with one bulbous eye, a grimacing mouth of long teeth, and no noticeable nose. When worn, the mask fills the wearer's mind with hideous whispers and images of murder and violence. It heightens his ability to sense fear. He can smell the cold sweat brought on by terror and hear the thundering beating of a frightened heart. Further, fresh blood glows brightly to him, to the extent that he can see the shimmering traceries of living circulatory systems pumping away in the bodies of those around him. These enhancements grant +2 competence bonuses on Listen, Search, and Spot checks made against creatures that aren't immune to fear. Further, the ability to see so plainly the map of a target's arteries and veins grants the wearer a +1 profane bonus on damage with slashing weapon attacks made against living creatures. Wearing a *skinsaw mask* leaves hideous mental scars; when the mask is donned, the wearer takes 1 point of Charisma damage as his thoughts become tangled with images of murder.

CONSTRUCTION

Requirements Craft Wondrous Item, *deathwatch*; **Cost** 750 gp, 60 XP

Eavesdropping on Cultists

While this adventure assumes that the PCs learn about Ironbriar's connection to Xanesha by looking through his belongings, or perhaps following the messenger birds to the Shadow Clock (see page 49), freeing Ironbriar from the lamia's charm is a much more dynamic way to lead the PCs into the climax of "The Skinsaw Murders" and offers them a chance for some entertaining roleplaying as they negotiate with the reprehensible cult leader. Of course, unless the PCs make their Sense Motive checks when they talk to him, chances are good that they won't realize he's being controlled.

If you want to drop some hints to your PCs, it's a simple matter to have them overhear conversations between cultists. Of course, this only works if the PCs are being somewhat stealthy, but if they can make a DC 0 Listen check (remember to account for distance and the intervening sounds of mill machinery), they might overhear intriguing snatches of conversation between cultists, who have started to wonder about their leadership. These conversations could revolve around doubt in Ironbriar's leadership, worry that the visions he's been having aren't what Father Skinsaw wants, or even theories that he's been seduced by "that vamp from the Clocktower." As long as you plant the seeds in the PCs' minds that there might be more to Ironbriar than meets the eye, they'll be more likely to pursue this angle and discover the truth.

—James Jacobs

Feats Improved Initiative, Martial Weapon (war razor)
Skills Balance +6, Climb +5, Hide +6, Knowledge (local) +4, Knowledge (religion) +1, Listen +2 (+4 masked), Move Silently +6, Search +4 (+6 masked), Sleight of Hand +6, Spot +6 (+8 masked), Tumble +6
Languages Common, Infernal
SQ spontaneous casting (*inflict* spells), trapfinding
Other Gear leather armor, masterwork war razor, *skinsaw mask*, 20 gp

D4. Lumber Collection (EL 5)

This large storeroom is filled with stacks of timber, firewood, and other finished lumber products waiting for shipment. A network of pulleys on tracks covers the ceiling, ropes dangling here and there to aid in the shifting of inventory as needed. Machinery churns along the south wall, while nearby two chutes fitted with winches allow lumber to be hauled up from the holding pools below. Four openings in the ceiling lead to the upper floor; chutes extend through each of these from the log splitters in the room above. Under each opening is a collection bin.

Creatures: Except during sermons, this area is populated by four Skinsaw Cultists who busy themselves inspecting lumber, arranging product, and preparing shipments. Like their fellows in the undermill, they react to intruders with smiles as they slowly work themselves into flanking positions before attacking; they do not wear their masks or robes, but they do keep their razors hidden throughout the room. At night, the cultists and their razors are out on the city streets, stalking prospective victims.

Skinsaw Cultists (4) **CR 2**
hp 12 each; see page 44

D5. Log Splitters (EL 6)

The floor of this room has a thick carpet of sawdust, penetrated by two large log splitters and saws set up over openings in the floor. Another pair of openings is fitted with winches and ropes to raise and lower uncut lumber from below.

If the waterwheels are functioning, these log splitters and saws thunder away at stacks of lumber. The cacophony imparts a –4 penalty on Listen checks to all creatures in this room.

The log splitters are powered by the waterwheel machinery; each splitter consists of a chute in the floor with blades that split logs as they are fed in. A character can clamber onto a log splitter with a DC 5 Climb check, but must make a DC 5 Reflex save to avoid being caught by the whirling blades. A character who falls into a square (or is pushed into it) can avoid being caught by the blades with a DC 15 Reflex save. Once a character falls into a working splitter, he takes 6d6 points of slashing damage and is then dropped into the collection bin 10 feet below in area **D4**.

Creatures: During the day, four Skinsaw Cultists toil in this room, loading lumber into the the log splitters with care and precision. They react to intrusions as their brothers in areas **D3** and **D4** do, with warnings that this is a "dangerous place" and eventual razors.

Skinsaw Cultists (4) **CR 2**
hp 12 each; see page 44

Treasure: The closet in the northeast corner of this floor contains two dozen robes used by the skinsaw cultists during ceremonies or for their prowls through the nighted streets. A barrel at the southern end of this closet contains a fair amount of loot harvested from their victims; the cultists maintain a community pool of stolen goods and coins for use as the need arises. The barrel contains three bags of 100 gp, three *potions of barkskin +3*, a beautiful crystal decanter set with an obsidian stopper worth 300 gp, and a tiny wooden box containing three poorly cut diamonds worth 200 gp each.

D6. Workshop (EL 3 or 10)

A thick layer of sawdust covers the floor, mounded nearly a foot deep in places. Workbenches sit here and there in the room, their surfaces cluttered with saws, hand drills, planers, and other woodworking tools.

This room serves the cultists not only as a place for them to work on various projects, but once a week as a place for them to gather to hear Ironbriar's sermons and share his visions. Lately, the cultists have taken to capturing victims alive and returning here to watch Ironbriar perform the Sihedron ritual upon the bodies before they are slain—disposal of these bodies generally falls to two lesser cultists while the rest clean up the place. Nonetheless, a DC 15 Search of this room finds numerous places where blood stains sawdust-covered floorboards, or bits of gristle remain caught in tools. The two smaller side rooms in this area are both unused storerooms.

Creatures: During the day, two cultists work on this floor, planing timbers or creating custom-sized lumber for customers. As with the other cultists in the mill, they react to intruders with feigned concern for their safety before donning masks and drawing razors.

Skinsaw Cultists (2) **CR 2**
hp 12 each; see page 44

Development: If the PCs decide to wait for a cult meeting or ritual and infiltrate the sawmill at that point (these meetings take place at midnight every Oathday), they'll find the lower floors of the mill abandoned—all 13 cultists are instead in this room, where they've pushed aside the tables to make room to stand in a semicircle around Ironbriar, who leads them in prayer before murdering his latest victim (an unconscious gambler) after performing the Sihedron ritual. The cultists are unlikely to notice the PCs' arrival—give the party automatic surprise if they attack the group during this time of unholy prayer. Of course, a battle with 13 Skinsaw Cultists and Justice Ironbriar at the same time is an EL 10 encounter—very difficult, but not impossible, for a group of 6th-level characters.

D7. Ironbriar's Office (EL 6)

The walls of this room bear macabre decorations—human faces stretched flat over wooden frames by strips of leather or black twine. Each face grimaces in a slightly different expression of pain, looking down on a cramped room that contains a desk, a high-backed rocking

Justice Ironbriar

REAPER'S MASK

Aura moderate enchantment; **CL** 7th

Slot head; **Price** 12,000 gp

DESCRIPTION

This disturbing mask appears as a single long strip of pliant human skin, stitched into a widening spiral by black thread. Gaps between the stitching allow the wearer to see and breathe through the unsettling mask. A reaper's mask functions identically to a *skinsaw mask* (see page 45), but also allows the wearer to cast *confusion* twice per day.

CONSTRUCTION

Requirements Craft Wondrous Item, *confusion, deathwatch*; **Cost** 6,000 gp, 480 XP

chair, and a low-slung cot heaped with scratchy-looking blankets. A ladder in the southeast corner of the room leads up to a trap door in the ceiling.

Creature: For the past several decades, after Vorel Foxglove vanished, an elven cleric of Norgorber named Ironbriar has led the Skinsaw Cult. His appointment to Magnimar's Justice Council only strengthened the security of the cult, but his recent magical seduction by the lamia matriarch Xanesha has perhaps damaged his reputation with his followers beyond the point where it can recover.

Justice Ironbriar keeps a home in the Alabaster District of Magnimar but is rarely there, leaving its care to a small army of servants and entertaining guests only as his role as a Justice requires. The rest of his time he spends here, stalking the streets, or visiting his mistress Xanesha at the Shadow Clock.

Ironbriar is one of the Forlorn—elves raised outside of elven communities by humans. Like most of the Forlorn, Ironbriar grew up on the streets; in this case, in the city of D'jansibar in the Spice Islands, an archipelago known for its sweltering heat, misery, slavery, and opiate dealers. On the streets of D'jansibar, he quickly learned the laws of Norgorber, and by the time his travels brought him to Magnimar, he was already a practicing priest of the god of murder.

Today, Ironbriar is a stern-faced man who believes he's finally found love, when in fact he's actually just been charmed by the object of his affection. He keeps Xanesha's identity secret from his followers, more out of jealousy that they might try to steal her away than anything else.

Ironbriar prefers to let his cultists handle any intruders, but once they start fleeing up to area **D6** with stories of the PCs causing problems downstairs, he puts on his *reaper's mask* and seeks them out personally—he looks forward to bringing their framed faces to Xanesha as trophies. He's not interested in speaking to the PCs, but if they can engage him in even a few rounds of conversation, a DC 25 Sense Motive check is enough for the PC to realize that Ironbriar is affected by a charm effect.

JUSTICE IRONBRIAR **CR 7**

Male elf rogue 1/cleric 6 (Norgorber)

NE Medium humanoid

Init +6; **Senses** low-light vision; Listen +8, Spot +8

DEFENSE

AC 23, touch 19, flat-footed 17

(+4 armor, +3 deflection, +6 Dex)

hp 40 (1d6+6d8+7)

Fort +6, **Ref** +10, **Will** +7 (+2 against enchantment)

Immune sleep effects

OFFENSE

Spd 30 ft.

Melee *+1 war razor* +11 (1d4/18–20)

Special Attack rebuke undead 4/day (+1, 2d6+7), sneak attack +1d6

Spells Prepared (CL 7th)

3rd—*bestow curse* (DC 15), *cure serious wounds, suggestion*[D] (DC 15)

2nd—*bear's endurance, cat's grace, cure moderate wounds, invisibility*[D], *undetectable alignment* (already cast)

1st—*charm person*[D] (DC 13), *command* (DC 13), *cure light wounds, divine favor, shield of faith*

0—*cure minor wounds* (2), *light, mending, read magic, virtue*

D domain spell; **Domains** Charm, Trickery

TACTICS

Before Combat Ironbriar prepares for combat by casting *bear's endurance, cat's grace, shield of faith*, and *invisibility*; the effects of these spells are included in his stats.

During Combat Ironbriar prefers to let his cultists fight in melee, himself hanging back to use his spells at range. Once he's cast his ranged spells, he casts *bestow curse*, holds the charge, and steps in to touch the PC who seems to be the most dangerous, after which he fights with his magic war razor.

Morale As long as he remains under the effect of Xanesha's *charm monster* spell, Ironbriar fights to the death. If the charm effect ends, he suddenly realizes how the lamia matriarch has been using him and immediately offers the PCs a deal, as detailed under Development. If the PCs refuse to deal with Ironbriar, he does his best to escape into the city—he abandons his life here and attempts to flee Varisia aboard a trade ship bound for the distant south.

STATISTICS

Str 8, **Dex** 22, **Con** 12, **Int** 14, **Wis** 14, **Cha** 12

Base Atk +4; **Grp** +3

Feats Combat Reflexes, Martial Weapon Proficiency (war razor), Weapon Finesse

Skills Bluff +11, Concentration +5, Decipher Script +6, Diplomacy +13, Forgery +6, Hide +10, Intimidate +7, Knowledge (local) +6, Knowledge (religion) +8, Listen +8, Move Silently +10, Search +4, Spot +8

SQ spontaneous casting (*inflict* spells), trapfinding

Languages Common, Draconic, Elven, Infernal

Combat Gear *wand of cure moderate wounds* (12 charges); **Other Gear** mithral shirt, *+1 war razor, reaper's mask*

SPECIAL ABILITIES

Charm Domain (Ex) Once per day, Justice Ironbriar can boost his Charisma by 4 points. Activating this power is a free action. The Charisma increase lasts 1 minute.

Treasure: The faces of Ironbriar's victims are ghoulish but worth little. The large footlocker, however, is filled with oddments that Ironbriar has collected from his many victims over the years. A fair number are of a historical nature, including books, sea charts, etchings of vast rock formations and dolmens accompanied by maps, several pamphlets discussing a "forgotten" school of magic known as The Alchymyc, and a fine painting depicting a city carved from a vast frozen waterfall with towering ice cathedrals and domes (this painting is worth 200 gp).

Near the bottom are several books. The first of these is a wizard's spellbook emblazoned with two entwined snakes (one red, one green) that contains the following spells: all cantrips, *blink, cat's grace, chill touch, enlarge person, fox's cunning, grease, haste, lightning bolt, mage armor, magic missile, scorching ray, shocking grasp, shrink item, spider climb,* and *web*. The second book is an old and beautifully filigreed tome containing numerous hand-drawn illustrations and titled *The Syrpents Tane: Fairy Tales of the Eldest*. The book presents tales of the Tane—goliaths of war and madness dreamt and stitched into being by the Eldest, the most feared of a group of notorious fey known as the Twisted. The Tane are said to be terrible to behold, and the stories speak of them stumbling into mortal lands, where they ravage kingdoms by creating firestorms, crushing keeps with their feet, and eating dragons. Specific Tane described include monstrous creatures like the Jabberwok (a thing of thorns and fire and crushing fury the size of a castle), the Thrasfyr (also known as the Dreaming Hill of the Dark, a barbed thing of iron and hooks and blades that the book claims took part in the Three-Thousand-Year War of the Eldest), and the Sard (the Storm of Insanities, a thing of boughs and briars and misery, an ancient Wychwood Elm given life and hate by the Eldest, a mad creature apt to pull a roc in two or fell a castle at a blow). This fine and rare tome is worth 500 gp.

Finally, a slim volume near the bottom of the chest serves double-duty as a ledger and journal for Justice Ironbriar. He's recorded everything in the journal in a cipher he painstakingly invented himself using a mix of Draconic, Elven, and Infernal characters. A character who can read all three of these languages can make a DC 25 Decipher Script check after 2d4 days of study to untangle the complex cipher. If a PC deciphers it, enough evidence exists in the book to put Ironbriar in the gallows. If the PCs haven't already determined that Ironbriar wasn't the mastermind behind the murders, his journal makes it clear enough that someone he refers to as the "Wanton of Nature's Pagan Forms" has stolen his heart and provided him with a new method of murder. There's not much information about Xanesha in the journal, but the book does reveal that he's visited her dozens of times at the Shadow Clock.

Although the PCs are unlikely to follow up on it, the ledger also indicates that Ironbriar has received payment from the Red Mantis for delivery of "Vorel's Legacy." This refers to the deadly fungus harvested from area **B37** of Foxglove Manor, sent to a sinister group of assassins based in Cheliax. For now, this lead is a red herring, but it plays a significant role in the next *Pathfinder* Adventure Path, Curse of the Crimson Throne.

Development: If released from Xanesha's *charm monster*, all of Ironbriar's rage is suddenly directed at the lamia matriarch. He offers the PCs a deal—he tells them that Xanesha is responsible for all of the murders, both those in Sandpoint and the recent spate here in Magnimar, and that she was using the Brothers of the Seven as patsies for her own plans (Ironbriar's careful to try to blame the "cult" aspects of the situation on her influence, and does his best to leave Norgorber out of it). In return for looking the other way for 12 hours (long enough for Ironbriar to escape Magnimar), he promises to reveal to them not only the location of Xanesha's hideout, but the strength of her forces and guardians. He only reveals this last if he thinks he can trust the PCs. He knows about the Scarecrow and how many faceless stalkers Xanesha keeps in the tower (three in all), and can even provide a brief description of the lamia matriarch's abilities.

D8. Rookery

A timber cabinet sits against the northern wall here, its doors made of iron mesh. Inside perch three strangely silent ravens. A table nearby holds a tall narrow bucket of birdfeed, a quill, and a vial of ink, as well as several thin parchments weighted down by a polished rock.

These are messenger ravens, as a DC 12 Handle Animal check or DC 15 Knowledge (local) check can reveal. Ironbriar uses them to communicate with Xanesha; if the PCs use *speak with animals*, they can learn as much for the price of a few bird snacks offered from the bucket on the table. If the ravens are released, they fly unerringly north at a speed of 40 feet; if the PCs can keep up and keep them in sight, the ravens lead them directly to the Shadow Clock. Chasing them requires DC 15 Spot checks every few rounds to keep them in sight.

PART FIVE: SHADOWS OF TIME

Known to some as the Wanton of Nature's Pagan Forms, Xanesha is a lamia matriarch who, for many years, dwelt in the hoary spires of the lost city of Xin-Shalast. She was honored to be among those chosen by Karzoug and sent south to begin the harvest of souls of greed. While other matriarchs went to places as diverse as Riddleport, Janderhoff, Korvosa, and the orc strongholds of Belkzen, Xanesha ended up in Magnimar. She took her time seeking the perfect agent to perform the Sihedron ritual, and exceeded her expectations in catching Justice Ironbriar.

Now, the lamia matriarch is free to explore the city and discover new greedy candidates for murder, while leaving the actual work of the slayings to her new underlings. Her current goal is to engineer the sacrifice of Lord-Mayor Haldmeer Grobaras, one of the greediest men in Varisia; although this plan is still in its early stages of planning, Xanesha could eventually bring Magnimar to its knees.

Xanesha was drawn to the part of Magnimar known as the Shadow for its lawlessness and sociological turmoil—here was a place where she could dwell without constant fear of discovery. Her chosen lair was the Shadow Clock, one of several failed attempts to bring order to this ramshackle region.

The Shadow Clock

Hidden beneath the grimy blackened goliath that is the Irespan, the lesser works of men huddle like weeds at the foot of the great trees that are the ruined bridge's stone supports. Near one of these supports leans a decrepit and sagging clocktower, a dying structure of weathered stone, wood, and rusted metal supports that teeters to an unlikely height of nearly one hundred and eighty feet. High above, near the tower's roof and barely fifty feet from the Irespan's stony belly, a tangle of scaffolding sits near a section of the structure that has fallen away. The tower's clock face is frozen in time, defiantly (and falsely) proclaiming it to be three o'clock, while above, a stone statue of an angel, her wings crumbling, leans precariously, almost as if she were preparing a final leap from her decaying perch.

The Shadow Clock is a minor marvel of engineering. The locals in the region half expect it to collapse any day, and several Shadow taverns have long-standing betting pools on how many structures it will crush and people it will kill when it finally falls. The tower itself is made mostly of limestone, with a tangled skeleton of wooden supports buttressed here and there by iron bands. The stone walls are etched by wind, rain, and grime. While this pitted surface might seem to make for a relatively easy climb, the fact that so many of the stones are loose makes such a stunt dangerous—it's a DC 25 Climb check to scale the tower's outer walls. Inside, it's not much safer; the crumbling wooden steps are known as the "Terrible Stairs" to the locals. After the tenth unfortunate death when someone tried to climb these stairs several years ago, the city ordered the tower closed.

Yet the locals of the Shadow know better. They whisper stories that someone has moved into the clocktower. Many claim to have seen a serpentine shape slithering out of the gap near the roof, slinking through the night sky into regions unknown, while others tell of a shadowy bulk twice the size of a man sometimes seen lurking in the darkness at the clock's base. No one has dared enter the tower to confirm these rumors, yet most who live in the Shadow do not doubt their veracity.

The Shadow Clock is currently inhabited by Xanesha, three charmed faceless stalkers, and a self-aware flesh golem known as the Scarecrow. Each section on the map is twenty feet higher than the prevous one.

E1. The Scarecrow's Lair (EL 8)

The air inside the clocktower is dusty and dry. Swaths of rubble and mounds of plaster lie in heaps on the stone floor, particularly in the southwest corner, where a large mound has gathered. A single wagon sits to the north, and six partially collapsed offices line the northern and eastern walls, their doors hanging askew and their ceilings caved in. A wooden staircase winds up into the cavernous space above. Well over two hundred feet overhead, four immense bronze bells hang from sturdy crossbeams.

The collapsed rooms were once used as barracks, workshops, and storerooms, but nothing of value remains here now. A DC 15 Survival check made by someone with the Track feat reveals that, despite the place's general appearance of ruin, a fair amount of foot traffic has been through the area—the floor bears several Medium humanoid footprints and a pair of enormous misshapen prints that defy classification. This second pair of prints has been left by the room's guardian.

Creature: A thing of horror, a monstrosity created decades ago by none other than Vorel Foxglove (one of many favors he performed for the Brothers of the Seven before his unfortunate end), dwells in this area—a being known only as the Scarecrow. This misshapen monster is a thing from a child's nightmares—a flesh golem who, through an accident of magic, gained sentience many decades ago when its elemental spirit went berserk. A jumbled mass of body parts incorporating as much cow and horse as man, the Scarecrow's considerable girth is topped by an idiot head that leers and drools like a grotesque baby. Its face is cruelly stitched, the lips sewn together. It is dressed in straw and dung-covered rags which give off the sickly sweet smell of decay. A trio of what appear to be carved pumpkins hang from cords on its belt, but a second glance reveals these to be horribly bloated human heads with a sick yellow tinge. The Skinsaw Cultists often use the Scarecrow to do minor dirty work in the city, terrifying the local slum populace with appearances every so often. When Xanesha learned about the golem from Ironbriar, she had him bring it before her and quickly added it to her collection of charmed minions.

When at rest here in the mill, the Scarecrow bides its time in the northeast corner of the loading bay, the *cloak of elvenkind* it wears increasing its ability to remain unseen. If it notices intruders, it remains motionless and hidden for several rounds before moving to attack once any of the PCs comes more than halfway into the room or once most of the group has moved along upstairs.

THE SCARECROW **CR 8**

Lifespark elite flesh golem (MM 135; *Advanced Bestiary* 159)

CE Large construct

Init +1; **Senses** darkvision 60 ft., low-light vision; Listen +1, Spot +1

DEFENSE

AC 20, touch 10, flat-footed 19

(+1 Dex, +10 natural, –1 size)

hp 79 (9d10+30)

Fort +3, **Ref** +4, **Will** +4; –2 against mind-affecting effects

Defensive Abilities construct traits; **DR** 5/adamantine

OFFENSE

Spd 30 ft.

Melee +1 *scythe* +14/+9 (2d6+11/×4) or

2 slams +12 (2d8+7)

Space 10 ft.; **Reach** 10 ft.

TACTICS

During Combat The Scarecrow does not pursue foes up the stairs, but it does chase after anyone who tries to escape into the Shadow district.

Morale Although a construct and loyal to the cult, the Scarecrow values its life as well. If brought below 20 hit points it tries to escape into the ocean, where it remains for days until it feels brave enough to emerge and seek out someone it can bully into repairing its damage.

STATISTICS

Str 25, **Dex** 13, **Con** —, **Int** 12, **Wis** 13, **Cha** 10

Base Atk +6; **Grp** +17

Feats Martial Weapon Proficiency (scythe), Power Attack, Stealthy, Weapon Focus (scythe)

Skills Climb +19, Hide +16, Move Silently +15

Languages Common, Infernal

SQ open mind

Gear *+1 scythe, cloak of elvenkind*

SPECIAL ABILITIES

Immune to Magic (Ex) The Scarecrow is immune to any spell or spell-like ability that allows spell resistance. Any magical attack that deals cold or fire damage slows the Scarecrow for 2d6 rounds (no saving throw). Any magical attack that deals electricity damage breaks any *slow* effect on the Scarecrow and heals 1 point of damage for every 3 points of damage the attack would otherwise deal; excess hit points are gained as temporary hit points.

Open Mind (Ex) Unlike standard flesh golems, the Scarecrow is self-aware and possesses a personality, and it does not have a chance of going berserk. It is not immune to mind-affecting attacks, and in fact takes a –2 penalty on saving throws against mind-affecting effects.

Treasure: A DC 20 Search check of the mound of debris in the southwest corner uncovers a moldy leather sack containing 125 gp, 309 sp, a tarnished silver ring worth 75 gp (labelled "To AV, with love"), and a silver mirror worth 50 gp.

E2. The Terrible Stair (EL 5)

The inner wall of this vast space is traversed by a winding wooden stairway supported by an intricate network of wooden beams but lacking, at many stretches, a handrail or other enclosure. In certain places, two or even three stairs at a time are partially missing or gone altogether.

This stairwell looks treacherous—and it most certainly is. The rotting wood can support no more than one Medium creature in any pair of adjacent squares. If the wood is overloaded, it creaks and sways alarmingly for 1d4+1 rounds. If at the end of this time the section is still overloaded, it cracks and falls away, dropping anyone on that section into area **E1** below. Anyone in a crumbling section can grab onto nearby remaining stairs with a DC 15 Reflex save, otherwise taking the appropriate falling damage. The Scarecrow never climbs the stairs and Xanesha navigates the tower by flight, leaving only the faceless stalkers to use the stairs with any frequency—and they're always careful to stay at least 10 feet away from each other.

Trap: If the faceless stalkers in area **E3** above notice the PCs, they wait until the party is halfway up the stairs before they make their move by cutting several intentionally weakened ropes supporting the bells above. At this point, the PCs are still about 100 feet away from area **E3**, and a DC 10 Listen check allows them to hear the sudden sounds of ropes snapping and timbers splintering above.

Once the ropes are cut, the southeasternmost bell gives way, causing the immense bronze bell to ring for the first time in years as it swings down then tears free with a tremendous crash. The bell tumbles and smashes along the walls, tearing through the section of stairs just below it (and leaving a 10-foot-wide gap) before crashing its way down into area **E1** below. Along the way, it has a chance of striking 1d4 of the characters—randomly determine which ones have a chance of being struck. Any character who didn't hear the ropes and timbers snap is considered flat-footed against the bell's attack.

Note that this trap can only be disabled from area **E3**; characters approaching from below likely won't have a chance to prevent this dangerous event from being triggered.

Falling Bell — **CR 5**

Type mechanical
Search DC 20; **Disable Device** DC 20

EFFECTS

Trigger manual; **Reset** repair
Effect Falling bronze bell, targets 1d4 characters in area **E1** or **E2**, Atk +15 (6d6 bludgeoning damage). The bell breaks stairs in a 10-foot-long swath wherever it hits a PC. A character damaged by the bell falls into area **E1**, taking the appropriate falling damage, unless he makes a DC 15 Reflex save to cling to the stairs.

E3. The Bells (EL 7)

Four immense brass bells hang from timbers here, affixed by rusting lengths of chain and thick ropes. Above the bells are immense gears and clockworks, although they seem both rusted and scavenged, as if many of the smaller components are missing entirely. The rickety wooden stairs wind up and around them but don't quite reach the ceiling above, coming to an end at an opening in the wall. Here, the stairs continue up the exterior of the tower to a room that must lie just beyond the ceiling directly above the bells.

The rickety stairs lead up and over themselves out through the hole in the wall to area **E4** above.

Creatures: The three charmed faceless stalkers that guard the Terrible Stair spend most of their time waiting patiently here for intruders to attack. Their first gambit is to drop a bell on intruders; they haven't prepared any of the other bells for such an assault, and once they drop the first one they lurk here, waiting to attack anyone who progresses further up the stairs.

Faceless Stalkers (3) — **CR 4**

hp 42 each; see page 88

Impaler of Thorns

Aura moderate enchantment; **CL** 7th
Slot — (held); **Price** 9,000 gp

DESCRIPTION

The *impaler of thorns* is an ancient weapon dating back to Thassilonian times, where it was often used by city guards to aid in breaking up civil unrest. An impaler's shaft is made of darkwood, its head a thorn-like, wide-bladed barb. When used in combat, successful critical hits are accompanied by an unsettling screech, as of some wild beast in anger.

Once per day as it strikes a foe, you can trigger it (as a free action) to unleash a 30-foot-radius burst of despair that affects all creatures not wielding an *impaler of thorns*. Creatures affected must make DC 16 Will saves or become overwhelmed with sadness and despair, suffering a –2 penalty on attack rolls, saving throws, ability checks, skill checks, and weapon damage rolls for 6 minutes. The target struck when this effect is triggered must also make a second DC 16 Will save to resist becoming nauseated with despair for 1 round.

CONSTRUCTION

Requirements Craft Magic Arms and Armor, *cat's grace, delay poison*; **Cost** 4,500 gp, 360 XP

E4. Clocktower Rookery

A timber cabinet with a mesh door sits against the southern wall of this room, while a boarded-up door stands in the wall to the east.

The cabinet contains a single black messenger raven (plus any additional ravens that the PCs might have released from area **D8**). Xanesha uses these ravens to send messages to Ironbriar on the few occasions she feels the need to do so.

E5. Clockworks

This large and cluttered room is filled with immense gears and clockworks. Most of them appear to have rusted into place.

Whereas the stairwell leading up the inner walls of the clocktower is quite rickety, the wooden floor of this chamber is solid. The clockworks themselves have long since fallen into ruin—it would take many months of repair work by gifted tinkers to rebuild and restore the clock. Although the room looks sinister and dangerous with all its gears, there's nothing to be found here.

The Shadow Clock
E1
E2
E2
E2
E2
E2
E3
E4
E5
E6
N
One Square = 5 Feet

E6. The Angel (EL 10)

The smoky, filthy rooftops of the Shadow sprawl below this dizzying perch. The conical roof supports an onyx statue of an angel. Towering like a god, her weathered features are caked with grime, making her seem almost demonic in countenance. At the far end of the hollow space under the roof, in the angel's shadow, is a nest of cushions, silk sheets, and other incongruously fine bits of decor.

Creature: The lamia matriarch Xanesha has selected this area as her lair, both for the unparalleled view of Magnimar's poorest district and for the isolation afforded by its remote location. She comes and goes via flight, usually making sure to become invisible before doing so to prevent curious eyes from noticing her. She often spends her nights in other parts of the city, in her human guise and in the arms of charmed lovers who strike her fancy during her walks among the enemy. Many of these "lovers" pine for her company for weeks or months after she abandons them, but they are the lucky ones who aren't murdered and brought back here to serve as food. In many ways, Xanesha is a predator living hidden among her prey. She has grown fond of her position in Magnimar over the years and is content to leave the actual work of harvesting greedy souls to the Skinsaw Cult. Recently, she's been contacted with recurring frequency by Mokmurian or his agents—she realizes that the time of Karzoug's return is close at hand and has decided to spur on the cult in its work. Recruiting Aldern was actually Ironbriar's idea, but Xanesha prefers to think of it as her own. Once the PCs make their move against the Skinsaw Cult, she holes up here to prepare herself against their inevitable arrival.

XANESHA **CR 10**

Lamia matriarch sorcerer 2

Always CE Large monstrous humanoid (shapechanger)

Init +6; **Senses** darkvision 60 ft., low-light vision; Listen +2, Spot +2

DEFENSE

AC 26, touch 16, flat-footed 20 (+1 armor, +1 deflection, +6 Dex, +9 natural, –1 size)

hp 142 (12d8+2d4+48)

Fort +11 (+13 against poison), **Ref** +15, **Will** +16

Immune mind-affecting effects; **SR** 18

OFFENSE

Spd 40 ft., climb 40 ft., swim 40 ft.

Melee *impaler of thorns* +20/+15/+10 (2d6+9/19–20/×3 plus 1 Wisdom drain) or touch +18 (2d4 Wisdom drain)

Space 10 ft.; **Reach** 5 ft.

Spell-Like Abilities (CL 10th)

At will—*charm monster* (DC 21), *ventriloquism* (DC 18)

3/day—*deep slumber* (DC 20), *dream*, *major image* (DC 20), *mirror image*, *suggestion* (DC 20)

Spells Known (CL 8th, +18 ranged touch)

4th (4/day)—*dimension door*

3rd (7/day)—*fly*, *haste*

2nd (8/day)—*invisibility*, *scorching ray*, *silence* (DC 19)

1st (8/day)—*cure light wounds*, *divine favor*, *mage armor*, *magic missile*, *shield*

0 (6/day)—*acid splash*, *dancing lights*, *daze* (DC 17), *detect magic*, *ghost sound* (DC 17), *mage hand*, *mending*, *prestidigitation*

TACTICS

Before Combat If she realizes the PCs are near (as is the case if the faceless stalkers drop a bell), Xanesha casts *fly*, *mage armor*, and *shield* on herself. If she has a chance just prior to combat (as is the case if she hears the PCs approaching her lair) she also casts *mirror image*, *haste*, and *invisibility*, and then *silence* on a timber near the entrance to her lair. These effects are incorporated into her stats.

During Combat Xanesha activates her *Sihedron medallion's false life* ability and casts *divine favor* (enhanced by Silent Spell if necessary) on the first round of combat. If she's still invisible, she casts a *major image* to make an illusory flying demon

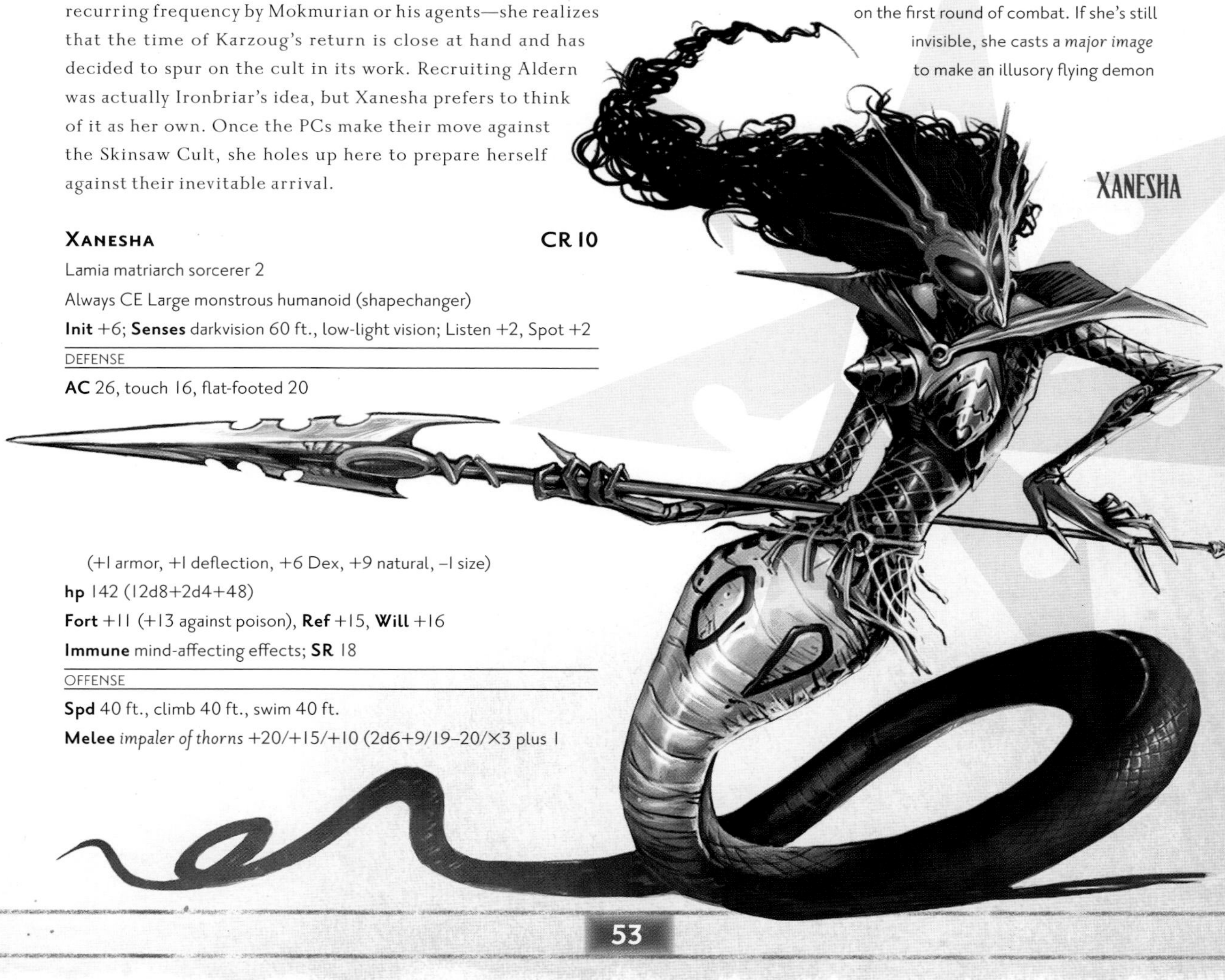

XANESHA

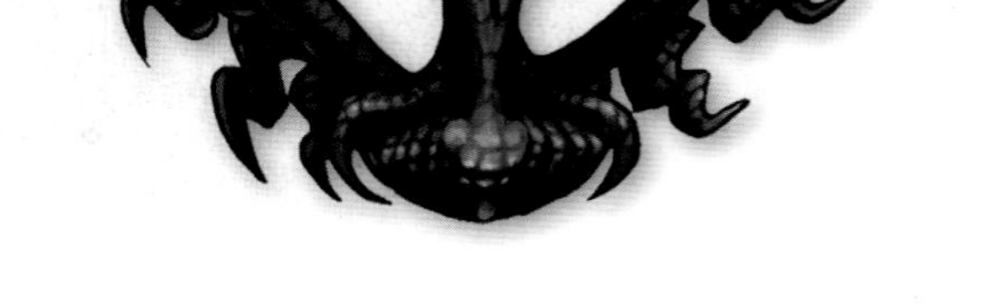

Medusa Mask

Aura moderate transmutation; **CL** 11th

Slot head; **Price** 10,000 gp

DESCRIPTION

This intricate mask is made of gold-plated iron. The eyes are two dark lenses of crystal, while surrounding these are the writhing tails of snakes radiating up from the mask itself, almost as if they were medusa-like hair. The mask grants you a +4 bonus on all saving throws against visual effects, including gaze attacks and many illusions. Once per day as a standard action, you can cause the lenses to glow with pale green light, at which point you may target any one creature within 30 feet. The targeted creature must make a DC 15 Fortitude save or be petrified for 1 minute, as if by *flesh to stone*.

CONSTRUCTION

Requirements Craft Wondrous Item, *flesh to stone, resistance*; **Cost** 5,000 gp, 400 XP

Snakeskin Tunic

Aura moderate abjuration and transmutation; **CL** 8th

Slot torso; **Price** 8,000 gp

DESCRIPTION

A *snakeskin tunic* is a tight, form-fitting shirt crafted from the scales of a giant snake. When worn, it grants a +1 armor bonus to your AC, a +2 enhancement bonus to your Dexterity, and a +2 resistance bonus on saving throws against poison.

CONSTRUCTION

Requirements Craft Wondrous Item, *cat's grace, delay poison*; **Cost** 4,000 gp, 320 XP

appear in a cloud of smoke that then begins to circle the top of the tower. On round three, hopefully as the PCs are distracted, she attempts to petrify a PC near the edge using her mask; this, of course, makes her visible. After this attack, she prefers to fight in melee. She may try to topple a petrified PC off the edge to smash into fragments on the ground 160 feet below. If reduced to less than 60 hit points, she flies out into the sky around the tower to continue the fight using her spells.

Morale Xanesha attempts to flee Magnimar, abandoning her plot and the scroll hidden in her nest, if she's reduced to 20 hit points or less. If she escapes, she cuts ties with her kin and Mokmurian, afraid of the punishment for failure. She grows obsessed with the PCs, seeing their capture as the only way she can redeem herself to Mokmurian—in this case, she becomes a recurring villain who might ally with any number of foes the PCs find themselves up against in the next adventure.

STATISTICS

Str 22, **Dex** 23, **Con** 22, **Int** 16, **Wis** 14, **Cha** 25

Base Atk +13; **Grp** +23

Feats Extend Spell, Improved Critical (spear), Power Attack, Silent Spell, Weapon Focus (spear)

Skills Bluff +19, Concentration +18, Knowledge (arcana) +15, Knowledge (local) +14, Spellcraft +19, Tumble +15, Use Magic Device +24

Languages Abyssal, Common, Draconic

SQ alternate form

Other Gear *impaler of thorns, medusa mask, Sihedron medallion* (+1 resistance bonus on all saves, *false life* as free action 1/day at CL 5th; see *Pathfinder #1* 55), *snakeskin tunic, ring of protection +1*

SPECIAL ABILITIES

Alternate Form (Su) A lamia matriarch has a single humanoid form that she can assume as a standard action—most lamia matriarchs have human, elven, or half-elven alternate forms. Their appearance in this form is identical from the waist up to their serpentine form, yet in humanoid form the lamia matriarch is Medium sized (–8 Strength, +2 Dex, –4 Constitution), cannot use her Wisdom drain attack, and has a base speed of 30 feet.

Wisdom Drain (Su) A lamia matriarch drains 1d6 points of Wisdom each time she hits with her melee touch attack. If she strikes a foe with a melee weapon, she drains 1 point of Wisdom instead. Unlike with other kinds of ability drain attacks, a lamia matriarch does not heal damage when she uses her Wisdom drain.

Skills Lamia matriarchs have a +4 racial bonus on Bluff, Tumble, and Use Magic Device checks.

Spells Lamia matriarchs cast spells as 6th-level sorcerers, and can also cast spells from the cleric list. Cleric spells are considered arcane spells for a lamia matriarch, meaning that the creature doesn't need a divine focus to cast them.

Treasure: An interesting object hidden in her nest can be found with a DC 10 Search check. This object is a long scroll bearing an extensive list of names and professions, many of which have been crossed out. The list bears the heading "Sihedron Sacrifices." Some of these names are of folks from Sandpoint, but the majority are people who live in

Magnimar—all of them merchants, moneylenders, gamblers, adventurers, and thieves—greedy souls hand-selected by Xanesha. Crossed-out names indicate murder victims. If any of the PCs are particularly greedy, their names appear on the list as well.

The most prominent name on the list, though, is that of Lord-Mayor Haldmeer Grobaras. In addition, it would seem that Xanesha has been taking extensive notes on the lord-mayor's habits—when he takes his meals, who he visits, his favorite taverns, and even the hours he sleeps. It shouldn't take much effort to determine that Xanesha was planning to assassinate the ruler of Magnimar. Nowhere in these documents does Xanesha give any indication why she was organizing the murders of so many souls—the PCs might piece together her pattern, but for now, the motive remains a disturbing mystery of its own.

CONCLUDING THE ADVENTURE

With Xanesha's defeat, the murders that have plagued Magnimar and Sandpoint cease. When Lord-Mayor Grobaras discovers that the murderers were planning his assassination, he faints. When he recovers, he invites the PCs to attend a feast at his home, Defiant's Garden. Grobaras is hardly a scion of virtue, but he is nonetheless a powerful man, and in reward for defeating the murderers he grants each PC 6,000 gp.

The PCs have, at this point, braved a haunted house, defeated a dangerous cult, and saved the leader of Magnimar, yet they should feel as if there is yet more brewing behind the scenes. The recurrence of the Sihedron Rune should trouble them as well. Unfortunately, even in Magnimar, little can be learned about Thassilon—a fact that has frustrated many scholars who have tried to decipher the mysteries of the ancient ruins of Varisia.

Whether the PCs realize it or not, the time draws near when they will learn all they need to know about Varisia's ancient past. It begins as Lord-Mayor Grobaras, freshly pleased with their work against the Skinsaw Cult, contacts them with a job. It seems that little has been heard from the rangers stationed at a remote fort at the edge of Magnimar's direct holdings—even *sendings* directed at the fort's leader have gone unanswered. The fort is a good distance away, and although several members of the city's Council of Ushers have been pressuring him to send someone to reestablish contact with the rangers of Fort Rannick near Hook Mountain, until now he's not had someone he cared to spare for the task. The PCs would be perfect for the job, yet when they arrive, they find themselves not at a border fort, but at a massacre.

MAGNIMAR

CITY OF MONUMENTS

Built in the shadow of megaliths, Magnimar endlessly endeavors to surpass the overwhelming scale and grandeur of the ancient wonders that litter the Varisian landscape. A place of great opportunity, social stress, and cold beauty, the city exudes the airs of a southern metropolis, seeking to rise above its ignoble beginnings as a refuge for Korvosan outcasts to become a beacon of culture and freedom in an unforgiving land. Yet its towering monuments, elegant gardens, ostentatious architecture, and elaborate sculptures form but a cracked mask over a struggling government and a desperate people in need of heroes.

Magnimar's sprawling slate rooftops and marble avenues stretch from the foundations of the unignorable Irespan—a ruined stone bridge of impossible size—to beyond the western banks of the Yondabakari River. A sheer cliff, the Seacleft, cuts through the city's heart, dividing Magnimar into its two major sections: the Summit, upon the cliff's top, and the Shore, below. A third district, the Shadow, lies beneath the Irespan, a place where the sun rarely reaches and the city's failures and corruption hold blatant reign.

The second largest city in Varisia, Magnimar wages an open war of coins and lies with Korvosa to the east. Both city-states vie for control over vassal communities, natural resources, and trade with the cosmopolitan south. This rivalry stretches back to a time even before the city's founding, as droves of Korvosan dissenters, unwilling to blindly kowtow to foreign despots after the fall of the Chelaxian Empire, departed for the Lost Coast. Ever since, Magnimar has welcomed those who would shape their own fates by the sweat of their brows and keenness of their wits, regardless of race or beliefs. To this end, the city has opened its gates and harbor to all comers, encouraging traders from many lands to discover the wonders of Varisia away from the excessive taxes and regulations of Korvosa, yet in greater safety than that offered by pirate havens like Riddleport.

Today, more than 16,000 people make their homes in Magnimar, with the majority of that populace consisting of humans of Chelish decent. It also boasts the largest semi-settled population of Varisians in the world, with approximately 2,000 such residents—significantly fewer in the spring and summer travel months. Aside from the region's native nomads, Magnimar hosts a second transient population: thousands of regular traders from far-flung foreign locales, particularly Absalom, Cheliax, and Osirion. Many of these merchants, emissaries, and adventurers have homes that they reside in while passing through but that otherwise remain empty. As a result, whole city blocks—particularly along the Shore—appear deserted for months out of the year. Should every homeowner coincidentally be in the city at the same time, Magnimar's population would increase by almost half again its current number.

MAGNIMAR

Large City conventional (mayor); **AL** N

GP Limit 40,000 gp; **Assets** 32,856,000 gp

DEMOGRAPHICS

Population 16,428

Type mixed (81% human, 5% halfling, 4% dwarf, 4% elf, 3% gnome, 2% half-elf, 1% half-orc)

AUTHORITY FIGURES

Haldmeer Grobaras, lord-mayor (N male human aristocrat 9); **Verrine Caiteil,** spokeswoman of the Council of Ushers (NG female elf aristocrat 5/bard 2); **Lord Justice Bayl Argentine,** leader of the Justice Court (LN male human aristocrat 6/fighter 3); **Remeria Callinova,** leader of the Varisian Council (CG female human expert 4/rogue 2); **Lady Vammiera Symirkova,** mistress of the Gargoyles (NE female human aristocrat 2/rogue 6/sorcerer 4); **Princess Sabriyya Kalmeralm,** de facto ruler of the Bazaar of Sails (CN female human rogue 12)

GOVERNMENT AND POLITICS

Since the establishment of a formal city government in 4608 AR, Magnimar has been led by two political bodies: the Council of Ushers and the Office of the Lord-Mayor. When the city was established, this egalitarian arrangement was meant to assure that no one man would have too powerful a voice in the city-state's governing. After more than a hundred years, though, this noble effort has become embroiled in officialism, paper shuffling, and the ambitions of its members.

Supposedly the most powerful political institution in Magnimar, the Council of Ushers is defined by its charter as an assembly of the eldest, most experienced, and most influential of the community's leaders, overseen by an executive moderator. As the city has grown, so too has this legislature, and what began as a group of the city's 15 most active and outspoken family leaders has bloated into a delegation of 117 members, rife with bored nobles, scheming power-seekers, and greedy merchants. For all the assembly's corruption, though, many honest business leaders and political activists passionately (and often, frustratedly) seek to serve the will of Magnimar's citizenry. From its impressive chambers known as Usher's Hall, the council debates matters of city-wide import and makes decisions regarding the area of influence outside Magnimar's walls—effectively governing the city-state as the fledgling nation it's becoming.

Undisputedly the most politically powerful man in Magnimar, **Lord-Mayor Haldmeer Grobaras** (N male human aristocrat 9) is a paunchy, self-serving politico more concerned with his own comforts than the needs of the underprivileged he hears so much about. Having managed Magnimar for the last seven years, Grobaras handles the immediate needs of the city, indifferently settling matters relating to the distribution of city funds, use of the city watch, and the concerns of countless citizens groups, all while welcoming bribery and lavish gifts. Although the finest Chelish fashions and his numerous chins make the lord-mayor's self-indulgent foppishness blatantly apparent, they hide a silver tongue and the private wealth to give nearly any promise form. While his station would have him uphold the mandates of the Council of Ushers, he often ignores such duties, proving much more attentive to whether or not his personal declarations are enforced. Grobaras's mandates are rare, but—without the need for council review—sometimes prove grossly biased or potentially damaging to the city. Fortunately, the secretary of the lord-mayor, Grobaras's personal assistant and messenger **Valanni Krinst** (NG male human noble 1/rogue 3), personally—and quite illegally—vets many of the orders from the lord-mayor's office.

A third political body operating outside of the city government is the Varisian Council. Formed at the request of the city's elders more than 80 years ago, the Varisian Council assures that the Magnimarian government does not infringe upon the rights and traditions of Varisia's native peoples—peripherally including the Shoanti—who live in close-knit neighborhoods and transient tent and wagon communities throughout the city.

LAW & CRIME

As a city founded by those who refused to live under the reign of tyrants, Magnimar has relatively few laws. From its barracks within

HELLKNIGHTS IN MAGNIMAR

In 4682 AR, Queen Domina of Korvosa courted several orders of Cheliax's feared law keepers, the hellknights, in the hopes of buying militarily weak Korvosa the strength the city-state needed to dominate southern Varisia. Denied by such powerful bodies as the notorious Order of the Rack, genocidal Order of the Scourge, and devil-blooded Order of the God Claw, she was finally able to coax the stern Order of the Nail to her lands, promising them vast endowments and a fortress of their own: Citadel Vraid in the foothills of the Mindspin Mountains south of Korvosa. Fast upon their relocation to Varisia, Queen Domina began entreating the hellknights for aid, particularly in attempts at intimidation and minor raids against the growing mercantile power of Magnimar. The knights, however, bluntly refused, seeing no lawlessness in the success of their patron's rival—much to the spurned queen's ire.

Ever since, hellknights have patrolled the lands of southern Varisia, enforcing the laws of their orders and the nearby city-states, exterminating threats to civilization, and quelling uprisings among the Shoanti. While only the foolish don't rightly fear the black-clad knights, much that is now tamed and cultivated would still be wild if not for the efforts of Citadel Vraid, its veteran commander Lictor Severs "Boneclaw" DiVri—a still intimidating man despite his obvious maiming—and its relentless Mistress of Blades, the centaur Maidrayne Vox. While King Erodred of Korvosa and his council have little direct association with the hellknights—seeing them as ungracious and untrustworthy since their rejection of Queen Domina's "hospitality"—the Justice Court in Magnimar has ironically invited a detachment of hellknights, under the leadership of Paralictor Darean Halst, into its halls, welcoming their severity, their efficiency, and the fear they inspire in all lawbreakers.

the Arvensoar, the towering fortress of Magnimar's small military, the city watch patrols the length and breadth of the city—although Lord-Mayor Grobaras's decrees see that the richest quarters of the Summit receive the most attention. When the law falls into dispute or cannot be meted out by patrolmen, quarrels are taken before the esteemed Justice Court. Thirteen justices—led by **Lord Justice Bayl Argentine** (LN male human aristocrat 6/fighter 3)—form the highest court in the city, settling arguments and deciding the guilt or innocence of those who come before them. The worst of the confirmed guilty are sentenced to time in the Hells, several levels of sweltering dungeons beneath the Pediment Building.

For all the efforts of the city's law enforcers, numerous criminal elements operate throughout Magnimar. The oldest of these groups, the Night Scales, see themselves as the rightful masters of the city's criminal underworld. With operations focused along the Shore, especially in Beacon Point and Rag's End, the thieves' guild—under the command of its even-tempered, one-armed leader, **Therhyn Raccas** (LE half-elf rogue 9)—contents itself with smuggling, extortion, petty theft, and the occasional break-in.

Above the pickpockets and rackets of the Shore, the 80-year-old **Lady Vammiera Symirkova** (NE female human aristocrat 2/rogue 6/sorcerer 4) directs the Gargoyles, a coterie of peerless cat burglars. Her rarely seen "daughter," **Mizmina Symirkova** (CE female human rogue 8/assassin 3)—an icy young woman seemingly no more than 18 years old—personally leads the group on their most daring heists.

The Varisian criminals known as the Sczarni also operate in great numbers in Magnimar. While the con-artists and thieves typically work together, the number of Varisians in the city has birthed numerous gangs, each taking names like the Creepers, the Tower Girls, or the Washside Wringers, adopting criminal specialties and operating in locally known turfs. **Jaster Frallino** (CE male human fighter 5/rogue 4), an aging, merciless tough with thick scars around his neck, leads the largest and most influential group, the Gallowed, from a caravan of wagons almost directly below Lord-Mayor Grobaras's palatial home, Defiant's Garden.

ARTS & ENTERTAINMENT

In an attempt to elevate the city-state beyond merely an aggrandized trading post, the local government has done much to encourage education and the arts. The majority of its contribution to city-wide enlightenment goes to the Founder's Archive and Museum of Ages. Occupying a small campus just north of Usher's Hall, several grandiose structures house the histories, findings, and private collections of some of the city's most esteemed citizens. Of particular note are three of the museum's permanent displays: the ancient

Eye of Rakzhan, the Gemstone Regalia of King Chadris Porphyria III (much to Korvosa's disdain), and the Lions of Siv. Esteemed scholar of Varisian history **Dr. Ernst Landis** (N male human expert 5/wizard 5) curates the Museum of Ages, while the stern, half-Shoanti **Madam Irba Demerios** (LN female human expert 8) practically rules the Founder's Archives (and holds the only key to the library's famed Forbidden Collection). The museum also funds the region-wide expeditions of renowned explorer, treasure hunter, and Pathfinder **Dr. Archisa Aparna** (NG female human bard 5), who frequently lectures on ancient Varisian monuments on the occasions she returns to the city.

Beyond these halls of learning, Magnimar also hosts several esteemed—and not so esteemed—houses of the arts. While the Summit's Triodea presents the grandest performances in western Varisia, the most popular public venue is easily the Serpent's Run. The city's largest structure, this gigantic hippodrome hosts decathlons, horse and dog races, displays of magic, circus performances, and—on rare occasions—small-scale naval engagements and mock-gladiatorial battles. Capable of seating a crowd of more than 5,000 cheering onlookers, its uppermost rim bears the shape of a gigantic serpent circling the entire arena—an homage to the heroics of the city's most beloved founder. **Jorston "Axetongue" Droaeb** (LN male dwarf expert 4/fighter 3), the hippodrome's aged but still spry Master of Games, organizes events and assures that all competitions are fair and safe.

BUSINESS

First and foremost a trade city, Magnimar owes its prosperity to the countless foreign merchants who readily make use of the city's reputedly safe and free port. Enforcing no taxes on harborage or imports, the city welcomes business from all lands and makes the bounty of Varisia available for trade. As a result, several of the most prestigious trading coasters, mercantile families, and shipping concerns do regular business in the city, with some having even established offices and private local shipyards. The most notable of these include a remnant embassy of Andoran's deposed Rousseau family, offices of the Hook and Hammer traders, and a lavish regional headquarters of the infamous Aspis Corporation.

RELIGION

Magnimar welcomes religions from all corners of the world, so long as they don't pursue any ongoing crusades or violate city law. The churches of Abadar, Iomedae, and Pharasma have the strongest city-wide followings, along with Desna well-represented among the Varisian population. Asmodeous and Calistria are also openly followed by many of the city's scheming merchants, thieves, and betrayers, while a small sect of Gozreh's devotees maintain and worship in the city's various parks. Tradition and local legends surrounding the Arvensoar have also attracted a number of celestial mystery cults, which practice strange rituals outside the public eye. Assemblies devoted to the empyreal lords Soralyon, Ashava the True Spark, and the Horseman of War are all known to gather in the city.

MONUMENTS

Two architectural marvels dominate the Magnimarian landscape: the ancient Irespan and the modern Arvensoar.

The Irespan

Visible for miles out to sea, the ancient basalt bridge known as the Irespan dominates Magnimar's coastline. Jutting from a prominent foundation upon the Seacleft, the Giant's Bridge, as it is sometimes called, soars more than 300 feet above the city below, giving the eclipsed area its name: the Shadow.

An obvious remnant of ancient Thassilon, few know that the Irespan once served as a vital travel route across the broken, mountainous terrain of Bakrakhan, the Domain of Wrath. This consecutive series of bridges formed an incredible highway of overpasses leading to the capitol of Xin-Bakrakhan, now known only as the strange island monument Hollow Mountain. Marking the northern and southernmost holdings of the Domain of Wrath, the foundations of the Irespan lie at the edge of Edasseril to the north and between Eurythnia and Shalast to the south. When Bakrakhan sank into the Varisian Gulf during Thassilon's final days, the Irespan shattered. All that survived was its southern foundation, numerous broken supports, and a few resilient stretches of bridge now spanning turbulent waters rather than airy heights.

A HISTORY OF DREAD

In 4623 AR, Magnimar's second lord-mayor, Varnagan Draston-Meir, ordered that stone for the newly planned city wall and rising Arvensoar be quarried directly from the Irespan. While the decision unnerved many—especially laborers faced with mining 300-some feet above the ground—work soon commenced in earnest. Within days of setting to work, quarrymen proved the long-held rumor that the Giant's Bridge was a hollow structure, revealing partially collapsed hallways at the span's end. The discovery, however, did little to stall the bridge's demolition.

Less than a week into the project, events occurred that ended any current or future intrusion upon the megalithic monument. Toiling with pick and hammer, workers revealed a vast, darkened chamber within the bridge. Mere moments after the discovery was made, a cacophony of shuddersome skittering heralded an outpouring of hundreds of ravening spider-legged things. Scrambling forth, the man-sized spidery monstrosities invaded the community. Hundreds of Magnimar's citizens were killed, maimed, and taken, as the ravenous things preyed upon them. Only the heroics of the twin wizards Cailyn and Romre Vanderale and an adventuring company known as the Eyes of the Hawk saved the town, rallying the local militia, driving the flame-fearing spider horrors back into the bridge, and collapsing the gap to the chambers within.

Ever since, all tampering with the Giant's Bridge or building within 50 feet of it has been forbidden by law. Still, historians and daring youths frequently report strange vibrations upon the Irespan and low, scraping sounds emanating from within.

In modern times, the Irespan has been a source of wonderment, mystery, and ill-fortune. Although the founders of Magnimar chose their community's location primarily for its natural harbor and proximity to the Yondabakari River, the ancient rubble of the Irespan that once littered the surrounding beaches proved an opportune source of building materials for the fledgling community. Today, many of Magnimar's oldest and most elegant structures boast foundations, supports, and statuary constructed of Irespan basalt.

The Arvensoar

The tallest structure in Magnimar and a wonder in a city of architectural feats, the Arvensoar stands approximately 400 feet tall, climbing the entire length of the Seacleft and extending nearly a hundred feet above. In the simplest senses, the great tower is the garrison of the city's watch and small military, as well as being a quick city-controlled connection between the Shore and the Summit. Beyond these mundane uses, the tower is a symbol of the city's unity, ambition, and history.

Commander Ismeir Odinburge (LG male human fighter 4/paladin of Abadar 5)—a competent, sober, honest, but inflexible man—serves as Lord of the Tower and leader of Magnimar's military forces. Several field commanders report directly to him, as does **Captain Acacia Uriana** (LG female human fighter 3/rogue 5), the fiery and opinionated head of the city watch. A military of 400 professional soldiers—most particularly well-trained in archery—stand garrisoned within the Arvensoar, patrolling its heights and the city walls. Should more fighters ever be needed, the city watch and a local militia can be rallied within an hour, supplementing the tower's forces with upwards of 900 additional lesser, but willing, warriors. Well positioned to defend the city, the Arvensoar boasts eight trebuchets capable of firing over the city and even past Outcast's Cove—though Fort Indros and the Wyrmwatch are far better positioned to defend the city harbor—and provisions to supply the city through at least a week-long siege.

Lesser Monuments

Along with the stone sentinels that dominate the Magnimarian skyline, several lesser monuments adorn the city. Some are mere decoration, but others are much more. These are but a sampling of Magnimar's best-known and most magnificent landmarks.

The Battle of Charda: A statue depicting the first and most famous battle between Magnimar's navy and Riddleport's pirates.

The Celwynvian Charge: A gift from the elves, this two-story tree-shaped sculpture is crafted from white wood and crystal. Real leaves bud and fall at the appropriate times of year.

Champion's Walk: A statuary-lined avenue leading to Serpent's Run and depicting the field's greatest champions.

The Fifth Wind: A massive stone weather vane visible along the docks.

The Floodfire: A beacon warning ships away from Kyver's Islet.

Founder's Honor: A monument to the city's heroic founder.

The Guardians: An arch depicting local twin heroes.

Angels of the Arvensoar

More than a century ago, an unusual limestone spire jutted from the sheer Seacleft cliffs. Varisian legends deemed the place a blessed resting spot for celestial messengers, and the wanderers would often visit in hopes of seeing an angel and gaining the good fortune such a portent presaged.

Soon after settlers began moving to Magnimar, the Varisians asked the foreigners to move their newly built homes south of the Yondabakari River and away from their holy grounds. Freshly settled and defiant, Magnimar's leaders all refused except for one, Mistress Ordellia Whilwren. Curious, Whilwren promised the wanderers that she and her followers would gladly relocate if they would show her an angel. In response, the Varisians mysteriously told her to look to the spire at dawn everyday for a week. Obeying, Whilwren did so, and on the week's final day she saw a radiant figure perched in the dawning sun. Awed and inspired, Whilwren kept her promise and moved south to the area now called Ordellia.

As Magnimar grew, relations with the Varisians worsened. Two years after the city's founding, a great storm racked the land and threatened to destroy all the settlers had created. Through the driving storm, Ordellia Whilwren prayed to the angel of the spire. In a blinding flash, a bolt of soundless white lightning struck the cliff's rocky perch, blasting it to nothing more than glass and rubble, but in so doing scattered the storm clouds to reveal starry skies.

Having heard Whilwren's prayers and seen the silent lightning, the townsfolk agreed to create a great tower to replace the fallen spire. As workers laid the first stones, local Varisians—seeing they now shared the same faith—joined in, and the Arvensoar began to rise. Although, it took more than 18 years to erect, the Arvensoar now stands as a symbol of Magnimarian-Varisian unity and an open invitation to goodly spirits.

Mistress of Angels: A sculpture of city leader Ordellia Whilwren, known for seeing celestial messengers upon the Arvensoar.

Our Lady of Blessed Waters: A bronze , strangely verdigris-free statue of the spirit said to linger within the Seerspring.

The Wyrmwatch: A lighted guard against dangers from the sea.

THE CITY

While the Seacleft and Irespan break the city into three obvious sections, the cityfolk and the government recognize 18 local communities: seven upon the Summit, ten along the Shore, and one in the Shadow. Each of these communities has its own distinct atmosphere, venues, and local personalities. Presented here is an overview of those districts and their most prominent features.

The Summit

The wealthiest of Magnimar's communities are found upon the Summit, along with the seat of the Magnamarian government, its most prestigious centers of learning and the arts, affluent businesses, and numerous meticulously kept parks and statue-lined avenues.

The Alabaster District: Formally called the Stylobate, the colloquially named Alabaster District is home to Magnimar's richest and most affluent citizens. Segregated from the lower districts by steeply canted, marble-inlaid walls, only a few prominent avenues allow ascendance to the statuary-lined streets above by way of long, well-guarded stairs. At the northernmost point, commanding a strategic position over Maganimar's coast, stands Fort Indros. Bristling with ballistae and trebuchets, the lofty fortress deters all but the most brazen pirate attacks. **Commander Wynmerd** (LG male dwarf fighter 5) oversees a garrison of soldiers, bowmen, and siege engineers here.

The Marble District: The residents of the Marble District hold only slightly less prestige than those in the Alabaster District. Well-appointed townhouses, small villas, and even the walled estates of several old Magnimarian families—most notably the Kaddren, Scarnettis, and Vanderales—find majestic views atop the Fogwall Cliffs.

SABRIYYA KALMERALM

Bridgeward: Although much of Magnimar's industry and trade takes place along the Shore, the dusty blocks that surround the Irespan ring with the noisy work of sculptors, jewelers, woodcarvers, and all manner of other artisans who work in rare mediums—even magic. One of Magnimar's best-known local industries is the Golemworks, a series of unremarkable, crow-haunted warehouses near the north edge of the Irespan. Nearly 30 years ago, local wizard **Toth Bhreacher** (N male human wizard 15) discovered that the stone of the Irespan proved particularly useful in spellwork. Since then, his studio has grown into a sizable and prestigious workhouse, dredging fallen segments of the Giant's Bridge from the Varisian Gulf to craft a range of constructs and simpler creations for wealthy buyers.

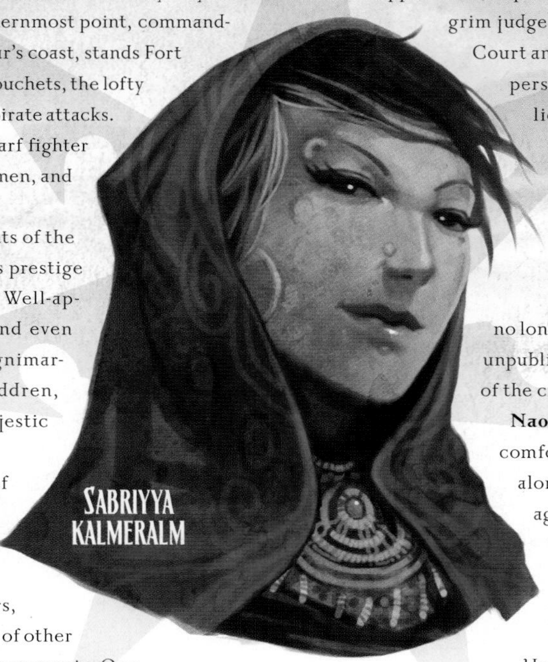

Nearby stands a 10-story, cylindrical monument called the Cenotaph. Created as a memorial to Magnimar's most beloved founder, Alcaydian Indros, the monument was meant to be an empty tomb honoring the local hero. As years passed and Indros's family members and friends passed on, an inordinate number requested to have their bones entombed near or within the monument. Begun as an honor to the great man, then a vogue, the practice has become a tradition and post-mortem status symbol for all who can afford burial beneath the stones of the surrounding Mourner's Plaza or in the later-constructed catacombs beneath the memorial.

The Capital District: Surrounding the bustling square known as Founder's Honor and the towering sculpture called "Indros cul Vydrarch" spread the high marble columns and ornate facades of the heart of Magnimar's government and political arena. Here, the elaborately sculpted Usher's Hall serves as the meeting place for the city's Council of Ushers. Anyone who wishes to meet with a councilmember must first meet with **Jacildria Quildarmo** (LE female human aristocrat 3/expert 2), the hall's Seneshal of Dates, a power-mongering, pinch-faced secretary who revels in her authority. Near the Usher's Hall stands the impassive gray stone fastness of the Pediment Building. While the impressive upper halls, replete with stern-faced gargoyles and grim judges, serve as the home of the Justice Court and the Halls of Virtue (each judge's personalized audience hall), beneath lie the sweltering halls of Magnimar's only prison, the Hells. Only the city's justices and most infamous criminals know how deep the prison's claustrophobic floors run, but rumors tell of one of the deepest halls where guards no longer patrol, sealed in response to an unpublicized uprising and left to the worst of the city's convicts.

Naos: The home to many merchants and comfortable families, the city stretch along the Avenue of Hours is disparagingly called the "New-Money District" by local nobles. Despite the disdainful comments of the elite, Naos is one of the most welcoming and well-kept parts of Magnimar. Upon Starsilver Plaza—where abalone shell inlays create a scene of thousands of stars—stands the Triodea, the most renowned playhouse and concert hall in Magnimar. This one building houses three performance halls: the Grand Stage for operas and plays, an acoustically perfect concert hall called the Stonewall, and the Aerie—a raised, rooftop stage for soloists. **Durstin Versade** (NG male human expert 5) currently owns the performance hall, but the Triodea's true master is **Kassiel Iylmrain** (NE male elf bard 7), a masterful dancer and alto, with a history of extraordinary fits of anger, jealousy, and promiscuity (especially when it aids his career).

Naos is also the home of two of the city's most eccentric citizens, esteemed hunters, explorers, and Pathfinders **Sir Canayven Heidmarch** (NG male human ranger 8) and his wife **Sheila Heidmarch** (LN female human fighter 3/monk 4). The world-traveling adventurers have recently retired to Magnimar, but have not been content to settle into the quiet life, opening their sizable manor to their society. The first Pathfinder chapter house in Varisia (just north of the Triodea) welcomes all members eager to explore the still relatively unknown land. Visiting members of the Pathfinder Society are welcomed to the manor by comfortable lodgings, a well-stocked library of far-flung lore, and its owners' sagely advice. Currently, two Pathfinders, aside from the Heidmarchs, use the manor as a base camp: **Almya Gorangal** (LE female human wizard 4), a sour Chelish explorer seeking to map the ancient ruins of the

Magnimar
1
2
3
4
5
6
7
8
9
10
11
12
13
14
15
16
17
18
19
N
0
640
FEET

A VIEW OF MAGNIMAR

The maps presented here show the general locations of Magnimar's districts and most prominent monuments. More maps of Magnimar showing exact district borders, avenue and plaza names, and the precise location of numerous locales can be found in the downloadable content for this volume, available at **paizo.com/pathfinder.**

1. The Irespan	11. Dockway
2. The Alabaster District	12. Lowcleft
3. The Marble District	13. Keystone
4. Bridgeward	14. The Marches
5. The Capital District	15. Beacon's Point
6. Naos	16. Rag's End
7. Vista	17. Silver Shore
8. Grand Arch	18. Kyver's Islet
9. The Arvensoar	19. Ordellia
10. The Bazaar of Sails	20. Underbridge

Mushfens, and **Joadric Heimurl** (NG male human barbarian 2/fighter 3), a bombastic man of barbaric descent bent on organizing an expedition into the Malgorian Mountains.

Aside from their home, the Heidmarchs also curate the Lord-Mayor's Menagerie, a public park where they display many of their taxidermy trophies and live captures, most notably a blinded ruby-eyed basilisk (its eyes also on display), the viable egg of a millennia wyrm, and "Prince Mandali"—a seemingly tame 14-foot-tall ape.

Vista: High-class shops, restaurants, businesses, and the offices of globe-spanning mercantile concerns spread between the Avenue of Honors and the Seacleft. The Aspis Corporation—a conscienceless shipping, trading, and money-lending venture of Chelish descent—keeps its bronze-faced Varisian headquarters here.

Directly upon the Seacleft stand several estates of the city's more daring nobles, but even the most lavish of these are outshined by Defiant's Garden, diplomatic resort and home of Lord-Mayor Haldmeer Grobaras. Although the lord-mayor has traditionally kept a simple residence among the people, Grobaras moved into the lavish city-owned estate under the pretense of wanting to be more intimate with his work—and certainly not to take advantage of the small castle's eight fully staffed floors of sumptuous salons and comfortable lounges, usually reserved for visiting diplomats.

Grand Arch: The largest of the Summit's districts, Grand Arch stretches from the Twins' Gate to the heart of the upper cliff. Many of Magnimar's middle class and simple shop owners live comfortably here, but a surprising number of the area's homes stand unoccupied much of the time—the homes of foreign merchants and travelers whose business takes them elsewhere but who desire comfortable living upon their return. Just within Twins' Gate stands one of the city's larger monuments, the Guardians: 200-foot-tall colossi depicting the young heroes Cailyn and Romre Vanderale facing each other with touching weapons held high, forming a giant arch.

The Shore

The majority of Magnimar's working population lives along the Shore. Comprising more than just the coast and dockside portions of the city, the Shore extends from the base of the Seacleft out to Kyver's Islet and Ordellia, south of the Yondabakari River.

The Bazaar of Sails: A destination for traders the world over, the Bazaar of Sails is the largest free market in Varisia. Anyone with merchandise to sell is welcome to set up a tent, booth, or wagon among the hundreds of other ever-changing shops that fill the dockside plaza. Crops from local farmers, Varisian artifacts, Osirian spices, Chelish fineries, Andoran quartos, and more exotic goods from a hundred foreign ports fill the market, with the offerings of any day varying with the season, trade winds, and tides.

As merchants eagerly trade, competitions, rivalries, and all manner of criminal temptations arise. Although the market welcomes all comers, the ever-changing crowd, shouts of exotic traders, and generally raucous bustle make the place a nightmare for the local watch to patrol and mete out justice. Fortunately, the Princess of the Market, **Sabriyya Kalmeralm** (LN female human rogue 12), takes care of policing her own. The daughter of the first Prince of the Market, Nazir Kalmeralm, who disappeared nearly 28 years ago, Sabriyya is well-loved by most of the bazaar's regular traders and her "court"—a sizable gang of toughs and money collectors (N male human fighters 2). A passionate woman in her late forties, her quick wit, aristocratic bearing, and silver tongue are as famed as her fiery temper and unforgiving memory. While many in the city still see her as little more than an exceedingly public gang lord, those who frequent the chaotic maze of stalls and shops know the service she provides.

Dockway: The shouts and bustle of countless traders, fishermen, and foreign travelers stir the choppy waters of Outcast's Cove through all hours of the day and night. Along the seaside district of Dockway, salt-blasted storefronts and cramped businesses cater to the typically rough seafolk, while exotic inns and taverns serve as familiar welcomes to visitors from afar. The best known of these seaside sanctuaries is the Old Fang, a taproom and cheap inn built right on the docks and covered in barnacles and peeling white paint. **Ol' Mam Grottle** (NG female human commoner 4/fighter 1), a burly, no-nonsense matron, runs this favorite local watering hole, decorated with the nautical trophies of her late husband.

Lowcleft: At the bottom of the Seacleft lies one of Magnimar's most vibrant districts. Numerous small playhouses, pubs, brothels, hookah bars, dance halls, and a wide variety of other entertainments make Lowcleft—or "the Rubble," as locals typically call it—a home to the city's artistic and avant-garde community. Among the best known of the district's nightspots is the Gilded Cage, a garish nightclub built into the face of the Seacleft and run by **Jayleen "Morning Dove" Mordove** (CN female human bard 5), a former prima donna of the Triodea who retains her connections to the city's artistic elite.

Keystone: Seerspring Garden, a park boasting a spring of crisp, clear water, marks the center of the Shore's central district. While impressive and intimidating buildings line the four avenues

THE WYRM AND THE WARDEN

In 4584 AR, a paladin of Aroden named Alcaydian Indros led an expedition into untamed western Varisia. After months of travel, he and his men discovered the Irespan and the placid harbor they dubbed Outcast's Cove. Tired from their travels, the scouts made camp nearby. Their respite was short, though, broken by the guards' screams. Watchful Indros alone saw a black shape knotted around his panicked men, dragging them into the darkened waters. Without hesitating, he unsheathed his sword and strode into Outcast's Cove, clad in the full armor of a Knight of Aroden. For long minutes the rush of the waves was all the scouts heard and hope began to turn to dread.

Then the cove explored in venom and stinging brine as the Vydrarch rose. A sea dragon the size of a castle tower, the beast was all fangs, and fins, and poison quills. Wrapped in its crushing coils, Alcaydian Indros wrestled with the monstrous thing. Steel met scale, fangs rent armor, but in the end, Indros cleft the serpent's head and twain, loosing a gout of blood and venomous bile. Walking from the surf, the paladin carried with him his saved men. Reaching shore, he dubbed himself the new master of all the waves he could see and named the place Magnimar, "Stone of the Sea" in his order's ancient tongue.

radiating out from the area's heart, behind them lie the townhouses and close streets of Magnimar's common people. The fortress-like temple of Iomedae—under the offices of **Chaplain Tira Ronnova** (LG female human cleric of Iomedae 7/paladin 2)—stands here, sounding the daily call to glory and preaching of honor, sacrifice, and spiritual rewards to the layman.

To the south of Seerspring Garden stands Magnimar's most esteemed school of wizardry, the Stone of the Seers. The spring that still bubbles at the heart of Keystone is said to have once been home to an oracular water spirit who departed decades ago but promised to one day return. In the tradition of that strange sibyl, **Master Leis Nivlandis** (NG male half-elf wizard 11) began a school of the arcane with a focus on abjuration and divination magics.

The Marches: The entrance to Magnimar for many traders and travelers, the Marches's Castlegate is where those locals who would bring their wares to the city must first pass. Many simple and largely contented folk live in this sizable district, but despite its size and population, the Marches receive little extra in the way of city funding to maintain the area and protect its people. While this has caused a rise in Sczarni theft and cons, the churches of Abadar, Erastil, and Iomedae all maintain presences to aid the city and perhaps win a few converts.

Beacon's Point: Comprising the western rim of Outcast's Cove and ending at the statue-studded point called the Wyrmwatch—a lighthouse said to overlook the spot Alcaydian Indros battled the Vydrarch—Beacon Point is a raucous home to traders; sailors; and hardworking, hard-living families of all sorts. Numerous warehouses, shipping concerns, and other businesses fill the area, as do numerous simple but boisterous festhalls and taverns.

Rag's End: Only the poorest and most deprived of the city's working class make their homes in the cramped, maze-like knot of alleys called Rag's End. Temporary laborers, crippled dockhands, drunks, and the sorely out-of-luck scrape by on coin earned from begging, performing odd and often demeaning jobs, and the charity of the city's sympathetic religions. Much of Rag's End is owned by Slumlord **Rassimeri Jaijarko** (CE male human fighter 2/rogue 2), a greasy half-Varisian drug dealer with ties to the Sczarni gang the Gallowed.

Silver Shore: The wealthiest district below the summit, Silver Shore is home to several well-to-do business owners, council members, and nobles who seek to live close to their work, the people, or the beauty of the river. At the northernmost part of the district stands a spherical building of metal and glass shaped something like a diving helmet, a curious diversion called the Aquaretum. The proprietor, **Nireed Wadincoast** (CG male gnome expert 5/ranger 2), opens this home and personal collection of large aquariums, captured fish, embalmed sea creatures, and sunken discoveries to any with a silver piece and the time to tour. Although an expert on life beneath the water, his tales of

whole cities lying at the bottom of the Varisian Gulf are largely discounted as "typical gnome enthusiasm."

Kyver's Islet: This small island at the mouth of the Yondabakari river is given over almost completely to lumbermills, shipwrights, and noisy workshops best situated away from homes and quieter businesses. From the northernmost point of the islet rises the Floodfire, a small lighthouse that warns ships away from the shallow waters and half-submerged sandbars of the river.

Ordellia: Long a hotbed of dissension and governmental criticism, Ordellia perhaps best embodies the untenable spirit of freedom and leaderless rule Magnimar was founded upon. Many in the district consider themselves a town apart from Magnimar, taking pride in organizing their own small community militia and council apart from the city's. The unofficial "capitol" of Ordellia is the Rose and Rake theater, an open-air, circular playhouse known for its scathing social satires and ribald political commentaries.

The Shadow

The area directly beneath and to the west of the Irespan holds but one city district, formally known as the Underbridge. Due to the eclipsing bridge above, light only reaches the streets below for one hour in the morning and two in the evening.

Underbridge: Seedy taverns, poorly run brothels, and rat-infested gambling dens compete with salt-blasted tenement buildings and cheap flophouses in Magnimar's most dangerous district. While the Magnimarian government champions cleaning up the Shadow as one of its most important long-term goals, many council members realize that the vices of the slum attract a certain amount of business to the city and that truly clearing away the "bridge trash" could significantly impact the local economy.

Although the submerged rubble and jagged, ruined pylons of the Irespan make sailing beneath the Giant's Bridge a treacherous prospect, a few docks line the trash-strewn Underbridge shore, serving as the entry point for all manner of contraband. At the end of one such dock slumps the Friendly Merchant, a dilapidated tavern frequented by thugs, con-men, deviants, and worse. The friendly merchant himself, **Siov Cassimeel** (NE male elf sorcerer 7), is a scheming but ultimately cowardly criminal involved in a variety of petty crimes. He eagerly rents out his private dock for exorbitant prices, but offers discounts to the Night Scales and generally keeps his ears open for the thieves' guild.

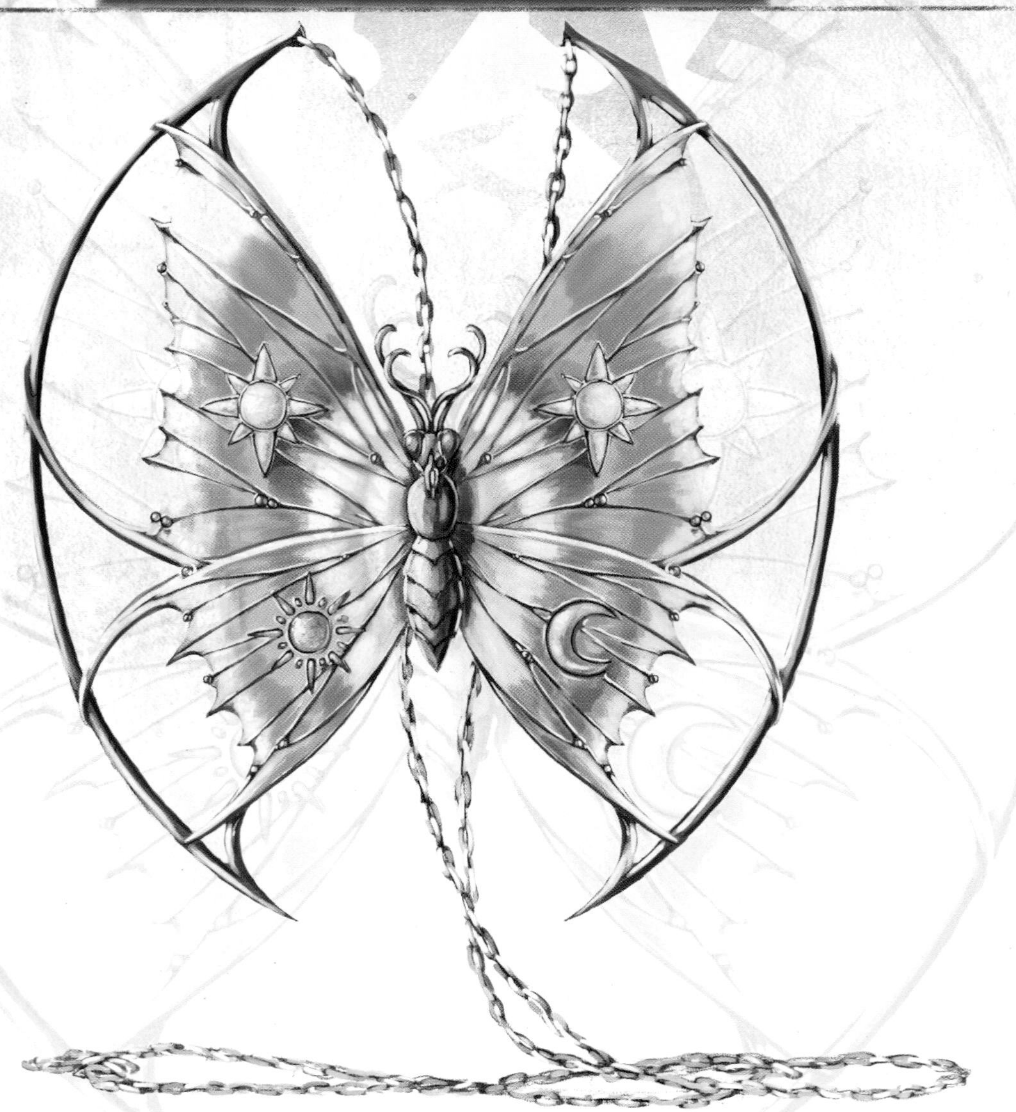

DESNA

THE SONG OF THE SPHERES

Blessed is the long road, the destination, the homeward path, and all who make the journey. Let each dream be a bright star in the night sky of your mind, and let it light your path in the day. Do not be troubled if your dream falters, for there are countless stars in the sky and countless dreams to experience—pick a new one and change your course.

—Prayer to Desna, carved on the wood of Riverrook Shrine near Magnimar

Desna (DEZ-nuh) is an impulsive and aloof goddess who delights in freedom, discovery, and mystery. Her aloofness stems not from arrogance, but from confidence in her own abilities and her desire to be unburdened by troubles. She is a collection of contrasts—an ancient goddess who dislikes predicting the future, a traveler who cares nothing for her destination, a carefree creature of instinct haunted by a past stretching back eons, and a peaceful deity forced to battle with old enemies, eternally young despite the weight of ages and stars upon her.

Some believe Desna is flighty, frivolous, and easily distracted, but she has a hard, cold side that few see, born of loss, tragedy, and battle. As a luck goddess, she always believes there is a chance for success. She knows that people fear the unknown, that dreams can turn to nightmares and a bright destiny can become a dark fate; these opposites in her own nature define her and give her things to strive against. She challenges those who would corrupt her domain or who have wronged her friends or followers, striking at them with burning starlight, bad luck, and energies alien to Golarion.

Although her dominion over dreams and stars means that many seers, diviners, and mystics revere her as an informal goddess of prophecy, she delights in the freedom of people to choose their own destiny and only uses her power to help others make good choices, avoid troublesome outcomes, and achieve happiness. She believes that "doom and gloom" prophecies or those that seem to guarantee or self-fulfill horrible acts are distasteful, and she only hands out such messages in the direst circumstances. She prefers to use prophecy as a tool for exploration and creating choices, not for limiting action and snuffing hope.

Primarily interested in travel for its own benefit, Desna watches over those who sojourn for any reason. Trailblazers, scouts, adventurers, and sailors all praise her name. (Although most sailors revere Gozreh, he is a temperamental deity and a little luck from Desna often comes in handy during a storm.) Her influence over luck makes her a favorite among gamblers, thieves, and others who rely on fortune for shady dealings.

Desna teaches her followers to indulge their desires, experience all they can, and trust instinct as a guide. Her followers are often wide-eyed, exuberant people, embracing the world in all its strangeness, and willing to jump in with both feet. Desnans aren't afraid to get their hands dirty, their feet wet, or their knuckles (or faces) bloodied while living life to its fullest. Critics call them hedonists, but that is an exaggeration, as worldly experience, rather than pure sensation, is their true goal. Ascetics, hermits, and meticulous planners are unknown in her church. Her faithful teach it is better to ask forgiveness than permission, as sometimes a unique opportunity requires a split-second decision, whether to touch a dragon's egg, savor a rare fruit, or passionately kiss the mayor's daughter.

Desna encourages her worshipers to believe in themselves and express their inner strengths, often in the form of music, dance, or theater. Many songs penned by her faithful become popular tunes for dancing and gatherings, and several "old favorites" are attributed to long-dead Desnan bards, their musical legacies persisting for centuries. Many believe that

the custom of a traveling bard paying for his lodging with a song stems from Desna's church and, like bards, wandering followers of Desna encourage young folk to sing and dance in the hopes of discovering hidden talents.

When the goddess has a message for one of her faithful, she prefers to intervene in the form of dreams, sending simple impressions, visions, or even prophecies that the sleeper clearly remembers upon awakening. If a member of her faith is in duress and prays to her before sleeping, she might send them encouraging dreams. In the most dire circumstances, or situations in which Desna takes a direct interest, a follower in need might awaken with the benefit of a helpful spell (such as *aid, magic vestment, prayer, protection from evil,* or *remove fear*) that persists throughout the day. When dreams are unsuitable or time is short she indicates her favor with flights of swallowtail butterflies, sparrows, dragonflies, geese flying in a four-pointed star shape, or the timely arrival of messenger birds. She typically shows her disfavor with a dreamless sleep that fails to refresh the sleeper (as if the person had not slept at all), sore feet, messenger animals losing their messages, and minor travel accidents.

When Desna manifests an avatar in the mortal world, she normally takes the appearance of a beautiful but coy female elven acolyte of her faith. In this guise she aids people in need or suggests relevant excerpts from her holy writings, the Seven Scrolls, as a way to lead the faithful on the correct path. She is not above singing to lighten dour moods or dancing with those in need to reinvigorate their confidence. When Desna wishes to reveal her true nature, she transforms her common clothing into a billowing silken gown and grows brightly colored butterfly wings on her back, although in somber situations her wing colors are pale and moth-like.

Desna is chaotic good, and her portfolio is dreams, stars, travelers, and luck. Her domains are Chaos, Good, Liberation, Luck, and Travel, and her favored weapon is the starknife. Her holy symbol is a butterfly with images of stars, suns, and moons upon its wings. Most of her clergy are clerics, although about one-third of her priests are bards or rogues, with a number of neutral good druids or rangers choosing her as their patron. She is called the Song of the Spheres, the Great Dreamer, Starsong, and the Tender of Dreams.

THE CHURCH

While an ancient faith—known even in the age of storied Thassilon—Desna's church is extremely disorganized with few actual temples or settled priests and no formal chain of command. Physical and magical might are respected, as are knowledge and experience, with personal expertise in a field trumping mere combat prowess or spellcasting ability. For example, when dealing with a basilisk's attacks on a frontier town, a low-level cleric who survives an encounter with the creature is accorded greater authority than a high-level character who has never faced one. This structure means that Desnans have certain ideas about what they consider "informed" authority; they feel free to ignore nobles, politicians, and other "meritless" leaders if more knowledgeable folk are on hand to provide better advice. Although they can be competitive with others inside and outside the church, these are friendly rivalries; they prefer to move on if a disagreement is going to turn ugly—after all, there is an entire world of wonder to explore, so there is no sense wasting time in an unhappy argument.

Desna's priesthood has no regalia or vestments beyond bright colors—sometimes in patterns like butterfly wings—and their goddess's holy symbol. Worshipers typically have little problem recognizing each other, as they often work Desna's symbol into jewelry, clothing, tattoos, or her holy weapon, the starknife. Even if their faith isn't prominently displayed, the like personalities of Desna's followers often attract one to another.

Services dedicated to Desna include singing, dancing, storytelling (especially of unusual dreams), footraces, and music. Some use exotic substances, herbal drinks, alcohol, or animal venom to spark unusual dreams or (for the very lucky) to create lucid dreams. Many rituals involve sand because of its relation to sleep and the comparison of grains of sand to the number of stars in the sky. Dust made from crushed rose quartz (which can have a starry pattern when illuminated from behind) is used in the faith's rare ceremonies and blessings instead of water or sacred oil; Desnan priests carry holy quartz dust in glass flasks instead of holy water. Some luck-seeking faithful carry dice or other luck talismans carved of rose quartz.

TEMPLES AND SHRINES

Desna keeps few temples, preferring unattended shrines at crossroads and places of secluded beauty, like hilltops or peninsula points. Although unmanned, these shrines often hold simple provisions and a place to scrawl notes or feelings if visitors are so inspired. Her association with the stars and night sky means that her temples sometimes double as celestial observatories, or at least have one room partially open to the sky. In many cases, these observatories have markers on the walls or windows to indicate the positions of important stars on holy days (one-room churches might have a single hole in the ceiling to show a particular star's position, kept covered on other days to keep out rain or snow). Temples in

LIBERATION DOMAIN

Granted Power: You gain a +2 morale bonus on all saving throws against enchantment spells or effects.

Liberation Domain Spells

1 *Remove fear*
2 *Remove paralysis*
3 *Remove curse*
4 *Freedom of movement*
5 *Break enchantment*
6 *Greater dispel magic*
7 *Refuge*
8 *Mind blank*
9 *Freedom*

large cities often take the form of tall towers with observatories at their tops, and with small libraries of astronomical and astrological charts. More common rural temples usually incorporate an inn or stable as a service to travelers. As Desna maintains good—or, at least, non-conflicting—relationships with most good-aligned and civilized deities, it's not uncommon for her faith to be found among those worshiped in communal temples.

Butterflies and moths (as well as their caterpillar young) congregate at her holy sites; legends say the priests can call upon these creatures to defend the temple, devouring cloth and leather to leave would-be thieves naked but unharmed. Some temples maintain colonies of silk-producing moths, creating hardy and beautiful silk for use and sale by the temple. Every temple protects a small chest of silver coins (usually no more than 300 sp), which it uses to help fund journeys by the faithful. Needy travelers can petition the temple for financing (up to a number of silver pieces equal to the supplicant's level squared). This funding is normally only available for frontier exploration or travel to exotic locations (a trip to the next town might merit only a silver for water, bread, and a spare blanket) and those who exploit this generosity tend to suffer bad luck in the long run.

A PRIEST'S ROLE

Priests of Desna—cleric, bard, rogue, ranger, or the rare druid—go where they please, earning money by telling fortunes, providing entertainment, and interpreting dreams as messages from the goddess. They help people where they can, but they prefer to make their acts seem like luck, coincidence, or the blessings of their goddess.

A typical day for a Desnan priest involves travel, often just from one shrine or temple to another, collecting stories and spreading the word of the goddess. If a holy site needs maintenance or repair, the priest takes care of what is needed or hires a skilled person to do it. Many caravan masters like to hire a priest of Desna to accompany their wagons (as they believe it brings good luck, especially in regard to warding off attacks from beasts), and this gives the priest an excuse to travel when she has no other pressing matters.

Many of Desna's faithful are talented artists, writers, and entertainers, and the church expects all priests to at least be familiar with contemporary music, theater, and literature (even though a particular priest might have no talent for playing instruments, acting, or writing). Those with skill should share it on a regular basis, usually with performances at festivals, open local venues, gatherings such as weddings, or public parties thrown specifically for that purpose. These latter events endear the church to the public, even if the offered fare is no more than cheese, warm bread, and watered wine. Those with no personal ability in these areas should learn to recognize such gifts in others and encourage them to explore those talents.

Some Desnans are skilled fortune-tellers, using their gift of reading people to entertain and inspire hope. Like their goddess, they oppose the use of divination to create fear or despair, and brush off unhappy requests such as when the listener or one of his enemies might die. The goddess expects her diviners to challenge any speaker who prophesies ill, misfortune, or doom, and when they hear of magical auguries predicting bad times, they actively intervene to make sure those events do not come to pass.

In addition to soothsaying, some Desnans learn to interpret dreams in order to ease troubled minds and mend other wounds of the psyche. Recurring or shared dreams are of particular interest, as they often stem from inner traumas or external magical sources. Those plagued by insomnia or nightmares call on Desnan priests for aid, for their healing spells or even just a soothing touch are often enough to bring a tranquil night's sleep. Her priests oppose night hags—which Desna particularly hates, and who equally despise the goddess—and similar creatures that prey on sleepers, as well as mages who use *nightmare*, going so far as to destroy spellbooks and magic items that use the spell. Her feud with Lamashtu means her priests are charged with protecting the common folk from dangerous beasts (especially intelligent beast-like creatures such as worgs), although they hold no hatred for wary predators that avoid mankind.

Elder priests whose bodies can no longer handle physical travel tend to use magic to visit the minds of others (using the *dream* spell), remote parts of the world (using scrying and *traveling dream* spells), or even distant planes (using the *astral travel* spell). Some use herbal or

GHLAUNDER

Ghlaunder (GLON-der) is a demigod of parasites and infection. His origin is unknown, but he might be a corrupt spawn of an evil deity or something that once grew on the corpse of a slain god. His natural form is said to be that of an immense mosquito-like creature with a dozen wings and proboscises and parasitic prehensile worms that act as his limbs. He is associated with stirges, giant mosquitos, faceless stalkers (see page 88), fungoid creatures, and vampires. His holy symbol is a blood-fat mosquito.

Ghlaunder's primary doctrine is that parasites and infection are necessary, lest the weak and old overrun the world. Cultists of Ghlaunder usually live in secluded communes and travel in secret, concealing their true devotion for fear of being shunned or attacked. Only in areas ravaged by disease do they make themselves known, preaching salvation from afflictions for the small price of eternal worship of their blood-drinking god. They only use spells such as *remove disease* on those of their faith, convincing many of the terminally ill to convert. The faith has a strong rivalry with Desna, as she actively hunts its followers. Few religions consider themselves allies of Ghlaunder, although followers of Rovagug hold that Ghlaunder is one of the Rough Beast's spawn.

Alignment: CE. **Domains**: Air, Animal, Chaos, Destruction, Evil. Clerics and druids of Ghlaunder may use animal-oriented spells (such as *animal shapes*, *detect animals or plants*, and *hide from animals*) to affect vermin instead of animals, although a vermin's natural immunities may render certain spells useless for this purpose.

alchemical substances to enter a dreamlike state to explore higher levels of consciousness or to commune with dream entities. A few such Wakeless Ones are so strong-willed that they have remained asleep and dreaming for years, not even waking to eat or drink, sustained by faith, will, and dream-food. Unlike battle-oriented faiths, it is considered a noble end for a Desnan to die in her sleep, as it makes the first step of the spiritual journey to the goddess that much easier (although not necessarily making the remainder of the journey simple or easy, as there is no challenge or wonder in that).

There are at least two bardic colleges founded by Desnan priests: Taldor's Baumont Conservatorium and Polyhymnia's Hall of Andoran, with alumni of each considering themselves the best in a long-standing rivalry. Many semi-retired Desnan musicians and actors hold private study for handfuls of students; some of these masters are graduates of a specific school and teach in a similar style, while a handful reject more orthodox teachings to use their own methods, often inspired by far-distant cultures or ancient lore. Nobles who want their children educated and protected sometimes hire a Desnan priest for this purpose. It is a comfortable living, especially as the noble usually has the priest on retainer for more adventurer-worthy duties, such as escorting the scion through a dangerous area, giving him a taste of battle, or staving off the amorous advances of a rival family's heir.

A typical day for a priest involves an early prayer (often spoken in bed moments after waking), recording remembered dreams in a journal, breakfast, study (the arts if so inclined, geography or the culture of a foreign land if not), and any duties assigned by an elder priest if one is present. After a light lunch the priest should go for a walk or ride, either to someplace new or by taking a new path to a known place; because there are usually only a limited number of routes between any two cities and local dangers might prevent serious exploration on these journeys, a priest might compromise by treating the left, right, and center parts of the road as "new" paths. Once at their destination they attend to their duties there, help passersby who require their skills, possibly entertain at a local gathering spot, seek a place to stay for the night, dine, pray, and sleep. Divine priests prepare their spells during morning prayers, while Desna's bard-priests generally prepare spells after those prayers.

Because they consider an uninterrupted sleep a kind of prayer to their goddess, traveling Desnans never volunteer for a middle watch during the night; first or last watch is preferable to them. If a priest believes he won't get as much sleep as he likes that night (for example, if his comrades plan a midnight battle), he tries to fit a nap or two into his schedule for the day rather than "toughing it out" and being short on sleep.

Desna's priests have a tradition of exploring distant places and leaving a mark indicating someone of the faith has been there. This "found-mark" might be as simple as the goddess's symbol scratched on a flat rock or tree trunk, as elaborate as a small shrine, or anything in between. Often, the explorer leaves a personal glyph or a note indicating who they are; in this way they gain fame in the church, and someone who has marked many sites in this way is called a Founder—a title with no formal powers but high esteem among the faithful, especially as other explorers discover their found-marks. Although Desnans constantly seek to make new discoveries, some particularly remote or hard-to-reach locales—such as mountaintops, islands, or the tops of ruined buildings—have become holy sites in their own right, with the mark of the original Founder being surrounded by dozens of personal runes or butterfly symbols left by those who have followed in his path.

THREE MYTHS

As Desna's faithful delight in storytelling, her worshipers find the greatest enjoyment in telling tales of their goddess. Here are but a few of their favorite and best-known myths.

Ghlaunder's Hatching: Legends tell how Desna wandered the Ethereal Plane and discovered a strange cocoon that pulsed with magic. Curious about its contents, she broke it open and released a mosquito-like being called Ghlaunder, which immediately attacked her. She easily fended off its attacks, but the resilient creature managed to escape before she could destroy it. Now Ghlaunder plagues the mortal world as a demigod of parasites and infection. Desna still hunts the godling and his cults in the hope of wiping them from the world or perhaps turning his power to a more positive end, just as leeches can aid certain ailments and

HERALD OF DESNA

Desna's herald is the night monarch, a butterfly-like outsider with a body the size of a dragon. Its wings may be brightly colored like any variety of mortal butterfly, muted like a moth's, or branded with starlike patterns of black and silver. Ancient and wise, it does not speak, preferring to communicate through dreams or a limited telepathy usable only when the monarch touches its antennae to a listener's head. Its stats are similar to an advanced 12 HD celestial giant eagle (CR 8), but once per round it can spray an adhesive at a single target that is equivalent to a tanglefoot bag (Reflex DC 19). The monarch's flesh is poisonous (equivalent to arsenic poisoning), affecting any creature that bites it or ingests part of its body.

Sometimes non-celestial versions of this creature, called star monarchs, emerge from pristine hiding spots and begin long journeys across the world. Spotting a monarch (mortal or otherwise) is a sign of good luck and Desna's favor. Killing such a creature is abhorrent to her worshipers, who go to great lengths to avenge such a death.

HERALDS OF THE GODS

The deities of Golarion are active in the lives of their followers and, in the most dire of situations, make their will directly known. In such cases, a god might send his herald—a unique servant and messenger—to inspire faith, lead his followers, and smite his enemies. While not always the most powerful of outsiders, these divine beings are living symbols of their deity's dogma and, in times of great need, priests might call upon the aid of these holy beings. Nearly every deity of Golarion has a herald, and witnessing one—an exceedingly rare incident—should inspire awe second only to encountering an actual avatar of a god.

maggots can cleanse infected wounds. The moral of this myth is that every life contains mistakes and bad choices, but it is better to live, make those mistakes, and accept the challenges they present than to hide away from the world and do nothing.

Lamashtu's Trap: In her earliest days as a goddess, Desna's mentor was Curchanus, a mostly forgotten god of beasts, travel, and endurance, and Desna spent many nights listening to stories of his travels. Curchanus's enemy was Lamashtu, an equally ancient goddess of monsters, madness, and nightmares who longed for his control over beasts. Lamashtu set a trap for Curchanus, leading him on a strange wandering path into her realm, where she swarmed him with horrible monsters, finally attacking in the guise of a great deformed jackal, tearing his beast-dominion from him. This wound was too great for the elder deity, and as his last act he willed his power over travel to Desna. Since this theft, wild animals have treated mankind as an outsider and an enemy rather than a part of nature, and Desna has searched far and wide to find a way to force Lamashtu to surrender Curchanus's stolen power. The faithful use this story to remind them of Lamashtu's treachery, to honor Curchanus's gift to Desna, and to remind them that failure is just a setback, not an end.

The Stair of Stars: This long and convoluted myth tells of the journeys of a priest who explored the world for many years, placing found-marks at the tops of mountains and in the deepest forests. As he sensed the edges of the world closing in on him, he lamented the end of discoveries and wonders. That night he dreamed he walked to the shore of a great ocean, and upon that shore he saw a stairway made of glittering stars. In the dream, he trod upon the stair and saw that it led to infinite worlds in the sky and beyond. He awoke, praised the goddess for this inspiration, and spent the rest of his days seeking this stairway and the other worlds it promised. This myth teaches that there are always new things to discover, even after a lifetime of journeys. Some faithful believe that the stars in his dream represent the countless people of the world and how getting to know each of their stories is a great journey in itself—that the need to explore and discover refers to people as well as places.

HOLIDAYS

Given their lack of unified structure and penchant for spontaneous celebrations, the church of Desna has few formal holidays. Two major festivals stand out from the dozens of minor events.

Ritual of Stardust: This celebration takes place on the summer and winter solstices, bracketing the shortest and longest nights of the year (and thus the best day to travel and the longest night to view Desna's stars). A great feast starts at dusk with several large bonfires throwing sparks into the darkening sky. When dusk turns fully to night, the faithful sing until the fires burn down to glowing embers, then throw handfuls of sand laced with star gems (star rubies, star sapphires, or rose quartz) on the coals or into the air downwind of the festival. Pledges of friendship and journeys follow the stardust ritual, with the winking speckles of sand mirroring the stars in the sky and representing Desna bearing witness to the words. Some cultures include prayers for good harvests or safe winters, depending on the season.

Swallowtail Release: Legends tell of one of Desna's avatars plummeting from the Heavens after a great battle with Lamashtu. A blind orphan nursed her avatar back to health, and to thank the child, the goddess transformed her into an immortal butterfly. In this form, the child could forever fly in the day and night, seeing all the wonders of the world. In honor of this event, the church raises swallowtail butterflies, releasing them from a netted wagon on the first day of

Autumn in front of a crowd of the faithful. These "children of Desna" fill the air for the rest of the day's singing, feasting, and storytelling. Those of the church believe it is good luck for a butterfly to rest on them during the festivities. Because of this event, larger temples sometimes have enclosed gardens where they raise the caterpillars for eventual release; smaller temples or those in climates averse to butterflies might release dry leaves or cornhusk fragments painted to look like butterflies.

RELATIONS WITH OTHER RELIGIONS

Desna remains aloof from most deities for she is a loner and a wanderer, and her sometimes-tragic history has left her cautious about leaving herself vulnerable to others. While coyly unreceptive, she is aware that some find her remoteness enticing, and she encourages even godly paramours to explore and discover new things while trying to court her. Recently, the young god Cayden Cailean has made attempts to woo Desna, a flirtation she finds endearing and that reminds her of her own youth.

For a deity who keeps her distance, Desna has several enemies, most from long-standing feuds or old grudges. She battles Zon-Kuthon (god of envy, pain, and darkness), for she wants the night to remain a time of wonder rather than of fear and oppression. Rovagug (god of wrath, disaster, and destruction) contests for the void of space, which she considers her realm—for it contains the stars—while her pursuits of Ghlaunder and Lamashtu are ongoing. The goddess also watches for signs of numerous mostly-forgotten and departed deities from ages long past, guarding against their unlikely but ever-possible return.

Desna's only sources of comfort among the deities are Sarenrae, who tends her wounds after battling the evils of the night, and Shelyn, who ever reinvigorates her spirits and creates new wonders to be explored.

RELICS OF THE FAITH

Consummate artisans and lovers of beauty, followers of Desna create a variety of holy items to honor their goddess and spread her mysteries.

Monarch Talisman: This mithral medallion is shaped into an elegant, gemmed image of Desna's symbol. Crafted long ago by a Desnan priest (some believe by the unnamed priest of the Stair of Stars myth), the wearer is protected by *endure elements* at all times and shrouded in fresh breathable air as if she were wearing a *necklace of adaptation*. By concentrating on the medallion, the wearer can determine which way is north (or a comparable reference point while on another plane), create a flame as if using a tindertwig, or cause the medallion to glow as dimly as a candle or as brightly as a torch. When unattended, the medallion floats several inches into the air and hovers whimsically. This item changes hands often and tends to turn up in unusual places. The church owns several lesser (non-artifact) versions of this item that duplicate some but not all of its powers (typically *endure elements, water breathing,* and *light*).

The Starhand: This slender piece of darkwood is topped with a star-shaped crystal with a handle wrapped in the silvery hair of an elven woman. It has all the powers of a *ring of shooting stars*. When held, it increases the wielder's base land speed by 10 feet (as if using the *longstrider* spell). As a standard action, the wielder can fire a *magic missile* (one missile only for 1d4+1 damage, but caster level 20) from its tip. A spellcasting wielder can use a standard action to channel one of her own 1st-level spells through the *Starhand*, transforming the energy into a *magic missile* spell at the wielder's caster level, even if *magic missile* is not on her spell list or one of the spells she knows (for example, a 9th-level druid could use one of her 1st-level spells to cast a *magic missile* spell at caster level 9th, creating five missiles at 1d4+1 damage each). Currently this item is believed to be in the hoard of a Numerian spine dragon, traded by a Desnan priest for his freedom.

NEW DIVINE SPELLS

Desna's clerics and druids may prepare the *dream* spell as a 5th-level spell, rangers as a 4th-level spell. The following new spells are available to any divine spellcaster who worships Desna.

Dream Feast

Conjuration (Creation)
Level: Cleric 1, Druid 1, Ranger 1
Components: V, S, DF
Casting Time: 1 standard action
Range: Touch
Target: Creature touched
Duration: Instantaneous
Saving Throw: Will negates (harmless)
Spell Resistance: Yes (harmless)

The next time the target sleeps (within 8 hours), she dreams of a rich feast with her favorite food and drink. When she awakens, she is sated as if she ate and drank a nutritious meal, regardless of what she dreamed she ate. The target must sleep for at least 1 hour to gain the benefits of this spell. Being awakened during this period interrupts the spell and cancels its effects.

If you sleep with this spell prepared, you may automatically expend it while you sleep to gain the spell's benefit. This expenditure does not count as spellcasting for the purpose of determining available spell slots (you could go to sleep at midnight, expend this spell during an 8-hour period of sleep, and still prepare your full allotment of spells in the morning).

Traveling Dream

Divination (Scrying)
Level: Clr 4, Drd 4
Components: V, DF
Duration: 1 hour/level (D)

This spell functions like *arcane eye*, except as noted above. Upon casting this spell you fall asleep for its duration, creating an invisible magic sensor (called a dreamscryer) that is the exact size and shape of your body, is recognizable as you, and cannot pass through spaces that your body cannot enter. Unlike the invisible sensor created by *arcane eye*, children (no older than 10) of any race and animals can see your dreamscryer. Sleeping creatures can sense its presence and might incorporate your image into their dreams. Force effects and any abjuration spell that wards out creatures (such as *magic circle against evil*) are effective barriers against a dreamscryer (regardless of your creature type, alignment, or other specifics). If you dismiss the spell or the dreamscryer is dispelled or destroyed, you awaken.

SPHEREWALKERS

A spherewalker is one who embraces the philosophy of Desna: travel far and wide, fight for your dreams, and indulge your desires. Spherewalkers explore extreme locales, dream fantastic dreams, and press their luck (good and bad) to make their lives interesting and noteworthy. They are known for founding cities, discovering lost civilizations, and going places where none have ever trod. They may choose to walk the distant paths alone or try to understand the mysteries of the mind and soul and become great leaders. Above all, spherewalkers seek adventure, with all the risks and rewards that such endeavors bring.

Spherewalkers are often multiclassed characters, as they tend to dabble in various classes to suit their adventuring needs. Their versatility adds extra depth and utility to combat-oriented characters (barbarians, fighters, rangers), their unusual magic appeals to spellcasters, and their special abilities make it easy for nonmagical characters to get out of tight spots.

Requirements

To qualify to become a spherewalker, a character must fulfill all of the following criteria:

Deity: Desna.

Base Attack Bonus: +5

Skills: 5 ranks in any two of the following skills: Climb, Knowledge (geography), Knowledge (nature), Knowledge (religion), Perform, Ride, Survival, or Swim.

Feats: Martial Weapon Proficentcy (starknife), one survivor feat (Great Fortitude, Iron Will, or Lightning Reflexes), one explorer feat (Acrobatic, Agile, Athletic, Endurance, Run, or Self-Sufficient).

Special: A spherewalker-to-be must have journeyed far in his lifetime, visiting two locations sacred to Desna that are at least 200 miles apart.

SPHEREWALKER

HIT DIE: D8

Level	Base Attack Bonus	Fort Save	Ref Save	Will Save	Special	Spells per Day
1st	+0	+2	+2	+0	Landmark, longstrider	+1 level of spellcasting class
2nd	+1	+3	+3	+0	Efficient sleep, star slinger	+1 level of spellcasting class
3rd	+2	+3	+3	+1	Dream link	+1 level of spellcasting class
4th	+3	+4	+4	+1	Divine luck	+1 level of spellcasting class
5th	+3	+4	+4	+1	Swarm form	+1 level of spellcasting class

Skills (4 + Int bonus per level): Balance, Climb, Concentration, Escape Artist, Handle Animal, Heal, Jump, Knowledge (geography), Perform, Ride, Spot, Survival, Swim, and Tumble.

Allies of Desna

Desna's clerics can use summon monster spells to call upon the aid of the following creatures in addition to those listed in the spells.

Summon Monster II

Lyrakien (CG)—see page 86.

Summon Monster III

Star monarch (CG)—same stats as a giant eagle.

Summon Monster VII

Young brass dragon (CG)—This creature has the extraplanar subtype but otherwise has the normal statistics for a creature of its kind.

Class Features

The following are class features of the spherewalker prestige class.

Landmark (Su): At 1st level, as a full-round action a spherewalker can create a mental landmark for her current location and thereafter take a standard action to note the general direction of that landmark. For example, if she sets her landmark in Magnimar and later travels to Korvosa, she can determine that Magnimar is roughly west of her current location. The landmark doesn't have to be a city or any kind of recognizable site—it could be in the middle of the ocean or even midair. This is a scrying effect.

A landmark location is one category more familiar for the purpose of teleporting ("studied carefully" becomes "very familiar" and so on). A spherewalker can have one landmark per class level. She can discard an existing landmark as a standard action and does not need to be at that location to discard it. Spherewalkers can take a minute to share a landmark with another spherewalker, and often do so to arrange meetings in unusual places without the need for maps or directions. A spherewalker can only detect the location of landmarks on her current plane, though they do not vanish if she leaves the plane and she can reference them if she returns to that plane.

Longstrider (Sp): At 1st level, a spherewalker may use *longstrider* once per day. Her caster level is equal to her character level.

Spells per Day: When a spherewalker gains a level, she gains new spells per day as if she had also gained a level in a spellcasting class she belonged to before she added the prestige class. She does not, however, gain any other benefit a character of that class would have gained. This essentially means that she adds the level of spherewalker to the level of whatever other spellcasting class she has, then determines spells per day and caster level accordingly.

If the character had more than one spellcasting class before she became a spherewalker, she must choose which class she adds each spherewalker level to for the purpose of determining spells per day.

If the spherewalker has no levels in a spellcasting class, she instead gains one 1st-level domain spell slot, which she may use to prepare spells from any of Desna's domains as if she were a cleric. Her caster level is equal to twice her class level. With each new spherewalker level, she gains a new spell slot for a spell level equal to her class level. A 5th-level spherewalker would thus have a spell slot for one domain spell from 1st to 5th level spells. The number of bonus spells and spell save DCs are set by the spherewalker's Wisdom score.

Efficient Sleep (Su): At 2nd level, a spherewalker gains a +4 sacred bonus to resist sleep effects and only needs 4 hours of sleep (or restful calm, for creatures that do not need actual sleep) instead of the normal 8 hours to become rested. Most spherewalkers prefer to sleep the normal amount, and if they use this ability they like to make up for it on later days by sleeping late.

Star Slinger (Ex): At 2nd level, any starknife a spherewalker uses in combat is treated as if it had the returning magic weapon special ability. Such weapons gain no additional enhancement bonuses or magical properties beyond this effect.

Dream Link (Sp): A 3rd-level spherewalker can form a mental bond with another willing intelligent creature as if using the *telepathic bond* spell. To do so, she and the target must spend at least 4 hours sleeping within 10 feet of each other. Either person in the link can end it as a standard action; otherwise it is permanent. If one person in the link dies, the other is stunned for 1 round and staggered until she can rest for 10 minutes. A spherewalker can only maintain one such link at a time, though she may be the recipient of multiple links. Married spherewalkers often link themselves to their spouses.

Divine Luck (Su): At 4th level, a spherewalker can add a luck bonus equal to her class level on an attack roll, skill check, or saving throw a number of times per day equal to her Charisma modifier (minimum 1/day). She may add this bonus after she has rolled but before she knows if the unmodified result is a success or failure.

Swarm Form (Su): At 5th level, a spherewalker gains the ability to transform into a swarm of Diminutive butterflies. In swarm form, she has a space of 10 feet (roughly filling the entire area) but can shape this space to fill four contiguous squares (such as a 5-foot-by-20-foot line, an L-shaped cloud, and so on) and can squeeze through any space large enough to contain one of her component forms. The swarm can fly at a speed of 40 feet (good). Like any swarm, it can occupy the same space as another creature regardless of its size.

Any creature that begins its turn sharing a space with a swarm must succeed on a Fortitude save (DC 10 + spherewalker level + Constitution bonus) or be nauseated for 1 round. Unlike most swarms, a spherewalker in swarm form does not do swarm damage to creatures she's swarming over. The swarm form is immune to weapon damage but is vulnerable to mundane fire attacks (torches, alchemical fire, burning oil, and so on), and energy attacks from weapon (such as flaming and frost) deal full damage even though the basic weapon damage has no effect. Although a swarm cannot make attacks, the spherewalker can cast spells as normal while in swarm form (although spells with material components could prove difficult).

A spherewalker can use this ability a number of times per day equal to her class level and remain in this form for up to one minute. While in swarm form, she may expend one use of this ability as a free action in order to remain in swarm form for an additional minute (rather than changing back to her normal form and activating it again). Changing back to her natural form before the effect ends is a standard action.

NPC PRIESTS OF DESNA

Here are but three faithful followers of the goddess of stars who might make good contacts for PC priests of Desna or who might encounter characters in their own travels.

Bodowen (CG male human bard 5) is a charming and talented Varisian singer, actor, and seducer. Rakish, with a pointed goatee and slicked-back black hair, he favors deep blue clothing with silver piping. He enjoys challenging thugs to duels, disarming them, and marking their weapon hands with quick slices. He has a fondness for elven wine and slender elven women, although he is not averse to beer and a husky human barmaid. Bodowen enjoys trading gossip, especially about people in power, and loves to travel, although he gets very seasick and therefore limits his sailing to emergencies. Bodowen left his nomadic clan, the Ralscarri, six summers ago—purportedly at Desna's urging—and has gone out of his way to avoid the Varisian east where they typically travel. Rumors hold that his father, the clan patron, asks after his wayward son wherever the family travels.

Krym (CN male elf cleric 8) is a mystic, always watching the horizon and trying to interpret subtle signs in the clouds and stars. He wears a simple white tunic and black pants with a silver belt, adding a large black cloak in the rain. His dirty blond hair is usually long and unkempt. He reads palms, interprets dreams, and writes bad poetry. He is also known to attract black and gray cats wherever he goes; they follow him while he walks and play or sleep at his feet when he stops. He claims not to know why the cats follow him, but has on occasion been caught examining a wrapped norn-crafted relic that he goes to great lengths to hide.

Hakkeshi (NG female human cleric 13) is a respected priestess, having traveled by foot, hoof, and sail over much of the known world and having placed her found-mark at the gate to the Sodden Lands ruin she dubbed the Seeping Silence. Currently recovering from a stubborn curse-induced injury to her leg, she teaches music and geography at a small college in Andoran called Torchpoint. Short, with black hair turning silver at the roots, she wears dapper vests, a silver circlet studded with small diamonds, and comfortable skirts to accommodate her splinted leg. Patient and friendly, with a barbed wit she only uses when among good friends or hated enemies, she is eager for recent news of the places she's explored, resenting the confinement her injury has forced upon her.

HOLY TEXTS

The faithful of Desna care little for heavy tomes of holy doctrine or arguments over the most righteous path. They prefer their religion concise, entertaining to read, and easy to carry.

The Seven Scrolls: These seven short scrolls contain all the official doctrine of the church, summerizing Desna's early days as a goddess, interaction with other deities, discovery of her powers, and the fixing of the stars in the night sky. The fifth scroll contains most of the church's words regarding the behavior of mortals, which sparks many friendly debates among the faithful. Desna is a goddess of inherent contradictions and not all of her dogma is absolutely clear. Fortunately, her faithful are not the sort to start fights over doctrinal differences, and her loosely organized church accepts all plausible interpretations of the scrolls that do not radically deviate from standard church teachings. The scrolls themselves are short enough that they all fit within two scroll cases (one if the writer's handwriting is particularly fine).

Shrine Writings: Wayside shrines to Desna are typically covered in graffiti, most perpetrated by travelling followers of the goddess. It is said that inspiration indulged at such a place is granted by the goddess herself and that adding to the artistry, scribbled verses, or life observations scrawled upon the shrine grants safe travels and good luck.

PLANAR ALLIES

Aside from Desna's herald and lyrakien (capricious minions of Desna—see page 86) the following outsiders serve the goddess of dreams and only willingly answer *planar ally* and similar calling spells cast by her worshipers.

Nightspear is a fierce avoral. His feathers are jet black except for spots of white on the tips, and his eyes are a bright silver that becomes dull and opaque when he's hunting or hiding. He is especially proud of his diving ability, able to snap out of a full plummet and turn horizontal with only inches to spare. He has an excellent singing voice and often belts out heroic songs of his own composing in mid-battle.

The Prince of the Night Sky is an arrogant djinn who once served Gozreh but joined Desna when he found her attitude more to his liking. He looks like a typical djinn except that he appears to be made of dense white smoke or inky black darkness dotted with bright stars (alternating between the two at whim). In either form, he has a long black beard which he keeps meticulously combed. For payment, he prefers jewelry and items that summon air elementals.

Sorrowbrand is an overly dramatic lillend composer and author. Her scales are a silvery black, and she wears dozens of black silk ribbons in her hair. While she enjoys helping in the mortal world, she constantly complains how it takes time away from her study and writing. She prefers payment in the form of bardic scrolls or long-lost songs.

The Journey Begins

To Shevala, Pathfinder Venture-Captain
Grand Lodge, Absalom

Hail from Magnimar, where the shadow of the Irespan drowns out the sun. You were absolutely correct that the City of Monuments has much to offer our organization, and it seems that our fellows here at the fledgling chapter house are uncovering new mysteries around every corner. Unfortunately, the surplus of projects has left little enough manpower to assist me in my own research. Although my initial investigation of Magnimar's esoteric shops has turned up few leads, one merchant of antiquities—a corpulent man named Belsir Trullos—informed me that he'd seen an ioun stone resembling the one we seek during his most recent visit to Kaer Maga. After I plied him with more than a few coins, he suggested that I speak with a man named Dakar in regard to the relic. No telling if the stone in question is authentic or one of the arcane reproductions that occasionally pop up, but there's only one way to find out. All that I have heard about Kaer Maga leads me to believe it a den of inequity, rife with criminals, outcasts, vice merchants, and worse. So, nothing I haven't seen before. I've chartered a boat and will leave on the morrow, and as always I shall send you updates as often as I am able. If there's truly an ioun stone for my wayfinder in Kaer Maga, I shall find it.

By my wit,
Eando Kline
Pathfinder

10 Gozran, 4707 AR

Riverboats are the only way to travel. After spending the morning lounging on deck and enjoying the gentle rocking of the boat, I can hardly bear the thought of the long ride ahead. I wish I could have left Redmare behind entirely, but as the captain has only agreed to take us as far as Wartle, she's currently corralled near the stern, where she whickers uneasily at each shift in the current. Poor girl.

I've never been aboard a halfling vessel before and am continually impressed by its efficient (if cramped) design. Captain Othlo is of a helpful disposition—as he ought to be, considering the exorbitant price he extracted for my passage—and has been happy to put up with my constant questions. Having spent most of his life traversing the Yondabakari, he's an excellent source of information on the peoples and dangers I might face on my journey farther up the river. His crewmen, for their part, are decidedly less sociable, spending much of their time tending to the craft and speaking with each other in the halfling tongue. Due to their occasional laughs and side-cast glances at me, I am sure they find my awkwardness aboard their tiny boat comical.

The river here is lazy, meandering in bends that stretch for miles on its long journey from the Mindspin Mountains down to Magnimar and the Varisian Gulf. In places it's sharply defined, cutting furrows through the rolling hills of the lowlands, while in others it almost blends completely with the boggy Mushfens to the south, merely a ripple of current through the endless patches of low trees and swamp lilies that threaten to swallow the incautious traveler. To our north, the Dry Way follows the river bends closely, allowing carts and horse-messengers access to settlements farther east. It's this that I'll eventually take to Kaer Maga, but for now, at least, I'm content to doze and let the miles slip quietly beneath me.

12 Gozran, 4707 AR

This morning, the wind kicked up and forced us ashore, the boat making little progress against the combined force of both air and current. Despite my rising impatience to be on my way, part of me secretly welcomed the chance to get off the boat and stretch my legs.

WAYFINDERS

Aura Faint evocation; **CL** 5th

Slot —; **Price** 500 gp

DESCRIPTION

This small magical device is patterned off ancient relics of the Azlanti, the first humans. *Wayfinders* are typically made from silver with gold accents, and function as compasses. Each bears four simple glyphs on its face, one for each of the cardinal directions, along with a spinning pointer that always points north, granting its user a +2 circumstance bonus on Survival checks to avoid becoming lost in the wilderness. In addition, all *wayfinders* include a small indentation designed to hold an *ioun stone*. While still granting the bearer their normal benefits, stones slotted in this manner frequently reveal entirely new powers due to the magic of the *wayfinder* itself. When no stone is in place, a *wayfinder* can be commanded to emit light as a standard action, as per the spell.

CONSTRUCTION

Requirements Craft Wondrous Item, *light*; Cost 250 gp, 20 XP

Othlo is a fine captain, though the halfling's boat is a bit cramped.

The longer we're on the water, the smaller Othlo's little cockleshell seems. The sparse woods near the river here are cluttered with game trails, so with an afternoon to kill, I saddled Redmare and set off for a quick hunt in the forest.

Not an hour into my journey, I heard a commotion up ahead, a strange cacophony studded with growls, whinnies, and hoots, as if a bear, a horse, and a monstrously huge owl were all engaged in a fearsome melee. Dismounting, I ground-hitched Redmare and drew my blade, creeping forward cautiously. On the other side of a large stone, a majestic stallion was facing off against a terrible beast combining the features of a bear and an owl. Seeing me, the creature let out a horrific growl-hoot, clicking its serrated beak shut with bone-shaking force. While impressive, the display proved to be its undoing, as the horse reared in terror and dropped its mighty hooves right into the beast's chest. The creature staggered, took a last swipe with its talons that opened the horse from withers to haunch, and went down, dragging the noble steed with it. For a long moment, nothing moved, the forest silent save for the frantic, blood-choked whinny of the horse. Speaking in a soothing tone, my sword before me, I approached.

Those talons are capable of opening a man like a ripe melon.

On the far side of the clearing was the horse's rider, or what little was left of him. The monstrous owlbear obviously struck from ambush, pulled the rider from his saddle, and ripped him asunder. The horse, an Uplands stallion that would have brought top dollar at the markets of Korvosa, must have remained to defend its master. A damn fine job it did of it, too—the last blow crushed the owlbear's ribcage, probably puncturing a lung. After making a quick sketch of the creature, I spent some time sifting through the mystery rider's trampled and ruined gear. He was an elf, and his raiment seemed of high quality, but beyond that there was little to identify him. From the road filth on his tack, he had been traveling for some time. Nestled at the bottom of his pack, carefully wrapped in a spare shirt, was a strange metal box with a puzzle for a lock. A simple incantation showed it to be magical in nature, but so far I've been unable to solve the locking mechanism. In truth, I'm not sure I want to—many of the designs on the box are unknown to me, but the engraved outlines of human skulls are disconcerting. Perhaps I'll hold onto it and let someone with more experience in such matters take a crack at it in the next chapter house I reach.

16 Gozran, 4707 AR

A simple meal, a hot bath, and a pleasant stroll around Wartle have made this one of the best days in recent memory.

We reached Wartle early yesterday morning, and Captain Othlo quickly set his crew to work unloading their Magnimarian goods and taking bids on cargo bound for the big city. Though I once again offered him a fair price to take me on to Whistledown, he would have none of it—apparently a business deal gone sour with the town's gnome residents left him unwelcome and prejudiced against the other little folk.

Despite a long history, the town of Wartle remains something of a frontier settlement, populated primarily by swampers and trappers. Aside from a few highly successful brothels, most of the buildings and boardwalks that rise on stilts above the murky swamp water are filled with dirty, bearded men who scratch out a living exporting peat, fungus, and furs to the "city folk" downstream. Still, they're a boisterous and fun-loving lot, easy to get along with so long as you don't put on airs. Most of last

DANGERS OF THE MUSHFENS

Numerous hazards and predators lurk in the Mushfens. What follow are just a few of the dangers travelers might expect to encounter when passing through the notorious bogs and fens.

Boggards: These savage frogmen are a deadly threat to any who wander the swamps (see page 84 for more information).

Faceless Stalkers: The ugothol, a race of degenerate shape-shifters, linger in the depths of the swamp, sparking tales of body snatchers (see page 88 for more information).

Fang Flies: Oversized flies sporting long proboscises breed by the millions in the swamps, latching onto larger animals and drinking their blood. Attempting to remove them with force generally results in the proboscis breaking off in the victim's flesh and possibly becoming infected. Instead, applying a small flame or hot object causes the flies to detach without harm. (These creatures have no stats, being little more dangerous than mosquitoes.)

Dragonwasp: Beautiful but dangerous, these Small insects come in a variety of iridescent colors and hunt in swarms, attempting to sting and lay their eggs in any suitable hosts. (Use the same stats as Small monstrous centipedes with fly speeds of 40 feet and perfect maneuverability.)

Marsh Giants: These hulking, misshapen brutes dwell deep in the Mushfens, adhering to a sinister animistic faith.

Moss Pigs: Similar to their forest counterparts, the flanks of these boars bear long strands of moss and fungus from rubbing on the sickly trees. (Use the same stats as a boar.)

night was spent in a precariously tilting dive known as the Lean-To, sampling the local liquor called Bog Grog. It's actually not so bad, once you get used to straining out the grit with your teeth, but it's generally a good idea to avoid drinking the dregs of the communal bottle. Needless to say, I got a late start today.

17 Gozran, 4707 AR

I left Wartle this morning astride Redmare after saying a surprisingly reluctant goodbye to the rowdy swampers. I miss the ease of the boat, but I won't deny that it feels good to be back on solid ground again. As I passed from the northernmost boardwalk onto the dirt of the road I encountered a small stone fountain marking the town's edge. Standing at the center of the fountain was a stone statue of a turtle, covered in a thick green moss, with water pouring from its shell. Perched on its nose was a single blue butterfly, and although I'm hardly a superstitious man, a momentary fancy took me and I tossed a copper coin into the water as I passed. You never know when Desna might be watching.

The Dry Way passes along the edge of the Sanos Forest, the Yondabakari drawing a surprisingly sharp border between the trees and the fens. Unfortunately, the swarms of tiny midges from across the water recognize no such demarcation, and more than once I had to stop to burn swaths of blood-bloated fang flies from Redmare's flanks. With such local fauna, few folk are willing to call these lands home, and on two separate occasions I approached a trapper's shack in hope of company, only to find a rotting ruin ready to collapse at the slightest breath.

As evening approached, the clear sky began to twinkle with a brightness rarely seen by city-dwellers. As the oppressive heat subsided, I decided to push on a bit into the twilight and was duly rewarded. In the distance, a faint spark came into view. Wary of will-o'-wisps and other hazards of the swamp, I dismounted and approached the site carefully, only to be greeted by the melodious plucking of a lute. No sooner had I heard it than a voice from the direction of the fire called out, "No point sneaking up on a minstrel, friend—I could hear your stomping a mile away. Come sit by the fire and warm your bones."

The rest of the evening flew by in a blur as Finnigar—a traveling storyteller of some skill—and I spent time sitting around the crackling fire, exchanging yarns and swigs of potent emerald liquor from his hip flask. One tale of note is recorded below—I would scribe more, but my quill grows heavy and the comfort of my bedroll beckons.

The Legend of the Whispering Tyrant

Long after the rise of Aroden, the Last Man, but early in the expansion of his empire, a band of his missionaries bound for points north encountered a tall, lonely tower on the banks of Lake Aletheia. In a single window near the tower's peak, a feeble light flickered. For days, the faithful had wandered through the barren lands, and the sight of habitation brought them much joy. Upon entering, however, they found only empty cobwebs and brittle bones slowly turning to dust. Climbing the dusty stairs to the tower's highest chamber, they discovered a single candle in front of the window, so freshly lit that the wax had barely begun to drip. Night fell as the missionaries waited uneasily for whomever resided in the barren tower to return, and as the darkness grew, so did their fear. Quietly at first, then slowly increasing in volume, sinister whispers rose, a low susurrus that tugged at the edge of their hearing, murmuring of wicked deeds and even darker delights. With prayers to Aroden for protection, they sought to flee the tower, but quickly found that the door they had entered through had disappeared, leaving a blank stone wall. As the hours passed, the whispers grew, and their urgings became commands. Minds cracked and broke under the strain of the vile suggestions, and those missionaries who resisted were set upon by those who had been claimed by the madness. In the darkness of the tower there was a carnival of unspeakable acts, the ruined monks cavorting in the blood of their fallen comrades, draping themselves with viscera and wallowing in perversion and depravity. Their shrieks echoed through the sinister tower, but only one of the former brothers was left alive to hear them, a missionary who had barricaded himself at the top of the stairs. Only by throwing himself from the candlelit window did he survive, but in doing so he left behind more than just his brethren. For the Tyrant of the Tower had demanded payment for his escape, and on quiet nights the pathetic mute can still hear a vague buzzing in his ears and feel a flutter in his throat as, far off in a forgotten tower, his voice is added to the tyrant's choir.

18 Gozran, 4707 AR

I awoke this morning to find Finnigar gone, along with the pair of coins I had left in my pouch. Removing the rest of my gold from my boot, I brushed down Redmare and continued on my way, peeved but unsurprised. Filthy bards.

20 Gozran, 4707 AR

Today's journey was swift and uneventful, and I passed only a single traveler making his way hastily toward Magnimar. The Dry Way remains close to the Yondabakari here, and the bugs are thick. Hopefully my campfire will keep the pests at bay long enough for me to get some rest. It is quiet here, and a warm fog has rolled in off the fens, bringing with it the strange calls of swamp life.

23 Gozran, 4707 AR

Perhaps that coin in the fountain bought more than I know, for surely it is only by Desna's blessing that I'm able to write this. Redmare is worse than dead, and I'm afraid it will take a dozen scalding baths to wash the stench of the Mushfens from my skin.

The trouble began three days ago, when I was awakened by the sound of Redmare whinnying in fright. No sooner had I sat up, grasping for my sword, than a sharp blow to the back of my head sent me back into darkness. When my senses returned, I found myself bound by tight reeds to a long pole carried by a pair of enormous frogmen. The creatures, known as boggards, are a serious threat to travelers in the fens, but are rarely sighted north of the river. It seems that my fire made me too tempting a target.

We traveled for what felt like hours, me slung underneath the pole, my back and neck raked by the tall thornweeds that infest the swamp. Another pair of boggards led Redmare along behind us, her nostrils foaming and eyes wide with fear. Despite my attempts to communicate, my captors seemed either unable or unwilling to speak to me. Instead, one of them actually stopped to pinch my side at one point, as if sizing up a succulent pig.

Soon after, we stopped at an immense mound made from mud, rotting wood, and swamp reeds, sculpted to resemble a gigantic

...I do not know what day it is, or even what time of day. I can't be sure, but the night carries strange sounds and I believe the creatures are giving chase. If anyone finds this journal, please send it to Venture-Captain Shevala at the Grand Lodge in Absalom.

The box is fascinating, but I'd rather not be the one who tries to open it.

frog with its maw open wide. There, sitting on a throne of alligator bones, was a monstrously fat boggard wearing the mud-stained regalia of a king. Upon his head was a crown of reeds bedecked with small stone fetishes, and about his neck hung a necklace of shells supporting a thick piece of amber above his breast. These, plus the obvious deference accorded to him by my captors, singled him out as their chieftain.

My pole was set upright, the bottom end jammed deep into the peat so that I might face their leader. After sizing me up for a moment, the king belched out a command and Redmare was brought before him. At the sight of my horse, his eyes glazed over with delight. The frogman then muttered a few croaks that sounded suspiciously like an invocation, and a host of gigantic dragonwasps the size of bucklers emerged from the swamp and made straight for Redmare, stinging her multiple times as she cried out in pain and terror. One of the boggards was nearly pulled from his feet trying to restrain her, but as the stings continued, her protests grew weaker. Every muscle in my body ached to break free and attack the boggards, but my bonds held firm, and I dared not reveal any of my other skills while so many of them stood ready to finish me off. Instead, I watched with burning eyes as my dear companion screamed, twitched, and gradually grew still, the red dragonwasps dancing about her prostate form.

Eventually the boggard chief gave a signal, and I was carried a short distance away, where my captors divested me of my gear, cut the bonds on my sore limbs, and dumped me into a shallow fen. The boggards then placed a lattice of stiff swamp reeds over the pit and secured it with heavy rocks, turning it into a soggy prison. No amount of ink can describe the stench that invaded my nostrils as I carefully treaded water, attempting to keep my face above the surface. Presently, the priest-king himself paid me a visit, pouring a bucket of foul-smelling oils into my pit while his long, sticky tongue darted about, probing the muck. Rumors hold that boggards prefer to marinate their food before dining, but I never imagined I would experience it firsthand.

In the gloom of the Mushfens, it's difficult to keep track of time, but it soon began to lighten and I was able to peer over the pit's edge and take stock of my surroundings. Most of my gear was only ten feet away, piled in a heap near where a single guard lazily devoured the carcass of a large dragonwasp like those that attacked Redmare. The drone of the ever-present fang flies was only overpowered by the cracking and slurping noises of my captor consuming his meal.

Fortunately, the wilderness is full of opportunity for those who know how to spot it. After an hour of patiently waiting, I was able to trap a cricket that had come to investigate my prison. From there, it was a simple enough incantation to put the boggard guard to sleep. With a low croak, the frogman tumbled to the ground and began to emit wet, snuffling snores. Using another minor spell, I was able to pull my dagger from its sheath across the way and into to my waiting hand, where I quickly put it to work cutting the reeds that made up the bars of my prison.

Within seconds I was free and dashing through the swamp with my most essential possessions, this journal among them. I caught only a glimpse of poor Redmare, now tied to the ground with a number of terrible bulges squirming in her belly, but that was enough. I shudder to think of the fate that befell her, but an attempted rescue would likely have had me back in the stewing pen, preparing to share her fate.

I covered a lot of ground in that first panicked stumble, and quickly became lost in the twisting meres and mangroves of the Mushfens, but here my wayfinder saved me, for even without its ioun stone, a compass is a handy thing. Two days later, feverish and weak from exposure, I stumbled out onto the banks of the Yondabakari, with the twinkling lights of Whistledown in the distance. I must have been a sight, staggering bloody and mud-coated between the quaint whitewashed houses, but the locals took pity on me and ushered me into the Azure Cup, a human-sized inn where I was barely able to rent a room before collapsing.

Outside my window, the tiny wooden chimes that swing from every eave catch the faint wind and create the subtle harmonies that give the town its name. Tomorrow I will undoubtedly begin re-provisioning for the next leg of my journey, but at the moment I haven't the heart. A soft bed and oblivion will have to suffice.

I am sorry, Redmare.

BESTIARY

SIZE COMPARISON

The majority of creatures in this month's Bestiary come from the demented pen of Richard Pett, author of "The Skinsaw Murders." This volume's murderous flock, avenging corpse, and sinister shapechanger form integral elements of his tale of reawakening horror. Aside from their use in the adventure, though, all of these creatures lend themselves well to their own tales of forgotten terror or deathless revenge.

Veteran gamers might recognize several of the other creatures on the following pages. For example, this is obviously not the first time a revenant has appeared in a roleplaying game, but the specifics of Iesha's betrayal, murder, and undying need for revenge make this the perfect place to resurrect such a classic undead horror. Lamias, too, find their origins deeply rooted in stories from the past—in this case from the myths of ancient Greece—with the new lamia matriarch drawing upon their fabled history. The lyrakien—angelic travelers inspired by Sean K Reynolds's treatise on the goddess Desna—might also sound familiar, as the name is an intentional corruption of "clurichaun" or "lurikeen," a mischievous Irish fairy similar to a leprechaun.

Finally, the boggards featured in this month's Pathfinder's Journal are expanded upon by author Jason Bulmahn, along with additional information on their barbaric society and foul amphibious deity.

NAMING MONSTERS

In general, monster names fall into one of two schools: what a creature calls itself or what others call it.

Fantasy names like aboleth, kolyarut, or sahuagin are all examples of names in this first school. By and large, they lack real-world root words and can be any combination of letters that sound cool. Such names work well for self-aware races that would attempt to define themselves through words or create a name in their own language.

More often, creatures are named by what others call them. Sometimes this reflects how a creature looks or what it does (obvious in cases like the ethereal marauder, owlbear, or rust monster) and often imply something new. Sometimes descriptive names aren't so simple, though, such as in the cases of names created by speakers of a different language. Basilisk, doppleganger, ettercap, and wight might sound like made-up names, but in their native languages the root words suggest a description: "little king" (Greek), "double walker" (German), "poison head" (Old English), and "man" (Middle English) respectively. Names, like all words, change as languages evolve, and gradually some names lose their association to their root words, gaining a distinctiveness all their own.

Thus, when naming a new monster, take a moment to consider a bit more than whether or not a name sounds cool.

—Wes Schneider

CARRIONSTORM

A swarm of rotting ravens takes awkward flight. Their lifeless eyes staring, their mangy wings rotting, the creatures open their beaks to call but make no sound. Bits of feather and flesh swarm around them, buzzing like flies.

CARRIONSTORM **CR 1**

Always NE Tiny undead (swarm)

Init +4; **Senses** darkvision 60 ft.; Listen +2, Spot +7

DEFENSE

AC 12, touch 12, flat-footed 12
(+2 size)

hp 13 (2d12)

Fort +0, **Ref** +2, **Will** +5

Defensive Abilities half damage from piercing and slashing; **Immune** swarm traits, undead traits

OFFENSE

Spd 10 ft., fly 40 ft. (good)

Melee swarm 1d6

Space 10 ft.; **Reach** 0 ft.

Special Attacks distraction

TACTICS

During Combat A carrionstorm has an unnerving preference for the flesh of humanoids, and while the swarm won't hesitate to attack other creatures, it generally seeks out humanoid targets before other victims.

Morale Carrionstorms fight to the death.

STATISTICS

Str 1, **Dex** 11, **Con** —, **Int** 2, **Wis** 14, **Cha** 6

Base Atk +1; **Grp** –12

Feats Improved Initiative

Skills Spot +7

SQ pallid bond, vulnerable to turning

ECOLOGY

Environment any near ghouls

Organization solitary, flock (2–4 swarms), or murder (5–12 swarms)

Treasure none

Advancement —

Level Adjustment —

SPECIAL ABILITIES

Distraction (Ex) Any living creature that begins its turn with a carrionstorm in its square must succeed on a DC 13 Fortitude save or be nauseated for 1 round. The save DC is Constitution-based.

Pallid Bond (Ex) A carrionstorm never initiates an attack on a creature that openly wears an unholy symbol of Urgathoa or is itself undead. If attacked first by such a creature, the carrionstorm's swarm attack only deals 1d3 points of damage rather than the normal 1d6.

Vulnerable to Turning (Ex) A successful turn undead check against a carrionstorm does not turn the swarm—rather, it destroys many of the individual birds, dealing damage equal to the result of the turning damage roll. A turn undead attempt that would normally result in the target's destruction destroys the entire swarm.

Where the dead walk, the carrion birds follow. In most cases, birds that feast on the remains of the undead simply grow diseased and die. Yet the flesh of some ghouls has an altogether different effect upon such scavengers, for when they die of the poisoned repast, they do not stay dead for long. Alone, the isolated undead crow or vulture is little more than a hideous mockery, but in rare cases where ghoulish activity is thick, entire flocks of carrion birds can succumb to undeath, retaining their flock mentality yet no longer seeking the flesh of the freshly dead to sate their hunger. Carrionstorms, as these flocks of undead birds are known, find brief respite from their morbid hunger only when their meals are warm and screaming.

Habitat & Society

Carrionstorms are typically found near graveyards, haunted structures, or abandoned villages where ghouls have been active. Many necromancers and cultists of Urgathoa have a particular fondness for carrionstorms, and since the birds have a strange respect for the symbol of the Pallid Princess, rookeries of them are often found roosting in the nooks of the god of undeath's macabre cathedrals.

BOGGARD

Although sitting on its haunches, this gray-green humanoid is still almost four feet tall. Two large, bulbous eyes sit on either side of its toad-like head, above a wide maw that holds a pair of sharp ridges instead of teeth. Countless tough warts cover its rubbery skin all the way down to its webbed hands and feet. The creature wears simple armor constructed from reptilian hide and turtle shells, and wields an immense spiked club.

Boggard **CR 2**

Usually CE Medium humanoid (boggard)

Init –1; **Senses** darkvision 60 ft., low-light vision; Listen +0, Spot +7

DEFENSE

AC 14, touch 9, flat-footed 14
(+2 armor, –1 Dex, +3 natural)

hp 22 (3d8+9)

Fort +3, **Ref** +2, **Will**+1

OFFENSE

Spd 20 ft., swim 30 ft.

Melee morningstar +5 (1d8+2) or
tongue +1 touch (sticky tongue)

Space 5 ft.; **Reach** 5 ft. (10 ft. with tongue)

Special Attacks sticky tongue, terrifying croak

TACTICS

During Combat A lone boggard opens combat with its croak before closing into melee. When attacking as part of a group, two boggards use their croaks, while the rest use their tongues to immobilize opponents. From there, they pummel opponents into submission.

Morale Boggards tend to flee a fight when reduced to 5 hit points or less.

STATISTICS

Str 15, **Dex** 9, **Con** 14, **Int** 8, **Wis** 11, **Cha** 10

Base Atk +2; **Grp** +4

Feats Toughness, Weapon Focus (morningstar)

Skills Hide –1 (+7 in swamps), Jump +15, Spot +7, Swim +10

Languages Boggard

SQ hold breath, swamp stride

ECOLOGY

Environment temperate marshes

Organization solitary, pair (2), or gang (3–12)

Treasure standard

Alignment usually chaotic evil

Advancement by character class; **Favored Class** barbarian

Level Adjustment +2

SPECIAL ABILITIES

Hold Breath A boggard can hold its breath for a number of rounds equal to four times its Constitution score before it risks drowning.

Sticky Tongue (Ex) A creature hit by a boggard's tongue attack cannot move more than 10 feet away from the boggard and takes a –2 penalty to AC while the tongue is attached (this penalty does not stack if multiple tongues are attached). The tongue can be removed by making an opposed Strength check as a standard action or by dealing 2 points of slashing damage. The boggard cannot move more than 10 feet away from the target while its tongue is attached, but a boggard can release its tongue as a free action. While attached, neither the boggard nor its target are considered grappled. A boggard's tongue attack is always considered a secondary natural attack.

Swamp Stride (Ex) A boggard can move through any sort of natural difficult terrain at its normal speed while within a swamp. Magically altered terrain affects a boggard normally.

Terrifying Croak (Su) Once per hour, a boggard can, as a standard action, emit a loud and horrifying croak. Any non-boggard creature within 30 feet of the boggard must make a DC 13 Will save or become shaken for 1d4 rounds. Creatures that succeed at this save cannot be affected again by the same boggard's croak for 24 hours. Creatures that are already shaken become frightened for 1d4 rounds instead. The save DC is Charisma-based and includes a +2 racial bonus.

Skills Boggards have a +16 racial bonus on Jump checks, a +4 racial bonus on Spot checks, and a +8 racial bonus on Hide checks made in swamps.

Often referred to as frogmen, boggards are human-sized creatures with a strong resemblance to their lesser amphibious cousins with their bulging eyes, wide mouths, and long sticky tongues. Any such comparison ends with physical characteristics, though, as boggards are cruel and capricious, caring little for other swamp-dwellers and even less for those who walk on the firm ground beyond their soggy realms.

HABITAT & SOCIETY

Boggards live almost exclusively in temperate swampy environments, but the occasional clan has been spotted in tropical rainforests, living on the banks of great rivers. Boggard villages are primitive affairs, with a number of crude mud mounds dotting a swampy clearing. Hut interiors are a mix of muddy ground and stagnant pools. Individual boggards rarely claim one such mound as a home and tend to move from mound to mound as space allows. In the center of a boggard settlement is the priest-king's mound. This impressive dome contains multiple chambers for the priest-king's guards, consorts, and followers.

Boggard society is a relatively fluid one, where one's status is dictated almost entirely by skill and accomplishments. Aside from such measures, size and weight also play an important role in finding a mate. Boggard clans are ruled over by a priest-king, who is a bit larger and stronger than the rest. Fed a rare blue dragonfly from birth, these priest-kings learn to speak to Gogunta, the corpulent goddess of the boggards. As they age and grow in power, these priest-kings continue to swell and grow, becoming more and more like gigantic frogs and less like humanoids.

Clerics of Gogunta have access to two of the following domains: Chaos, Death, Evil, Scalykind, or Water. Gogunta is chaotic evil and her favored weapon is the whip.

ECOLOGY

Boggards begin life as tadpoles, birthed from the fetid pools of their great brood mothers. It is here that they learn their first lessons in survival as they avoid the dangers of the swamp and compete with their siblings for food. After six months in this state, during which they grow to a length of three feet, adolescent boggards sprout legs and arms, a process that takes another three months. At the end of this time, the young boggards emerge from swamp pools and are pressed into gangs with young hunters who teach them all the necessary skills. After two years of training, young boggards must hunt and kill a sentient humanoid before becoming a full member of the clan. Boggards who do not complete this task within a month are cast out from the clan and rarely survive.

A boggard's diet consists of a mix of swamp plants, fish, smaller amphibians, and dragonwasps they breed specifically as food. These large insects are roughly two feet in length and are usually birthed from the corpses of dead humanoids or larger animals.

The average boggard stands nearly five feet tall, but has a crouching posture and appears much shorter. Most weigh about 200 pounds. Boggards can live up to 50 years old, but they often fall prey to swamp predators, fellow clansmen, or enemy humanoids well before this time. Most boggards have gray, green, or black skin, but brighter colors such as red or orange are not unheard of. As a boggard ages, its warts grow in size and thickness, and its color tends to fade. Especially venerable boggards are often bone-white and covered with knobby protrusions.

TREASURE

Boggards value objects that enhance their prowess in battle above all other things. Weapons and armor tend to be the most common treasure. They also value shiny metals that stand out in the gloom of the swamp. Such treasures are always carefully cleaned and maintained. Any other treasure in a boggard clan is kept by the priest-king at the bottom of a murky pond somewhere in his vast swamp mound.

BOGGARD PRIEST-KINGS

Rulers of entire clans of boggards, the appetites of the priest-kings know no bounds—be it for food, mates, treasure, or conquest. These corpulent monsters have feasted on the blue dragonflies of Gogunta and learned to hear her terrible croaks.

The following adjustments to a standard boggard represent a young priest-king. More aged varieties with even greater powers certainly exist.

—+2 natural armor.

—+4 Strength, +4 Constitution, +6 Wisdom.

—**Swamp Magic (Sp)** While in the confines of a swamp or marsh, a boggard priest-king can call on each of the following powers once per day as a spell-like ability: *fog cloud*, *jump*, and *summon swarm*. These spells are cast as a cleric of a level equal to the priest-king's total Hit Dice.

VARIANT BOGGARDS

Like the amphibians they hold obvious relation to, boggards are sensitive to their environments and have widely differing appearances and abilities. While the boggards of Varisia are green-brown and almost toad-like, those of the River Kingdoms have the greasy green look of frogs. In the Sodden Lands, numerous warring boggard tribes each have their own distinctive traits from the bright spots of tree frogs to the dead browns of cane toads. With these varied forms also come a variety of abilities such as harder skin, poison flesh, sticky hands and feet, and numerous other amphibious traits.

It is said that in the deepest swamps of the Hollow Morass, the Stinking Sink, and the Mushfens lurk the progenitors of the boggard race: the first priests, the Mobogo. Intelligent, primeval toads of gigantic size and incredible magic power, these swamp kings are said to be the offspring and harbingers of Gogunta herself, spreading her gospel of croaking doom.

LYRAKIEN

Amid a haze of queerly refracting light and the delicate song of a million rhythmically flapping butterfly wings hovers a tiny luminous figure. Beautifully androgynous with long, sharply pointed ears and transparent wings that split the light into countless tiny rainbows, the fairylike creature flits in the air, obviously unfettered by the physical laws of this world.

LYRAKIEN **CR 2**

Always CG Tiny outsider (chaotic, extraplanar, good)

Init +8; **Senses** darkvision 60 ft.; Listen +6, Spot +8

Aura *magic circle against evil* (10 ft.)

DEFENSE

AC 16, touch 16, flat-footed 12
(+2 size, +4 Dex)

hp 11 (2d8+2)

Fort +4, **Ref** +7, **Will** +6

DR 5/evil; **Immune** electricity, petrification

OFFENSE

Spd 20 ft., fly 80 ft. (perfect)

Melee slam +1 (1d2 –3)

Space 2-1/2 ft.; **Reach** 0 ft.

Special Attacks Desna's glare

Spell-like Abilities (CL 4th)

At will—*dancing lights*, *daze* (DC 15), *detect magic*, *ghost sound* (DC 15), *prestidigitation*, *summon instrument*, *tongues*, *ventriloquism* (DC 16)

3/day—*cure light wounds*, *lesser confusion* (DC 16), *silent image* (DC 16)

TACTICS

Before Combat Lyrakien prefer to flee rather than fight, seeking out servants of Desna more skilled in battle to deal with threats to her faith.

During Combat In battle, lyrakien prefer to use their powers to confuse their opponents and lure them into nearby hazards or ambushes.

Morale Unless their loved ones or those in their charge are threatened, lyrakien typically retreat after taking more than 5 points of damage.

STATISTICS

Str 5, **Dex** 19, **Con** 12, **Int** 15, **Wis** 17, **Cha** 21

Base Atk +2; **Grp** –9

Feats Improved Initiative

Skills Bluff +10, Diplomacy +7, Hide +17, Knowledge (any two) +7, Listen +8, Perform (any two) +10, Spellcraft +7, Spot +8, Tumble +9

SQ Desna's blessing, traveler's friend

ECOLOGY

Environment any

Organization solitary, band (2–6), or company (7–24 swarms)

Treasure none

Advancement by character class; **Favored Class** bard

Level Adjustment +3

SPECIAL ABILITIES

Desna's Blessing (Su) Favored of the goddess of travel, lyrakien are constantly affected by the spell *freedom of movement* and radiate a *magic circle against evil* (caster level 4th).

Desna's Glare (Su) As a standard action, lyrakien can momentarily tap into the divine radiance that surrounds their goddess, unleashing a blast of holy starlight to affect the area around them. All creatures within 5 feet of the lyrakien are affected by this ability and take 1d4 points of damage + 1 point for each step their alignment deviates from Desna's (chaotic good). For example, a chaotic neutral or neutral good creature would take 1d4+1 points of damage, a neutral creature would take 1d4+2 points of damage, and a lawful evil creature would take 1d4+4 points of damage. Chaotic good creatures are unaffected by this ability.

Traveler's Friend (Su) The performances and company of a lyrakien ease the burden of travel. Spending a minute listening to a lyrakien's song (or other performance) removes the effects of exhaustion and fatigue.

Divine musicians and messengers in the service of Desna, lyrakien wander the world aiding travelers, protecting their mistress's followers, and working the goddess's will. Whimsical creatures, they delight in fresh sights, new songs, and the simple joy of moving. When called to serve, though, they are staunch enemies of those who would hinder freedom, harm the innocent, or damage places of beauty.

Habitat & Society

While lyrakien can be found anywhere in Golarion, they tend to travel well-known paths and congregate in scenic spots where the stars can be clearly viewed. Hilltops, natural rock formations, and even the roofs of large buildings all make popular gathering spots. Beyond the mortal world, countless numbers of the tiny celestials attend Desna in her cosmic travels and dally in her star-veiled palace, the Sevenfold Cynosure.

Lyrakien enjoy the company of others of their kind and those who embrace the freewheeling nature of Desna, even if they're not of her faith. They eagerly engage in friendly competitions, ever seeking to outsing, outplay, outdance, and outshine friends and allies. Improvising the best song, reciting lengthy limericks, running wild races, and telling tall tales about past journeys are all favored games. Lyrakien delightedly reward those who beat them with their best secrets, usually in the form of rambling directions, knowledge of little-known shortcuts, and elaborate maps.

Ecology

Playful, gentle beings, lyrakien live at peace with the natural world and are especially protective of vistas of natural wonder in which they see their goddess's hand. Kindly, but at times mischievous, glistenwings—as they are sometimes called in children's tales and among gnome and halfling communities—resemble some races of light-hearted fey in appearance and personality, but these similarities are but coincidences stemming from Desna's impulsive yet kindly nature. While they have no need to eat or sleep, lyrakien often do so to celebrate the end of long journeys—a necessary enjoyment to close any travel.

Treasure

While lyrakien rarely carry treasure—enjoying the freedom of going unburdened—most range far and know much of the world around them. Without fail, a lyrakien can point toward the closest found-mark left by a worshiper of Desna (see page 70). Given the supplies, they also relish the chance to draw maps but are prone to artistic flourishes and seemingly irrelevant digressions that make beautiful pieces of art but difficult-to-decipher maps.

Gifts from the Goddess

As often as possible, lyrakien like to bestow gifts upon those who have captured their attention or who have acted in ways that please Desna. Enthusiastic dancers, accomplished travelers, or even simply those who look sweet while napping might receive a boon from a passing lyrakien. Such gifts are never costly and only sometimes prove particularly useful, being trinkets selected by the tiny outsiders for the sheer joy of giving. To the bafflement of those who receive their gifts, lyrakien often misunderstand some of the particulars of humanoid culture—age, gender roles, and tastes in food in particular. For example, a traveling knight who loses his helmet might awake the next morning to find a bonnet near his pillow, while a tramp who sings as he begs for food might inexplicably receive a heaping bag of oats. Lyrakien typically give their gifts at night, preferring to let people assume that their presents are boons from the goddess.

Conversely, those who displease Desna—homebodies, censors, mean-spirited critics, and the like—might receive unwanted gifts or have possessions misplaced or given to others. As lyrakien have little understanding of ownership, this tendency has more than once gotten those they seek to do right by accused of theft. Lyrakien are often baffled by what all the resulting fuss is about.

Lyrakien Familiars

Particularly creative priests of Desna who multiclass into classes that provide familiars are sometimes blessed by the company of a lyrakien. Flighty creatures, lyrakien often prove more independent and impulsive than other familiars and might even leave a master who they no longer find interesting or who forsakes the tenets of Desna's faith. For inspired and pious members of the goddess's clergy, though, those able to keep the tiny outsiders' attention by traveling far or performing well, lyrakien can be devoted allies and interpreters of Desna's will.

A chaotic good arcane spellcaster of 7th-level or higher can gain a lyrakien familiar through the use of the Improved Familiar feat (DMG 200).

Lyrakien in Varisia

Several lyrakien currently work Desna's will in Varisa. Here are but three that PCs might encounter or share parallel aims with.

Joidyrilli: Fascinated with instruments of all types, this purple-haired lyrakien (his hair purposefully stained with imem berry juice) currently wanders between nomadic Varisian and Shoanti settlements seeking new songs. He claims to know Desna personally and to have taught her several of her favorite tunes.

Kymryrcyl: A weirdly somber lyrakien, Kymryrcyl sulks about the grounds of Windsong Abbey. He never ventures far from the religious neutral ground and, if asked about his strangely settled life, pouts that he's waiting for someone but refuses to explain any further.

Novi: An inhabitant of the Sanos Forest, Novi helps protect the gnome community of Sipplerose. She eagerly entertains the local children with her tiny flute and joins in their games while protectively watching out for them.

FACELESS STALKER

This is a thing of skin and dislocation and horror. A featureless humanoid shape with hairless, scaly flesh like a dark crimson snake, its long stretching fingers twitch and writhe. Its form is horrifically human, and yet at the same time frightfully pliant, evident when its boneless arms stretch out unnaturally, grasping what should be out of reach.

FACELESS STALKER (UGOTHOL) **CR 4**

Usually CE Medium aberration (shapechanger)

Init +7; **Senses** darkvision 60 ft.; Listen +2, Spot +2

DEFENSE

AC 17, touch 13, flat-footed 14
(+3 Dex, +4 natural)

hp 42 (5d8+20)

Fort +5, **Ref** +4, **Will** +6

DR 5/piercing or slashing

OFFENSE

Spd 30 ft.

Melee mwk longsword +8 (1d8+4/19–20) or
slam +7 (1d4+6)

Space 5 ft.; **Reach** 10 ft.

Special Attacks sneak attack +2d6

TACTICS

Before Combat Given the opportunity, a faceless stalker prefers to enter combat in an assumed shape so it can revert to its actual form in the first round of combat to gain its morale bonuses as soon as the fight begins.

During Combat Most faceless stalkers aren't particularly gifted at hiding and so rely on flanking foes and using feints to maximize their sneak attacks. Faced with multiple targets, they prefer to fight foes armed with weapons that deal bludgeoning damage.

Morale Faceless stalkers generally retreat if brought below 10 hit points.

STATISTICS

Str 18, **Dex** 16, **Con** 18, **Int** 12, **Wis** 15, **Cha** 16

Base Atk +3; **Grp** +7

Feats Combat Reflexes, Improved Initiative

Skills Bluff +11, Disguise +11 (+21 when using change shape), Escape Artist +15, Sleight of Hand +13

Languages Aquan, Common; tongues

SQ change shape, elastic, faceless

Gear masterwork longsword

ECOLOGY

Environment any swamp or underground

Organization solitary, pair, or gang (3–9)

Treasure standard plus masterwork weapon

Advancement by character class; **Favored Class** rogue

Level Adjustment +4

SPECIAL ABILITIES

Change Shape (Su) A faceless stalker can assume the form of a Medium humanoid at will, although this transformation is somewhat painful for the faceless stalker. Assuming a new form takes 10 minutes of concentration—a faceless stalker generally seeks out a safe and secluded place before beginning to assume a new form. Once a new shape is assumed, the faceless stalker can maintain that form indefinitely. The creature can revert to its true form as a free action, its shape rippling and snapping back into its true shape instantly. For 1 round after reverting to its true form, a faceless stalker gains a +2 morale bonus on all attack rolls, weapon damage rolls, skill checks, and saving throws. The faceless stalker's actual statistics don't change when it assumes a humanoid form, and it retains all of its other extraordinary abilities. It does not gain any of the assumed form's abilities; it cannot gain a fly speed, the ability to breathe water, or any other extraordinary abilities either. Any items or gear worn by the faceless stalker when it changes form are not absorbed by the new form—they continue to be worn by its new shape. A faceless stalker that uses this ability to disguise itself as a specific individual gains a +10 circumstance bonus on its Disguise check.

Elastic (Ex) A faceless stalker's body is boneless and rubbery, affording it resistance to bludgeoning attacks and granting a +12 racial bonus on Escape Artist checks. It can extend the length of its limbs, providing it with a longer reach than most creatures of its size. A faceless stalker can slither through gaps as narrow as an inch wide, although it must leave behind most of its gear to do so—moving through a narrow space like this costs the faceless stalker 3 squares of movement per 5 feet traveled.

Faceless (Ex) In its natural form, a faceless stalker has no real facial features. Its eyes, mouth, nostrils, and ears are little more than tiny slits in the folds and whorls of flesh and color that decorate its head. A faceless stalker in its true form gains a +4 bonus on any saving throws made against visual attacks (such as gaze weapons), odor-based attacks, and sonic attacks.

Sneak Attack (Ex) A faceless stalker deals +2d6 points of damage when its target is denied its Dexterity bonus to Armor Class or is flanked. This ability works the same as the rogue ability.

Tongues (Su) A faceless stalker is under the constant effect of a *tongues* spell; this ability cannot be dispelled.

Feats Faceless stalkers are proficient with light armor and all simple and martial weapons.

The ugothols are a malevolent race of shapechanging aberrations whose methods and nature mark them more as parasites or diseases than actual residents of the environs they inhabit. Although their nomadic and savage natures certainly don't speak to it, the ugothols are among the oldest of Golarion's races. The first ugothols were created by the aboleths long ago, after the rise of the second aboleth empire, when the lords of the deep tried a stealthier method to curtail and destroy the development of air-breathing races after a full-scale invasion resulted in the collapse of the first empire. The ugothols were chameleons, elastic creatures of flesh and bone capable of adopting the shape of a diverse array of air-breathers, yet remaining under the complete control of the aboleths through the deep lords' use of master glyphs deep in the Arcadian Ocean. This invasion was much more successful than the previous one, and numerous burgeoning civilizations collapsed from within as they became infected with ugothol spies. It took the destruction of the master glyphs and the entire aboleth city of Voshgurvaghol to bring this incursion to an end. The aboleths have yet to mount a third offensive against the world above, and they've long since abandoned the ugothol to their own devices. Unable to breathe water, the ugothol did the next best thing—they fled to the swamplands of the world, and even into the dripping and dark tunnels of the world below, where they regressed over the millennia into the savage nomads known today as faceless stalkers.

Habitat & Society

Faceless stalkers have a rudimentary form of community—they enjoy the company of small numbers of their kind, but large concentrations invariably collapse into internal bickering, feuds, and power struggles. As a result, few faceless stalker communities have more than a dozen members. Nomadic in nature, they move from community to community, using their change shape ability to masquerade as the target community's dominant race and to pose as travelers, merchants, or pilgrims. Once established, the gang of stalkers systematically murders the village, leaving the bodies for scavengers while they enjoy the settlement's resources. Occupation by a gang of ugothols invariably leads to the settlement's ruin, as the faceless stalkers squander stores and resources, and ruin structures left behind. Once a settlement has declined to the extent that even the ugothols find it useless, they move on to their next target.

Ecology

Ugothols have no real mouths—their diets consist entirely of liquids (primarily blood) drawn into their bodies via a set of three long, hollow, rasp-like tongues. This gruesome method of feeding is too slow and delicate a process to serve the creature as an effective attack, but the sight of three or four ugothols squatting around a screaming, bound victim is sure to turn the stomach of even the bravest warrior. Ugothols greatly prefer to feed from living creatures—a feeding ugothol deals one point of Constitution damage per minute as its tongues burrow deeper and deeper in search of nutrition.

Religion

In the thousands of years since they were abandoned by their creators, the faceless stalkers have largely forgotten their genesis, remembering it only in their methods of raiding and supplanting villages. In an ironic turn of events, proto-memories of serving the aboleths have given rise to a faith, such that the ugothols—creations of a race of atheists—have developed strong ties to certain sinister deities. The god of parasites and stagnation is a particular favorite of faceless stalker clerics, with many believing that their kind were in fact created by the Tarnlord Ghlaunder (see page 70).

Treasure

Ugothols prefer light armor or none at all, finding it uncomfortable to transform while wearing heavy suits of mail. Their ability to wield any simple or martial weapon means that most ugothols carry, at the very least, masterwork weapons. Ugothols with class levels always have at least one magic weapon, with bladed weapons being favored over other types.

Faceless Hulks

Stories exist of much larger faceless stalkers capable of infiltrating giant societies with the same ease in which they infiltrate humanoid societies. A Large faceless hulk has 8 Hit Dice, while a Huge faceless hulk has 16 Hit Dice. Like their smaller and much more common kin, faceless hulks advance by character class levels, not by Hit Dice.

REVENANT

There is malevolence in the hate-filled eyes of this dead thing. Once a human, yet stripped of pity and remorse along with its life, its body is wasted, staggering in a spastic lope across the ground, as though only its evil intent keeps it walking upright.

REVENANT **CR 6**

Always LE Medium undead

Init +2; **Senses** darkvision 60 ft., sense murderer; Listen +11, Spot +11

DEFENSE

AC 19, touch 12, flat-footed 17
(+2 Dex, +7 natural)

hp 69 (7d12+24); fast healing 5

Fort +5, **Ref** +4, **Will** +6

Defensive Abilities undead traits; **DR** 5/slashing; **Immune** cold; **SR** 12

OFFENSE

Spd 30 ft.

Melee 2 claws +11 (1d6+10)

Space 5 ft.; **Reach** 5 ft.

Special Attacks baleful shriek, constrict 1d6+10, improved grab

TACTICS

Before Combat Knowing nothing besides its rage, a revenant attacks in the most direct manner possible.

During Combat A revenant single-mindedly attacks its murderer or the creature immediately in its way, ignoring all other distractions.

Morale A revenants never flees and fight until destroyed.

STATISTICS

Str 24, **Dex** 14, **Con** —, **Int** 6, **Wis** 12, **Cha** 16

Base Atk +3; **Grp** +10

Feats Cleave, Power Attack, Weapon Focus (claw)

Skills Listen +11, Spot +11

Languages Common

SQ reason to hate, self-loathing, unholy fortitude

ECOLOGY

Environment any

Organization solitary

Treasure standard

Advancement 8–21 HD (Medium)

Level Adjustment +6

SPECIAL ABILITIES

Baleful Shriek (Su) Once every 1d4 rounds, a revenant can use its baleful shriek as a standard action. All creatures within 60 feet of the revenant must make a DC 16 Will save or cower in fear for 1d4 rounds. This is a mind-affecting fear effect. The save DC is Charisma-based.

Constrict (Ex) On a successful grapple check, a revenant deals 1d6+10 points of damage.

Improved Grab (Ex) To use this ability, a revenant must hit with both claw attacks against a target of equal or smaller size. It can then attempt to start a grapple as a free action without provoking an attack of opportunity. If it wins the grapple check, it establishes a hold and can constrict.

Reason to Hate (Su) A revenant's undead existence is fueled by its undying hatred for the creature that murdered it. As long as this creature exists, the revenant exists. If this creature is killed, the revenant immediately drops to the ground and is destroyed as well. Note that a living murderer who becomes an undead creature does not trigger a revenant's death. If a murderer is brought back to life after dying (or later becomes an undead creature), the revenant returns to life as well unless its body has been destroyed completely.

A revenant's driving goal is to confront its murderer and slay him. When a revenant encounters its murderer, it immediately attacks, gaining the benefits of a *haste* spell (CL 20th) that lasts as long as its murderer remains in sight. Against its murderer, the revenant gains a +4 profane bonus on attack rolls, weapon damage rolls, grapple checks, and saving throws.

Self-Loathing (Ex) A revenant is filled with an overwhelming sense of self-loathing—the only thing that approaches its hatred of its killer is its hatred of what it has itself become. When confronted with a mirror or any object that was important to it in life (such as a recognizable and cherished possession or an old friend or family member), the revenant must make a DC 20 Will save to avoid becoming overwhelmed with remorse and self-pity. This condition renders the revenant helpless, and continues until the revenant is attacked or until it sees its murderer (or any iconic possession it recognizes as once belonging to its murderer), whereupon the monster emerges from its self-loathing to attack the source of whatever roused it from its helpless state. If a revenant makes its saving throw to avoid becoming overwhelmed with self-loathing, it becomes obsessed with the creature or object that triggered the saving throw and does everything it can to destroy it, treating the object as if it were its murderer and gaining the appropriate bonuses while the creature or object remains in sight (see Reason to Hate).

Sense Murderer (Su) A revenant can use *locate creature* at will (CL 20th), but only against the being that murdered it. If the murderer is outside of the revenant's range, it seeks out the closest location it recalls from life that it associates with its murderer and haunts the region until it is destroyed or its murderer dies. Against its murderer, a revenant has *true seeing* and *discern lies* in effect at all times (CL 20th); these abilities cannot be dispelled.

Unholy Fortitude (Ex) A revenant gains bonus hit points equal to its Charisma modifier times its Hit Dice, and a bonus to its Fortitude saves equal to its Charisma modifier.

Vengeful spirits bent upon the death of those who wronged them, revenants are creatures of pure animated hatred driven by the need to avenge themselves. They seek their enemy always, needing no rest or sleep and never halting until their revenge is fulfilled and they can be at peace.

In death they appear horrifically similar to how they did in life, but twisted, their faces masks of hate and torment, their limbs contorted. A foul graveyard stench accompanies them, and their voices are scathing hate-fueled venom.

Habitat & Society

Revenants are spawned from murder and the need for revenge. As such betrayals most likely happen in civilized lands, these rare undead are generally found in cities and on well-traveled roads as they seek out those they hold responsible for their deaths. Occasionally, a revenant might be encountered in the far-flung wilds as they trek over mountain and field tracking their fleeing victim. Possessed by their single-minded need for revenge, revenants have little to no interaction with those besides the ones who wronged them, and threaten only those who would impede them in their quests.

Religion

Wronged who worshiped the goddess Calistria in life return as revenants more often than those of any other faith. Priests of Calistria's church see revenants as divine crusaders, creatures that go beyond death to act as the goddess desires. As such, Calistria's flock aids revenants however they can and hold those the undead kill as honored sacrifices to their fickle goddess.

Treasure

Many revenants have a morbid sense of irony, and carry with them weapons similar to the one that ended their life. If possible, a revenant takes up the weapon that ended its life, eager to repay its murderer in kind.

Sample Revenants

Tales of the vengeful dead litter the repertoires of bards throughout Golarion. Here are but four storied revenants which GMs might use to inspire their own avenging undead.

Jikril "Handsome" Tods: Jikril scours the streets of Ocota for his Dubari murder and his lost (probably shrunken by now) head.

Lemara Romerri: The lover of a Korvosan noble, Lemara was killed by her paramour's jealous shrew of a wife. Nightly she besieges the walls of her murderess's manor, disappearing with the dawn.

Natash Endersan: A Taldorian merchant killed in Absalom by his treacherous partner and brother, Natash sneaks aboard ships he believes are headed to his home country in hopes of catching his murderous sibling.

Old Bones: His real name and the details of his death lost to history, this completely skeletal revenant wanders the length and breadth of Golarion. He's been witnessed making abrupt changes in his course, as if his nameless victim had swiftly and radically changed position.

Characters as Revenants

On exceedingly rare occasions, a player character who dies with a powerful need for revenge might return to life as a revenant. This can make an interesting final adventure for a character as she tracks down her murderer. A PC can only return as a revenant if the GM feels such a dramatic resurrection is warranted. If the character becomes a revenant, she must act as such a creature, single-mindedly hunting down the one to blame for her death. She uses the stats presented here instead of her own. While it might seem like this creature should be a template, a revenant is not the person it once was, but rather a corpse animated by hatred, possessing little of its former identity. More powerful or older forms of hate might spawn deadlier advanced revenants. Once the PC kills the one who murdered her, the revenant is put to rest and the character truly dies.

LAMIA MATRIARCH

Her chin raised and eyes narrowed in imperious scrutiny, this cold beauty accentuates her pale skin and finely toned curves with the scant jeweled fineries of a harem queen. Below her exposed midsection, though, all hint of woman vanishes, morphing into the powerful, deadly sleekness and iridescent black scales of a coiled asp.

LAMIA MATRIARCH **CR 8**

Always CE Large monstrous humanoid (shapechanger)

Init +4; **Senses** darkvision 60 ft., low-light vision; Listen +3, Spot +3

DEFENSE

AC 22, touch 13, flat-footed 18

(+4 Dex, +9 natural, –1 size)

hp 102 (12d8+48)

Fort +8, **Ref** +12, **Will** +13

Immune mind-affecting; **SR** 18

OFFENSE

Spd 40 ft., climb 40 ft., swim 40 ft.,

Melee +*1 scimitar* +14/+9/+4 (1d8+6/15–20 plus 1 Wisdom drain) and

+*1 scimitar* +14 (1d8+3/15–20 plus 1 Wisdom drain) or

touch +16 (2d4 Wisdom drain)

Space 10 ft.; **Reach** 5 ft.

Spell-Like Abilities (CL 10th)

At will—*charm monster* (DC 19), *ventriloquism* (DC 16)

3/day—*deep slumber* (DC 18), *dream*, *major image* (DC 18), *mirror image*, *suggestion* (DC 18)

Spells Known (CL 6th)

3rd (4/day)—*haste*

2nd (6/day)—*death knell* (DC 17), *invisibility*

1st (8/day)—*cure light wounds*, *divine favor*, *mage armor*, *shield*

0 (6/day)—*dancing lights*, *daze* (DC 15), *detect magic*, *ghost sound* (DC 15), *mage hand*, *mending*, *prestidigitation*

TACTICS

Before Combat A lamia matriarch prefers to send minions against her opponents, giving her time to cast spells like *haste* and *invisibility*.

During Combat Lamia matriarchs frequently use *charm monster*, draining the Wisdom of those who consistently resist the spell.

Morale Lamia matriarchs attempt to flee if reduced to less than a third of their total hit points, bartering for their freedom if escape is blocked.

STATISTICS

Str 20, **Dex** 18, **Con** 19, **Int** 16, **Wis** 16, **Cha** 20

Base Atk +12; **Grp** +21

Feats Extend Spell, Improved Critical (scimitar), Iron Will, Two-Weapon Fighting, Weapon Focus (scimitar)

Skills Bluff +19, Climb +13, Concentration +14, Knowledge (arcana) +13, Knowledge (any one other) +13, Spellcraft +15, Swim +13, Tumble +18, Use Magic Device +24

Languages Abyssal, Common, Draconic

SQ alternate form

SPECIAL ABILITIES

Alternate Form (Su) A lamia matriarch has a single humanoid form that she can assume as a standard action—most lamia matriarchs have human, elven, or half-elven alternate forms. Their appearance in this form is identical from the waist up to their serpentine form, yet in humanoid form the lamia matriarch is Medium sized (–8 Strength, +2 Dex, –4 Constitution), cannot use her Wisdom drain attack, has a base speed of 30 feet, and loses her climb and swim speeds.

Wisdom Drain (Su) A lamia matriarch drains 1d6 points of Wisdom each time she hits with her melee touch attack. If she strikes a foe with a melee weapon in addition to the weapon's normal damage, she drains 1 point of Wisdom instead. Unlike with other kinds of ability drain attacks, a lamia matriarch does not heal damage when she uses her Wisdom drain.

Skills Lamia matriarchs have a +4 racial bonus on Bluff, Tumble, and Use Magic Device checks. A lamia matriarch has a +8 racial bonus on any Swim check to perform some special action or avoid a hazard. She can always choose to take 10 on a Swim check, even if distracted or endangered. She also has a +8 racial bonus on Climb checks and can always choose to take 10 on Climb checks even if rushed or threatened.

Spells Lamia matriarchs cast spells as 6th-level sorcerers and can also cast spells from the cleric list. These cleric spells are considered arcane spells for a lamia matriarch, meaning that the creature doesn't need a divine focus to cast them.

ECOLOGY

Environment any

Organization solitary, pair, or cult (3–6)

Treasure standard coins, standard goods, double items plus two +*1 scimitars*

Advancement by character class; **Favored Class** sorcerer

Level Adjustment +6

The mothers and queens of a race consumed by bitterness, vice, and predatory instinct, lamia matriarchs mastermind all manner of foul plots in the hopes of breaking the cruel curse that afflicts their race. Possessing serpent bodies instead of their minions' leonine forms, they can move with shocking ease from silken-tongued temptresses to dervishes, striking with all the deadly precision of vipers.

Habitat & Society

Universally hated and distrusted, lamias lurk in the distant, dark places of the world among savages and beasts. Cults of lamias often form under the rule of a lamia matriarch or a powerful, willful warrior. These cults almost always gather with the intentions of avenging themselves against the goddess Pharasma or undoing her bestial transformation of their race. To that end, they seek out powerful magic-users and places of great arcane power that they might turn to their whims.

Ecology

Lamias are creatures of decadence and vice, their matriarchs even more so. Quick to covet, enslave, and overindulge, lamias

LAMIA IN MYTHOLOGY AND ART

In Greek mythology, Lamia was a woman of such beauty that Zeus took her as a lover. When Hera discovered the affair, she cursed Lamia, transforming her from the waist down into a snake and forcing her to eat her children. Much to the horror of Greek children, it's said that Lamia developed a cannibalistic taste for the young and sought out those who misbehaved.

Lamia is further immortalized in the art of John Waterhouse and Herbert Draper, but most famously in John Keats' poem of the same name.

She seem'd, at once, some penanced lady elf,
Some demon's mistress, or the demon's self.

—Excerpted from John Keats's "Lamia"

luxuriate in gory feasts, violent trysts, and bloody entertainments, reveling until their playthings are broken or they tire and move on.

Religion

Lamia matriarchs typically revere Lamashtu, goddess of monsters, although they'll venerate any deity they believe likely to bless their wicked plots. They hate the faithful of Pharasma and eagerly do them harm in vengeance for the curse the goddess of fate laid upon their race. Many lamias believe that their Wisdom-draining touch robs their victims of their destinies, and thus take special pleasure in depriving servants of Pharasma of their sacred paths.

Origins

In the days of the ancient Siv, the Shrine of the Fateless was among the world's most respected oracles. Deeply devoted to the mysteries of the goddess Pharasma, the Fateless forsook their own destinies to better divine the paths of those who sought their advice. For centuries, the ancient faith foretold plague and plenty and their words were irrefutable. Yet, over time, the Fateless grew greedy and arrogant. They exacted great sacrifices for self-serving lies cloaked by mysticism.

Displeased, Pharasma herself visited the Shrine of the Fateless, disguised as a sickly old wanderer, and begged to know her future. The leader of the temple, a beautiful sibyl known as Lamia of Avalos, dismissively demanded an offering for her insight. To the priestess's surprise, the stranger paid. Prepared to lie to be rid of the beggar, Lamia was instantly wracked with a vision—the first she had ever truly received. In it, she saw the old woman traveling a shining path, threatened on all sides by woods teeming with snakes, lions, and other deadly beasts, but at the road's end rose a tower of gleaming ivory. Speechless, Lamia quickly dismissed the vision and wickedly told the woman that she would receive great wealth if she travelled to the deadly Lands of the Horned Serpent.

Dismissing her disguise, Pharasma's aura of eyes filled the shrine, and in a booming whisper the goddess spoke: "I alone chose what perils lie upon the path to wonder! You who would speak and lie in my name, I renounce you and reveal you as kin in fate to the beasts forbidden to walk the path of destiny." With those words, the Fateless became as starving lions and Lamia's cries turned into the hiss of a pathetic snake. Pharasma banished the Fateless from her shrine, leaving them accursed things, forever wandering without destinies, half liars and half beasts.

Valeros

MALE HUMAN FIGHTER 4

ALIGN **NG** INIT **+7** SPEED **20 ft.**

ABILITIES

14	STR
16	DEX
12	CON
13	INT
8	WIS
10	CHA

DEFENSE

HP 30

AC 20
touch 13, flat-footed 17

Fort +5, **Ref** +4, **Will** +0

OFFENSE

Melee *+1 longsword* +8 (1d8+5/19–20) or *+1 longsword* +6 (1d8+5/19–20) and mwk shortsword +5 (1d6+1/19–20)
Ranged mwk comp longbow +8 (1d8+2/×3)
Base Atk +4; **Grp** +6

SKILLS

Climb	+6
Intimidate	+7
Ride	+10
Swim	+3

FEATS

Big Game Hunter[B], Combat Expertise, Improved Initiative, Two-Weapon Defense, Two-Weapon Fighting, Weapon Focus (longsword), Weapon Specialization (longsword)

Combat Gear *potion of cure light wounds* (2), *potion of cure moderate wounds*, *potion of shield of faith +3*; **Other Gear** *+1 breastplate*, *+1 longsword*, masterwork composite longbow (+2 Str) with 20 arrows, masterwork shortsword, backpack, lucky tankard, rations (2), silk rope, 50 gp

Seoni

FEMALE HUMAN SORCERER 4

ALIGN **LN** INIT **+2** SPEED **30 ft.**

ABILITIES

8	STR
14	DEX
12	CON
10	INT
13	WIS
16	CHA

DEFENSE

HP 12

AC 14
touch 13, flat-footed 12

Fort +2, **Ref** +3, **Will** +5

OFFENSE

Melee quarterstaff +1 (1d6–1)
Ranged dagger +5 (1d4–1/19–20)
Base Atk +2; **Grp** +1

Spells Known (CL 4th; 5th with evocation)
2nd (4/day)—*scorching ray* (+4 ranged)
1st (7/day)—*burning hands* (DC 15), *mage armor*, *magic missile*
0 (6/day)—*acid splash*, *detect magic*, *daze* (DC 13), *mage hand*, *prestidigitation*, *read magic*
Spell-Like Abilities (CL 4th)
1/day—*dancing lights*

SKILLS

Bluff	+10
Climb	+2
Concentration	+8
Listen	+3
Spellcraft	+7
Spot	+3

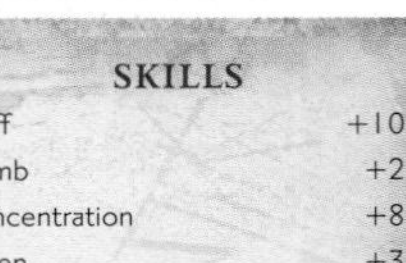

FEATS

Alertness (when Dragon's in reach), Dodge, Extend Spell, Spell Focus (evocation), Varisian Tattoo (evocation)[B]

FAMILIAR

Dragon (blue-tailed skink)

Combat Gear *potion of cure light wounds* (2), *wand of magic missile* (CL 3rd, 25 charges); **Other Gear** masterwork dagger, quarterstaff, *amulet of natural armor +1*, *ring of protection +1*, belt pouches (3), everburning torch, rations (4), 27 gp

Kyra

FEMALE HUMAN CLERIC 4 (SARENRAE)

ALIGN **NG** INIT **–1** SPEED **20 ft.**

ABILITIES

13	STR
8	DEX
14	CON
10	INT
16	WIS
12	CHA

DEFENSE

HP 23

AC 17
touch 9, flat-footed 17

Fort +6, **Ref** +1, **Will** +12

OFFENSE

Melee *+1 scimitar* +6 (1d6+2/18–20)
Ranged lt crossbow +2 (1d8/19–20)
Base Atk +3; **Grp** +4
Special Attacks greater turning 1/day, turn undead 4/day (+3, 2d6+5)
Spells Prepared (CL 4th)
2nd—*aid*, *bull's strength*, *heat metal*[D] (DC 15), *spiritual weapon*
1st—*bless*, *command* (DC 14), *cure light wounds*[D], *divine favor*, *shield of faith*
0—*detect magic* (2), *light*, *mending*, *read magic*
D domain spell; **Domains** healing, sun

SKILLS

Concentration	+9
Heal	+10
Knowledge (religion)	+7

FEATS

Country Born[B], Iron Will, Martial Weapon Proficiency (scimitar), Weapon Focus (scimitar)

Combat Gear *wand of cure light wounds* (25 charges); **Other Gear** *+1 chainmail*, heavy steel shield, *+1 scimitar*, light crossbow with 10 bolts, *cloak of resistance +1*, backpack, gold holy symbol (with *continual flame*) worth 300 gp, rations (4), 5 gp

Merisiel

FEMALE ELF ROGUE 4

ALIGN **CN** INIT **+4** SPEED **30 ft.**

ABILITIES

12	STR
18	DEX
12	CON
8	INT
13	WIS
10	CHA

DEFENSE

HP 17

AC 18
touch 14, flat-footed 14

Fort +2, **Ref** +9, **Will** +2 (+2 vs. enchantment)

Defense evasion, trap sense +1, uncanny dodge; **Immune** sleep

OFFENSE

Melee *+1 rapier* +8 (1d6+1/18–20)
Ranged dagger +7 (1d4+1/19–20)
Base Atk +3; **Grp** +4

Special Attack sneak attack +2d6

FEATS

City Born (Riddleport)[B], Dodge, Weapon Finesse

SKILLS

Bluff	+7
Disable Device	+6
Hide	+9
Jump	+8
Listen	+7
Move Silently	+9
Open Lock	+10
Search	+5
Sleight of Hand	+9
Spot	+7
Tumble	+11

Combat Gear *potion of cat's grace* (2), *potion of cure moderate wounds*, *potion of invisibility*, *potion of lesser restoration*, acid, alchemist's fire (2); **Other Gear** *+1 studded leather armor*, *+1 rapier*, daggers (12), rations (3), sunrod, masterwork thieves' tools, polished jade worth 50 gp, 17 pp, 3 gp

Next Month in Pathfinder

The Hook Mountain Massacre

by Nicolas Logue

No one's heard from the rangers of Hook Mountain for weeks, and the nearby town of Turtleback Ferry has been strangely quiet as well. Everyone knows that ogres live in the deep parts of the woods and atop the rugged peaks of the nearby mountains, but what if they've organized? What if someone—or some*thing*—has galvanized these brutish, inbred thugs into an army? Would anyone know before it was too late to mount a defense? A *Pathfinder* adventure for 7th-level characters.

Keeping the Keep

by Nicolas Logue

It's one thing to rescue a fortress from ogre occupation. It's quite another to get the same fortress back on its feet. What sort of problems await an industrious band of heroes who find themselves suddenly in charge of a remote mountain keep, and are they up to the bureaucratic nightmare of juggling visiting elven nobles, surly dwarven tradesmen, impish gnome entertainers, and the odd hungry troll while trying, at the same time, to remain adventurers?

Gazetteer of Varisia

by James L. Sutter

Take a journey through the wilds of Varisia in this in-depth gazetteer. Gaze into the bottomless pit of the Mobhad Leigh, and study the flickering ghosts of other worlds in the steel Forest of Mundatei. From the abandoned elven capital of Celwynvian to ancient Lurkwood where the seasons obey no calendar, from the steaming depths of Ember Lake to the iron-walled dwarven stronghold of Janderhoff, this guide details Varisia as never before.

Pathfinder's Journal

Eando Kline reaches the sinister streets of Kaer Maga, where his quest for an ancient *ioun stone* forces him into an uneasy alliance with one of the city's shadiest merchants. Surrounded by troll augurs, leech-covered bloatmages, and even stranger sights, just how far will Eando go to secure information for the Pathfinder Society?

Bestiary

Angry lake monsters, ravenous spawn of the goddess of madness, toothy undead menaces, haunted campfires, scorpions made out of skulls, and ogre love children!

Subscribe to Pathfinder!